SCHOLARLY PUBLISHING

Against the Grain
Special Millennial Issue

SCHOLARLY PUBLISHING

Books, Journals, Publishers, and Libraries in the Twentieth Century

EDITED BY

Richard E. Abel

Lyman W. Newlin

EDITORS-IN-CHIEF

Katina Strauch

Bruce Strauch

WILEY

A John Wiley & Sons, Inc., Publication

For ordering and customer service, call 1 (800) CALL WILEY.

Library of Congress Cataloging-in-Publication Data

Library of Congress Cataloging-in-Publication Data is available.

ISBN 0-471-21929-0

Contents

12

Appearance and Growth of Computer and
Electronic Products in Libraries   209
Ralph M. Shoffner

13

The Economic Crisis in Libraries: Causes and Effects   257
Michael Gorman

14

The Impact of the Library Budget Crisis on Scholarly Publishing   273
Jack G. Goellner

15

The Place of Scholarly and Scientific Libraries in
an Increasingly and More Widespread Competitive
Information Knowledge Marketplace   277
Charles Hamaker

Conclusion   293
Richard E. Abel and Lyman W. Newlin

Coda   301
Katina Strauch and Bruce Strauch

Foreword

Peter Booth Wiley

Soon after the dissolution of Alexander the Great's empire in 323 B.C., Ptolemy Soter, one of his generals, became the Egyptian pharoah. Ptolemy, like Alexander, was a student of Aristotle and thus a man committed to the broadening of human knowledge. So Ptolemy instructed Demetrius of Phaleron, the deposed ruler of Athens and another student of Aristotle, to build a great library in the city of Alexandria. Ptolemy's ambitions were truly global, at least in terms of the world as he knew it. Collect "the books of all the peoples of the world," he ordered Demetrius. Today with the Internet, technology fantasists are telling us that we could realize Ptolemy's dream of making the entire body of human knowledge available to each and every one of us.

Oddly this proto-Alexandrian library often looks more like the Tower of Babel, where we wander through a vast storehouse of information lacking a common key to decipher the code of human knowledge. We are virtually drowning in information—in a sea of bits and bytes of unrefined data. We are lost without a national consensus or adequate financial support for a strategy that would permit scholars, scientists, publishers, and librarians to collect, sort through, and refine this vast array of data and turn it into conceptual knowledge—knowledge that would be stored in our great libraries and ostensibly made available to everyone via print or the Internet. This is the problem posited by the editors and authors of this collection of essays about libraries and publishing.

The editors have asked a group of worthies—a collection of publishers, scholars, and librarians who have collectively spent more than two centuries laboring in the fields of knowledge—to share their views on this predicament. Besides describing the present state of the publishing industry and the

ix

modern library, the authors have noted a number of additional problems, including:

- a shift in library budgets away from collection development toward investment in electronic infrastructure
- the decline of the scholarly monograph, which was one of the principal means by which knowledge was refined, accompanied by a continuing increase in the number and cost of scholarly journals in the sciences and technology
- the hollowing out of acquisition budgets for the humanities, which is another consequence of the growth in expensive scientific journals
- the lack of a consensus about who will take on the task of sifting this vast new store of information and turn it into usable knowledge
- growing dependency on electronic media whose shelf life appears dangerously short.

Conversely, they have noted some other trends:

- a vast flowering of scientific and technical literature
- a concomitant growth in the capacity to search and store large amounts of information via the computer
- the expansion of niche publishing.

In this book the authors are challenging all of us, whether publisher, scholar, scientist, or librarian, to join the fight to increase funding to libraries, to find ways to publish materials that may not necessarily meet the profit objectives of commercial publishers, and to seek a proper balance between materials available in the humanities and social sciences and those available to the world of science and technology. Ultimately, their challenge is an ambitious one: to foster the development of a new generation of intellectuals who refine the vast deposits of raw data into the highest forms of knowledge. For almost two hundred years we at John Wiley & Sons have dedicated ourselves to the propagation of knowledge. We are proud to join the editors of this volume in continuing this important work.

Preface

Richard E. Abel and Lyman W. Newlin

It may prove useful to readers of this Special Millennial Issue of *Against the Grain* to acquaint them with the background and underlying principles which governed its creation and content. For those acquainted with Katina Strauch, the founder of the annual Charleston Conference as well as the founder and Editor of *Against the Grain*, it will come as no surprise that the initial inspiration for such a Special Issue sprang from her fertile and active mind about sixteen months prior to the appearance of this Special Issue. It seems particularly appropriate for an audience of publishers, booksellers, journal dealers, and librarians concerned with matters of comprehensiveness, accuracy, and consistency with respect to their mutual history, among other things, that the year in which she chose to have this Special Issue appear is, in fact, the millennial year.

Katina Strauch contacted Lyman Newlin to fly the idea past him. His enthusiastic assent began to give the Special Issue the promise of a concrete undertaking. Lyman Newlin recruited Richard Abel, as joint editor to the project adding further substance to the concept. It was agreed that the two joint editors of the Special Issue would spend most of their time at the 1999 Charleston Conference formulating and fleshing out the proposed contents and identifying authors for what would be the most extensive issue of *Against the Grain* published to date. It was further agreed that this proposed table of contents would be passed before Katina the day succeeding the closing of the Charleston Conference for her criticism and emendation. And so the project was advanced.

The joint editors spent six to ten hours a day throughout the course of the 1999 Charleston Conference in a hotel room thrashing out and formulating both the editorial principles we thought should be invoked and the content which we thought would best characterize the quite remarkable century through which the world of information and knowledge transfer and storage has passed. The exercise relating to the content initially led to formulation of twenty-one or twenty-two separate essays. Further reflection, however, exposed several redundancies or potential treatment conflicts which would lead only to confusion for the writers, as well as the readers. When these overlaps and conflicts were resolved by melding various topics into essays better suited to carry such substance, the joint editors concluded that they had the makings of a viable and coherent treatment of this sprawling expanse of traditional and new technologies, users, and uses. The result of this consolidating/synthesizing process led to the fifteen essays found herein.

The primary editorial principles summoned by the joint editors may be summarized as follows:

1. The principle objective of this Special Issue would be to offer readers at the turn of the twenty-first century as well-rounded and accurate an account as possible of the quite amazing and unpredictable sequence of interrelated events through which the information/knowledge transfer process involving books, journals, electronic, and other high-technology media, and libraries, has passed in the remarkable century just past.

2. While the information/knowledge transfer process in the entire span of the twentieth century was to be addressed by the writers, the principal focus of every essay should be the last five decades in which the most profound, intractable, and portentous developments in the conjoined worlds of the book, the journal, information technology, and the library occurred.

3. We asked every essayist to speculate briefly upon possible future outcomes impinging upon or likely to mark the particular subject content being dealt with by him or her. Given the present state of uncertainty, enveloping the entire process can hardly be thought of as an enviable request. Chuck Hamaker, never one to run away from an intellectual confrontation, was enlisted to tackle the even more unenviable job of prediction in the concluding essay dealing with the place of the traditional library in an increasingly competitive information/knowledge supply marketplace.

4. We defined the length of each essay. The primary motivating factor was, of course, the space constraints inherent in the form of the journal. In defining lengths we endeavored to respect the weight or role of the subject matter in the totality of the information/knowledge transfer process. Given the often indeterminate boundaries separating and dis-

tinguishing the various electronic forms of publication and their common reliance upon computer technology, it was necessary to impose upon that "electronics and information technology" war horse, Ralph Schoffner, who has been in the thick of these battles for nearly half a century, to adequately represent their fast-moving and kaleidoscopic evolution in the longest essay herein.

5. We created and provided to each writer an outline of topics within the subject purview of each essay which we thought might be usefully addressed. But none were confined to any or all of these suggestions. As will be noted shortly, the authors were selected on the basis of their long and intimate knowledge of the subject field being dealt with—they all served long and productive careers associated with the field. They had, inevitably, formed a number of distinct views growing out of these years of experience. So, it would have proved counter-productive for the joint editors to insist upon the necessary legitimacy of narrowly pursuing the suggestions and outline the joint editors had developed.

With the table of contents intellectually comfortably and defensibly in place, the joint editors turned their minds to identifying the best authors for each essay. Given the high editorial standards posited for the Special Issue, the selection of second-stringers would have been counter-productive. So, we racked our memories for the names of the foremost living players who had established superior reputations in the course of their careers. Our judgements of the writers we would solicit were formed only secondarily out of our personal experience, however, but rather, largely, as a reflection of their achieved status among the knowledgeable with respect to the discharge of their various roles in the worlds of books, journals, electronic media, and libraries. (The joint editors would be less than candid if they did not acknowledge that these selections were informed in substantial measure by their combined 125 years labor in the world of books, journals, and libraries.)

Within the confines of this overriding criterion we formulated the following principles of identification and selection:

1. Every writer had to have been playing in the game for a substantial number of years. And, as importantly, they had to bear the scars of fighting the good fight over those years. Most are retired, but all are still keeping at least a finger in the game. Those not yet retired have all achieved commanding presences in their respective pursuits.

2. We particularly wished to identify/select those who either:
   • had a genuine breadth of experience and could bring a sweep of perspective to their essay, or,

- had pursued an unusual/atypical career path and could bring a unique/creative outlook to their essay.

In short, the converse of the plodders.

3. We sought a degree of international perspective. It is true that the principal focus of this Special Issue is on the North American scene, for most of the dramas in the world of information/knowledge transfer have first been played out or have been played out with greater intensity here. But an understanding of parallel or alternative developments abroad would, even if not directly addressed, lend a measure of depth and nuance to the essays.

When we had identified two or three potential authors for each essay based on these criteria, we placed those names in priority order. Happily for the joint editors, and even more happily for the readers, almost uniformly every one of the first priority authors agreed to undertake the job.

The product of these several days of work was duly passed before Katina, who, in turn, had several useful suggestions which served both to sharpen the focus and to highlight various aspects of the substance of the coverage.

Some readers may conclude that the above recitation is really quite unnecessary, based on the argument that the principles and objectives recounted therein merely reflect one of the rational and systematic approaches to the structuring and organizing of such a collective issue as this. Fair enough. But it has been done for what the joint editors believe to be a legitimate purpose.

Consider: To the best of the joint editors' knowledge, no comparable effort to record the principal outlines and trends of the modern history of the information/knowledge transfer process in North America and the places and fates of the major players therein has been undertaken.

By contrast, several notable undertakings to identify the "major" or "most important" or "most influential" books of the century have been compiled and have enjoyed more or less wide circulation. By a related token, some brief accounts, most virtually a kind of discursive "shorthand" of some of the leading trends or patterns which have marked one or another sector of the information/knowledge universe—the book trade, the journal industry, the information technology sector, or the library world—have been compiled. None have sought to present the principal lineaments of the convoluted, interrelated, and uncertain courses of the quite radical mutations and transformations which affected/afflicted all the players, created seas of yet unresolved uncertainty, and led to the spilling of more unsupported conjecture and ink in the professional/trade literature than since early Victorian times. Nor, to the best of the joint editors' knowledge, has any other publication sought to recruit such a preeminent array of "heavyweights" who had been there and had had a major hand in the shaping of events they describe and as those events have been played out to date.

The joint editors are further of the understanding that no comparable effort to structure the contents of this Special Issue to provide a coherent and integrated presentation had been made elsewhere. The intent was, and remains, to provide a comprehensive and inclusive account which will draw together the often separated and dispersed threads of recollection and views characteristic of most of those involved in the information/knowledge transfer process.

Why all this concerted effort on the part of sixteen authors and the joint editors? The reason is quite straightforward. All involved have proved themselves over decades as committed to the life of the mind, and the maintenance and enhancement of the inherited culture. As such they have proved themselves dependable and level-headed observers and contributors to the ongoing endeavors to make sense of the often conflicting cross-currents characterizing the information/knowledge transfer process in the last five decades of the twentieth century. The joint editors believe these qualities and contributions by the authors will be fully evident to every careful and critical reader of this Special Issue.

If this expectation is realized, we, authors and editors alike, hope that this Special Issue might become the focal point around which and the springboard from which careful and rational discourses might evolve at the Charleston Conference 2001. But in a larger sense we hope it serves some of the same catalytic functions in the wider community of publishers, book and journal vendors, and librarians who are genuinely bent on formulating and putting into place a new paradigm of the information/knowledge transfer process for the next century.

Acknowledgments

The editors of this integrated body of essays, framed as a Special Millennial publication of *Against the Grain,* and devoted to the history and practices of the world of books in the last century—which has occupied each of our lives for over a half of that century—must extend our profound and heartfelt thanks to those several people and organizations which have collectively brought this undertaking to fruition.

First, we acknowledge with warm collegial gratitude the significant contribution to the recording and interpretation of the history of the world of books, journals, and libraries in the last century, one of the most momentous in the history of knowledge and culture, so willingly and thoughtfully advanced by the authors of these essays. Future historians of the world of information/knowledge must look to these essays by those "who were there and did it" as key evidence in, and contributions to, the evolving history of the world of learning.

Our profound thanks must next be extended to the old and honorable publishing firm of John Wiley & Sons, Inc., to whose distinguished list we trust this publication will make a modest contribution. Both editors have worked long and fruitfully with the Wiley firm and its people over two generations. So in a genuine and heartfelt sense this publication can be seen as the culmination of a relationship which ever warranted our respect and admiration.

We proposed this book to George Stanley, John Chambers, and the Wiley library sales team's Athena Michael, Trudy Lindsey, and Barry Champany. Their positive response and enthusiasm was contagious and encouraged us to suggest presenting the possibility of publishing to Peter Wiley and the Wiley family: Will Pesce, CEO, Stephen Kippur, President, Professional and Trade Division, and Eric Swanson, Senior Vice President, Scientific, Technical, and Medical Division. The acceptance by Wiley executives ensued in placing the enterprise into the hands of Janet Bailey, Greg Giblin, Camille Carter, Heather Haselkorn, Nicole Sette, Margie Schustack, and P J Campbell. These staff members have helped us gather, craft, and create what we all have hoped will be a unique and valuable addition to the literature of the vocation to which we are all dedicated.

To all those named above, we offer our sincere thanks.

And, lastly, we offer our deepest thanks to all those who contributed behind the scenes to one aspect or another of the framing, shaping, and publication of this book.

Lyman W. Newlin
Richard E. Abel

*   *   *

The framing, editing, and production of this book—the Special Millennial Issue of *Against the Grain*—would not have been possible without the contributions of countless people.

We would like to thank Peter Booth Wiley, whose family publishing firm has made the publication of this volume a reality.

Thanks also to Lyman Newlin and Dick Abel, who first proposed this project over two years ago. Lyman and Dick have worked tirelessly, indeed passionately, on this project, despite major personal setbacks.

More thanks are due to John Chambers for his willingness to follow this project through to completion, and to enlist John Wiley & Sons in the publication of this notable volume.

And, finally, we would like to thank Camille Carter, Director of Production and Manufacturing, Susan Walton, Copy Editor, Russell Till, Typesetter, and countless others at John Wiley & Sons who made this project their top priority.

Bruce and Katina Strauch

◆1◆

The Growth of Printed Literature in the Twentieth Century

Albert Henderson

Measuring and forecasting the growth of what we call the printed literature—the primary vessel of knowledge and culture since Gutenberg invented movable, reusable type—has been challenging, even contentious. Perhaps one day the dispute will become an icon of the twentieth-century perversity that Michael Gorman called "the treason of the learned," the betrayal by which cultural priorities are gladly sacrificed by their guardians (1994). In academic and professional disciplines, knowledge is the primary objective of investments of labor, money, and other resources. Formal publication of new knowledge and informed criticism is essential. It is the work product of research and intellectual analysis. It is the medium of transmission and study that propagates further research and up-to-date practice. Finally, formal publication is accepted as evidence of the author's competence. Universities, according to Vannevar Bush's conception of the government sponsorship of academic research, "are charged with the responsibility of conserving the knowledge accumulated by the past, imparting that knowledge to students, and contributing new knowledge of all kinds" (1990, p. 19). The result has been increasing numbers of journal articles, monographs, and patents that convey a healthy message of success and future potential. At the same time, it has generated the appearance of new publications, which calls for spending money on their acquisition, preparation, preservation, and dissemination. Campus libraries, many with multimillion-dollar requirements, particularly threaten common resources and redundant liquidity. They compete not only with the parochial self-interests of the programs that they support, but also with the academic bureaucracy and its boorish preoccupation with financial assets and self-promotion. The *Copyright Act of 1976,* which embraced "fair

1

use," blended with the proliferation of photocopiers to poison the growth of libraries. The combination provided a thin excuse to deemphasize library collections and services in favor of resource sharing (such as interlibrary borrowing), cost shifting (such as scholars' travel, personal document procurement, and, lately, the Internet), and weeding (the permanent removal of resources to forestall the expansion of facilities). Despite lip service given to "productivity," no thought has been given by university managers or the deans of science policy to the greater cost of poorly informed research and education. After the U.S. *Patent and Trademark Amendments of 1980* permitted universities to exploit inventions created with federal research and development funding, the academic bureaucracy tasted the sweetness of patent royalties, now in the hundreds of millions of dollars each year. It soon aspired to what it saw as copyright-derived profits achieved easily by commercial and association publishers (Shulenburger 1998). There is no advocacy of "fair use" by universities in connection with patents.

Therein lies the conflict that flared up in the mid-twentieth century, provoked by the late Fremont Rider, a Wesleyan University librarian (1944). It is about money, with little or no reference to knowledge. Rider noted that major academic library collections had increased exponentially for hundreds of years, doubling in size at sixteen-year intervals. Yale University possessed about 1,000 volumes in the mid-eighteenth century. Its collection grew to 2,748,000 volumes by 1938 with just over eleven sixteen-year doublings. Between 1831 and 1938, Yale and nine other top U.S. universities doubled their library collections 6.7 times. Such continued growth, projected into the future by Rider, incited conflicts over future resources. Yale University's collection would house 200 million volumes by the year 2040 and consume untold millions of dollars.

According to Rider, the benefit of vigorous growth lay in the role of the research libraries at the "heart" of every university as key disseminators of knowledge. His view that ever-increasing publications propelled library growth was bolstered in the 1950s by the late Yale University historian, Derek de Solla Price, who observed the growth of published science research (and of the number of scientists). Doubling every fifteen years over the long term, this constant pace tied in closely with Rider's observation of libraries and their critical contribution to the quality of education (1975). Then William Axford discovered that postwar library growth between 1946 and 1960 had fallen well below Rider's ideal (1962). He reemphasized Rider's warning that universities must double their collections every sixteen years or jeopardize their effectiveness. That, in fact, is what made Rider's conclusions most irritating: his implication that a measured escalation of library spending was necessary to maintain the quality of higher education and research:

Of course, what makes this rate of library growth a very real problem from the educational standpoint is that it is not a laboratory experiment, not a growth in a vacuum. There has always existed a direct correlation between the educational effectiveness of a college and the growth of its library, a correlation so close and so consistent that it cannot have been fortuitous. The various sources from which these tables are quoted give us the statistical history of a great many more libraries, and give it in much greater detail. And it is obvious, as one runs through them and traces the progress of any one library down through the years, that, whenever its growth slackened, its college was slipping with it. On the other hand, when any library spurted ahead of the sixteen-year average during any given quarter century, that library's college was, for one reason or another, taking on a new lease of life.

In fact, this may be asserted as almost axiomatic: unless a college or university is willing to be stagnant, unless it is willing not to maintain its place in the steady flow of educational development, it has to double its library in size every sixteen years, or thereabouts. When its library ceases to grow an educational institution dies. One may argue that this ought not to be so. All that can be said is that the statistical record shows clearly that it is so. Nor is it material whether our reasoning be that a strong college insists upon having a strong library, or that a strong library develops a strong college: the one clear fact is that the two go together (Rider 1944, pp. 8–9).

Thorstein Veblen noted long ago that university managers were infected by a tendency to relegate knowledge to a secondary status, to "overrate ways and means as contrasted with the ends which these ways and means are in some sense designed to serve" ([1918]1993, p. 34). They were fully revolutionized in the mid-twentieth century, first by the effects of the GI bill and federal research programs after World War II, then by the baby boom and Vietnam war politics. Echoing Veblen, perhaps, the former president of Columbia University noted, "a government contract becomes virtually a substitute for intellectual curiosity" (Eisenhower 1961). Other analysts mourned the impact of the new influences on the academic priority of knowledge and traditions of gold standards (Nisbet 1971; Shils 1975). Thanks to Sputnik, which caused the science policy establishment to confess to the mediocrity of information resources, federal attention turned to libraries and education. Library growth kept pace with research and development for one decade, until an American set foot on the Moon. Then, shielded by controversies over curriculum and politics, politicians looked the other way, and university managers devoted considerable energy to exorcising Rider's demon from their budgets. George Piternick attacked data on library growth as not uniform; he dismissed evaluations of universities as subjective (1963). A report funded by the National Science Foundation (NSF) known as the "Pitt Study" (that was promptly repudiated by the University of Pittsburgh Academic Senate and other library researchers) claimed that libraries spent too much money on publications that were rarely or never used (Borkowski and MacLeod 1979). In an article that was called by an Andrew W. Mellon Foundation report "the best critical overview" of library growth (1993, p. 11 note), Robert Molyneux ignored questions of effectiveness and offered a simpler argument—past growth is not indicative of the future (1986). Eventually, a media blitz was kicked off officially by Association of Research Libraries' (ARL) project on serials' prices, which accused researchers of "excessive publication" and publishers of profiteering (1989). Aside from innumerable references in the library literature, their report was echoed by *Science* (Koshland 1989), *The Scientist* (Kalfus 1989), *The New York Times* (Kingson 1989), and *Science and Engineering Indicators* (1989). Even the sensationalist television program *60 Minutes* aired academic instructors whining that "publish or perish" requirements filled miles of library shelves with trivial research that "nobody reads" (Stahl 1995).

None of these journalists bothered to check the accuracy of ARL's claims. They have no excuse. They had plenty of time. The literature of library impoverishment goes back to the 1970s (Fry and White 1975; National Enquiry 1979). U.S. Department of Education statistics show it (Talbot 1984). And there were also well-known criticisms of the failure of science policy to pay attention to dissemination (U.S. Congress. Senate. Special Subcommittee on the National Science Foundation of the Committee on Labor and Public Welfare 1975; U.S. Congress. Office of Technology Assessment 1989; McClure and Hernon 1989; White 1990).

Ironically, one of the mantras embraced by the media blitz was, "library expenditures have been increasing faster than inflation" (National Science Board 1989). Total postsecondary library spending actually plummeted by $110 million in fiscal year 1986–87, quietly undermining publishers' prices and laying the ground for the "library crisis." (I use the word "quietly" because the cut was not "announced" as it would have been in any other industry, and statistical evidence was not reported by the government for several years.) With fewer units sold, prices were forced to rise to cover high fixed costs that continued to rise with the publication of more articles. Statistics reported by colleges and universities indicate a more important trend. Between 1975 and 1995, library spending dropped from 3 percent to 2 percent of total revenue; academic profits (revenue minus spending) rose from 2 percent to 3 percent (U.S. Dept. of Education National Center for Education Statistics 1997a). World output of research articles tripled since 1970, while U.S. research universities increased spending on their libraries half that (in constant dollars to remove the effects of inflation). Moreover, ARL had been keeping, but withholding from publication, data on the declining share of university funding reported by their members for more than a decade (Advisory Panel for Scientific Publications. 1992). Following the report that these data existed, a sampling was made available in 1993 with a note of surprise by

ARL through the Andrew W. Mellon Foundation. Moreover, the standards published by the Association of College and Research Libraries (ACRL) have abandoned every finite goal by which to objectively gauge excellence.

Advocates of the anti-Rider persuasion remember Derek de Solla Price best for his insistence that growth must level off. Price was fond of predicting that the continued expansion of science would produce the absurd result of dozens of scientists per "man, woman, child, and dog." (1975) In one passage, he envisioned that the continued doubling of electrical engineering workers every ten years (from Ben Franklin in 1750 to "an even million by 1955") must end during the twentieth century. He boldly predicted: "At this rate, the whole working population should be employed in this one field as early as 1990" (1975, p. 181).

Arithmetic gives us only 17 million electrical workers by 1990, not close to the U.S. Department of Labor workforce of 100 million. However, the image was so impressive that Daniel Bell quotes this passage in *The Coming of Post-Industrial Society* as an example of "limits of growth" (1973, p. 181).

Some writers have "seen" the end of growth, often to justify reduced spending (but never revenue). Citing Price, Horace Freeland Judson claimed that peer review is being transformed by the "transition from exponential growth of the sciences to a steady state" (1994). David L. Goodstein, vice provost of California Institute of Technology, cited Price to support the end of financial support for students. He wrote: "The big crunch occurred around 1970. Science went from one phase of its history into a completely different kind of phase, and when it happened, around 1970, nobody noticed. We have spent the past 25 years in what I call the age of denial" (1995).

These writers must deny the reality that academic research and development spending increased 2.5-fold between 1970 and 1995 (in constant dollars). World production of journal articles increased threefold. The *Physics Abstracts* database grew even more, from 624,000 records to 2,852,000 records, doubling every ten years or so from 1970 to 1990. This record far exceeded Price's example of the fifteen-year doubling of the physics literature that he called the "modern normal rate" or "time-constant" from 1918 to 1955 (1975, pp. 170–173; 1986, pp. 16–17). What Goodstein called "the big crunch" of 1970 was the shift in the U.S. politics of the Cold War. Winning the space race and opposition to defense spending precipitated sharp cuts in the growth of research spending (Henderson 1999; Nichols 1971). Spending on certain sectors of academic research and development in the United States was affected dramatically. However, the effect was only temporary and not imitated in other nations, where the majority of research articles are authored. Total research and development spending in the United States never decreased, as library spending did. Nonetheless, the anti-Rider radicals managed to derail the traditional growth of libraries.

It is clear that research universities once had allocated 6 percent of their spending to their library (Barzun 1993, pp. 174, 196) Today, they allocate less than half that amount (U.S. Department of Education. National Center for Education Statistics 1997b, pp. 19–20). This decline is particularly important because research universities, while representing 4 percent of academic libraries, control about 40 percent of library-operations spending in the United States. They also monopolize sponsored academic research. They generate most journal articles. Presumably, they are also the heaviest users of the published literature. Library collections, as a foundation for sponsored investigations, appear to be crumbling under a deliberate doomsday policy demonstrated by projections of ARL statistics:

> If the curve were extended even further, by 2007 ARL libraries would stop buying books entirely, and only purchase serials; by 2017 they would buy nothing, and instead access everything. But in the near term, at least, this scenario is unlikely, for as Tom Shaughnessy, director of libraries for the University of Minnesota puts it, "You can't borrow, if no one owns it" (Okerson and Stubbs 1992).

Price revised his doomsday prediction, using a constant doubling every fifteen years rather than every ten years (1986). Making a specific reference to spending, he wrote:

> It is clear that we cannot go up another two orders of magnitude as we have climbed the last five. If we did, we should have two scientists for every man, woman, child, and dog in the population and we should spend on them twice as much money as we had. Scientific doomsday is therefore less than a century distant (1986, p. 17).

Labor economists Paula Stephan and Sharon Levin recast the terms more broadly, suggesting that "Price exaggerated slightly, but not by much. To place his prediction in some perspective, if the number of Ph.D.'s in science and engineering were to double every ten years, by the year 2097 there would be approximately 617 million scientists" (1992).

In the midst of such growth, economists who include Fritz Machlup and William J. Baumol investigated the cost-effectiveness of information. By ignoring their observations, mainstream managers and economists plunged headlong into the quicksand of a false paradigm and confounded themselves with the "productivity paradox"—their disappointment that information technology does not decrease input costs and increase profits, as mechanical technology had done (Harris 1994). A report by the Andrew W. Mellon Foundation described it this way: "The argument in favor of the wholesale adoption of the new information technology (IT) in universities, publishing houses, libraries, and scholarly communication rests on the hope—indeed the dogma—that IT will substantially raise productivity" (Quandt and Ekman 1999, pp. 2–3). Quixotically spinning contradictory evidence that IT produces no financial savings, the introduction to the report concludes, "Even though some costs at individual institutions may rise, we are confident that system costs will eventually fall" (p. 12). Long before the foundation embarked on its $12-million crusade to find profits in technology, Baumol and Blackman described the paradox, which they labeled "the cost disease," as an administrative weakness (1983). They explained that falling prices of computers in academic libraries stimulated costly new labor-intensive activity. All savings in calculation and distribution is quickly eaten up by the new opportunities to handle information differently.

Not surprisingly, the "cost disease" became an epidemic that substantially increased the administrative share of spending in higher education after 1970, according to National Council for Education Statistics (NCES). Table 1 illustrates the growth of higher education in current dollars and the rearrangement of priorities represented by changing shares of spending.

In contrast to the mirage of financial surpluses promised by IT, Machlup explained that in research and education, information improves outputs (1962). Information yields savings by reducing error and duplication. A famous example was given to Congress by the late Western Reserve University dean, Jesse H. Shera (1958). He noted that a Russian paper, "The Application of Boolean Matrix Algebra to the Analysis and Synthesis of Relay Contact Networks," was discovered only after $250,000 (more than $1 million in 1995 dollars) had been wasted duplicating research already reported. Another demonstration of the value of information was provided through a survey of 60,000 scientists and engineers, which showed that, annually, they used an estimated 13.7 million articles and technical reports (King et al. 1981). The report calculates a saving to the U.S. Department of Energy of $13 billion by eliminating unproductive work, based on readings costing $500 million.

To maximize the economies described by Machlup, scientists need more information, not less. They must comprehend the formal literature of primary reports of research, and then go beyond. This includes information that is never formally published (Garvey 1977, pp. 291–295; Weber et al. 1998). Informal communications are important. (Chemical Abstracts Service has only now begun to index preprints.) The reporting of negative results is vital to avoid repetition. Editors, however, readily admit a bias against publishing negative results. Ephemera (such as letters, notes, conference papers, oral communications, comments, and preprints), reference works (including data

TABLE 1
Changes in Revenue, Spending, and Profits 1970–1995
for All U.S. Institutions of Higher Education

FY	1970	1995	
Total Revenue	$21,515,242	$189,120,570	
Total Current Fund Expenditures	$21,043,110	$182,968,610	
Administration and General Expenses	$ 2,627,993	$ 25,904,821	
Instruction and Departmental Research	$ 6,883,944	$ 55,719,707	
Organized Research	$ 2,144,076	$ 17,109,541	
Libraries	$ 652,596	$ 4,165,761	
Plant Opereration and Maintenance	$ 1,541,698	$ 11,745,905	
Surplus (Revenue less Expenditures)	$ 472,132	$ 6,151,960	
	1970	1995	Change
Total Revenue	100.00%	100.00%	
Total Current Fund Expenditures	97.81%	96.75%	–1.08%
Administration and General Expenses	12.21%	13.70%	12.14%
Instruction and Departmental Research	32.00%	29.46%	–7.92%
Organized Research	9.97%	9.05%	–9.22%
Libraries	3.03%	2.20%	–27.38%
Plant Operation and Maintenance	7.17%	6.21%	–13.32%
Surplus (Revenue less Expenditures)	2.19%	3.25%	48.12%

compilations, bibliographies, glossaries, notification services, and indexes), and syntheses (such as reviews, compilations, surveys, notes, synoptics, abstracts, meta-analyses, and comments) join formal publications—journal articles, monographs, and patents—as essential markers of the information landscape.

What about the quality of research and the research literature? Ever-wider horizons and the proliferation of content present the fundamental challenge of modern science (Garvey 1977, pp. 105–113; Herring 1968; Huth 1989). Roughly 90 percent of all scientists who have ever lived are alive now (Holton, quoted by Price 1986, p. 1). Their output is more than overwhelming. The major cost associated with journals is the cost of scientists' time acquiring information—not the expenditures associated with the library (King, McDonald, and Roderer 1981, pp. 218–221). While cost per reading has not changed proportionately, the cost of acquisition has been shifted from university libraries to scientists and, in effect, to their sponsors (Tenopir and King 1996). A greater cost borne by sponsors springs from the gap between scientific output and the human capacity to understand it. This gap widens as research activity grows. It deepens as research and development spending outpaces investments in conservation and dissemination. This gap is the Achilles' heel of peer review and learned authorship. It is the real disease of science, diagnosed often, prescribed for with care, yet not addressed by any policy. Garvey described the problem for contemporary scientists: "even if they had perfect retrieval systems they would be presented with so many items that they could not assimilate and process them" (Garvey 1977, p. 107). A Canadian group demonstrated this dramatically, finding over 10,000 items in a search of MEDLINE for articles on whiplash-associated disorders (Spitzer et al. 1995, pp. 25–26S). Their task force screened out all but 294. Then teams representing different specialties read the remainder closely. Eventually, all but 62 articles—one out of four—were accepted (177 were rejected as lacking merit; 55 as not relevant). Automation cannot provide substitutes for knowledge and understanding, as it does for other types of human labor. The first, rather eloquent, and too quickly forgotten recommendation of the President's Science Advisory Committee was right on point:

> We shall cope with the information explosion, in the long run, only if some scientists re prepared to commit themselves deeply to the job of sifting, reviewing, and synthesizing information; i.e., to handling information with sophistication and meaning, not merely mechanically. Such scientists must create new science, not just shuffle documents: their activities of reviewing, writing books, criticizing, and synthesizing are as much a part of science as is traditional research (1963, p. 2).

Derek de Solla Price used a variety of exponential factors to measure the growth of science. His Malthus-like predictions, in fact, often turn on how one defines the arena of activity. Does one include the entire world, with a huge potential for growth in the Third World, or limit horizons to the United States? Current doctoral programs and corporate recruiters scour the world for candidates, which suggests that measures be all-inclusive. Does one include women? In Price's day, women were actively discouraged from careers in mathematics and science. Including women means doubling the universe as seen by Price. Nor are science and technology still the exclusive province of Ph.D.s; technical colleges, high schools, the armed forces, corporate training, and other programs annually admit tens of thousands to the growing skilled labor force. We may thank Price more for his investigation of indicators of the growth and propagation of science. He noted that counting volumes or titles of science journals is a poor measure of growth because the number of articles in a journal volume varies considerably. He also showed that discipline-oriented bibliographies reflect the worldwide nature of science, and that local events—even major wars—have little impact on long-term growth. Referring to *Physics Abstracts*, for instance, a production record that he called "a rather complete and significant selection" (1975, p. 171) he was able to plot an exponential curve running near the fifteen-year doubling from 1918 and an accumulation of 180,000 contributions to the literature by the year 1950. His comparison of inputs and outputs is often compelling, leading to economic dynamics of supply and demand. He also pioneered the study of citations that trace the intellectual roots of new scientific knowledge.

The growth of learned journals actually demonstrated by Price's measures contradicts his sensational predictions of growth leveling off during the late twentieth century. Spectacular growth can be found in biology, mathematics, and physics, which, respectively, doubled on average in periods of 12.5, 11, and 9 years. (See Figure 1.) The annual production of Chemical Abstracts Service continued to double, three times between 1940 and 1990, at the same fifteen-year rate that it maintained for decades before. EI (founded as *Engineering Index* with ten journals in 1884) took seventy years to reach its

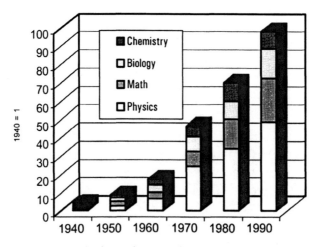

Figure 1. Growth of annual output of science abstracts, 1940–1990.

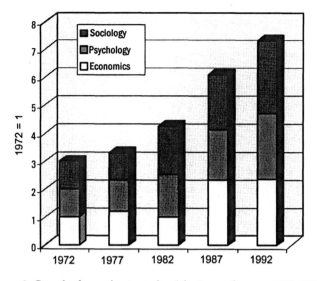

Figure 2. Growth of annual output of social sciences abstracts, 1972–1992.

first million records, thirty years to reach its second million, and passed the third million ahead of schedule. Social sciences (see Figure 2), music, and art also demonstrated no lapse in fifteen-year doublings over the past twenty years. The aggregate databases of the members of National Federation of Abstracting and Information Services exceeded 157 million records in 1994.

The conflict between the growth of research, its publications, and of resources allocated to dissemination reaches well beyond the size of libraries. It compromises the reliability of bibliographic statistics as indicators of research activity, undermines the effectiveness of information services, and frustrates the preparation of well-informed research. Kaser warned that many bibliographies narrowed their coverage in an attempt to remain affordable to impoverished libraries (1995). In 1989, for example, the publishers of *Mathematical Reviews* decided to hold future production at current levels (Bartle 1995). As we enter the twenty-first century, bibliographic information services are metamorphosing beyond the database format of the last forty years, raising new questions about what their production statistics reflect. Administrative bias, disinterest, and other influences may also interfere with the usefulness of bibliographies to measure growth. Some examples:

- The database of articles used by the National Science Board in its biennial *Science & Engineering Indicators* is a sample that is not meant to be comprehensive. Its meager growth is far from the rise reported by disciplinary databases. Its use to represent output of science activity is compromised. Comparing sharply increased inputs of money (in constant dollars to remove the effects of inflation) with apparently static outputs of publication and a declining share of U.S. authorship might easily mislead one to conclude that increased percentages of spending are wasted. (An effort to remedy deficiencies in coverage of dissemination was made by National Science Foundation in the mid 1970s under the title *Statistical Indicators of Scientific and Technical Communication 1960–1980* and abandoned suddenly after two years.)

- The 1879 *Index Medicus* covered the totality of the biomedical literature with some 20,000 citations; 100 years later, with an increase of ten times its original output, it covered only 12 percent (Corning and Cummings 1976, p. 729). If its coverage had kept abreast of the literature, at the fifteen-year doubling that Price called the "modern normal rate" (1975, pp. 170–173) it would have increased its output more than 120 times (seven doublings) during its first 100 years. The National Library of Medicine survey of periodicals received during a three-month period estimated that the total number of substantive articles is roughly double the number actually covered by the *Current List of Medical Literature*, then the largest medical index in the world (Brodman and Taine 1958). Notable as an example of how bureaucratic barriers arbitrarily exclude important sources, *Index Medicus* delayed eighteen months before deciding to cover the *Online Journal of Clinical Trials* despite its intrinsically germane peer-reviewed content, a star-quality editorial board, and the considerable reputations of its co-publishers, American Association for the Advancement of Science and Online College Library Center (Wilson 1994). The biomedical literature that is accessible through electronic searching of bibliographies today represents a fraction of all studies in a field (Scherer, Dickersin, and Kaplan 1994). Incidentally, this deficiency presents an insurmountable obstacle for authors inasmuch as standards followed by many publishers ask that new data be interpreted in the light of the totality of available evidence. Authors simply do not comply (Begg, Cho, and Eastwood 1996).
- BIOSIS, which covers the life sciences, has responded to regular growth of the literature it indexes with stepwise increases in coverage (Freedman 1995).
- A search of seven major life sciences databases for references to a common pest turned up only half the total found using nonautomated searching (Deitz and Osegueda 1989).
- Latin American scientists complained that bibliographic services ignore Third World science. They charged that one publisher demanded the purchase of a $10,000 subscription as a requirement for coverage (Gibbs 1995).

Development of Classes of Books—Trade Cloth, Trade Paper,
Mass-Market Paper, Text, STM PSP—That Trade Now
Commonly Aggregates Statistics

The conceptual linking of publishing with the printing industry frustrated the analysis of publishing as a separate activity for a long time. Less than 100 years ago, economists Day and Thomas puzzled over publishing saying, "No adequate figures are available for measuring production" (1928, p. 111). Part of the confusion is that publishing involves intangibles such as financial and intellectual capital, marketing, and goodwill. One need not be a printer to be a publisher. Other sources of confusion are contributed by inconsistent definitions of publishing, by import and export activities, by constant mergers, acquisitions and divestitures, by substantial revenues from licensing, and by the relative ease of entry into and disappearance from the business of publishing. John P. Dessauer pointed out a basic difficulty in adjusting statistical methodologies to accommodate publications by firms that the government does not considered to be publishers (1993). Measuring the economic activity of publishing is made more challenging by the size and diversity of an industry in which thousands of participants record total annual sales that appear minuscule compared to other industries—indeed, beside any giant corporation such as General Electric.

Publishing statistics generally do not include government publications and titles issued by nonpublishing corporations, foundations, hospitals, associations, libraries, museums, religious groups, and the like. The term "gray literature" is applied to titles not tracked by the trade bibliographies that happen to produce statistics as a useful byproduct. In the United States, virtually all foreign-language and government publishing might be considered "gray." The National Technical Information Service, which distributes unclassified reports for many federal agencies, processed 14,063 reports in 1965 and around 80,000 annually in recent years. Some other government agencies that publish include the United Nations, the U.S. Government Printing Office, the Patent and Trademark Office, and innumerable state and municipal agencies that appear in neither industry census data nor trade bibliographies such as *Books in Print*. "Gray literature" poses a great challenge to libraries, and it contributes to library spending and collection data (Gelfand 1997).

Such factors make it important to note that nearly all numbers must be considered estimates based on a narrow view rather than as indisputable facts (Winter 1992). Data from different sources can be impossible to reconcile. One must be satisfied that a given source provides some longitudinal consistency or that it notes the inevitable changes in parameters and process that affect the data. For example:

- *Books in Print 1997–98* reports 57,600 publishers in the United States, a little more than seven doublings in fifty years, from its first publication in 1948 covering 357 publishers. The present 1,350,190 active titles in print, a number that includes reprints, multiple imprints, and new editions, but excludes titles dropped, represent four doublings in fifty years from the original 85,000 titles listed. Peters gives us annual title output production reported to R.R. Bowker's *American Book Publishing Record*—from 2,097 titles in 1880 to 46,743 in 1990, or well over four doublings in just over 100 years (1992). More recent data indicate a sharp increase to the record of 68,175 set in 1996 (Ink 1999).
- The U.S. Census reported 666 establishments engaged primarily in book publishing in 1909 each with an average employment of 423 wage earners. An additional 163 publishers also produced printing. By 1997, the *Economic Census* found 2,684 establishments with a total of 89,898 paid employees. Little mention was made in 1997 of publishers who were printers or of numbers of titles published.

Official U.S. Census data started in 1810 (called the *Census of Manufactures* from 1909 to 1992 and *Economic Census—Manufactures* in 1997). The approach of the Census Bureau to book publishing changed as the industry grew distinct from job printing and as the view of economists became more sophisticated. Its primary focus remains on "establishments" rather than the formats, audiences, numbers of copies or titles, or distribution methods that characterize industry descriptions.

- Early statistics reported numbers of copies "published," while later reports itemized copies "sold."
- Textbooks, which were not recognized in 1909, accounted for 27 percent of book publishers' shipments in 1997. They were segmented into eleven subgroups. Many, such as standardized tests, were unheard of at the beginning of the century.
- Adult and juvenile trade publishers, perhaps the most visible market segment, accounted for 23 percent of 1997 shipments.
- Technical/scientific and professional publishers accounted for 12 percent of 1997 shipments.
- The revision of the Standard Industrial Classification (called the North American Industrial Classification System) continues to focus on establishments, but emphasizes content rather than form. Thus, it groups publishers with other media under "Information" rather than as a subset of paper and printing manufacturers.

U.S. economic census data are a basic referent for the statistics program of the Association of American Publishers (AAP), which began in 1970. Major publishers report annual data to AAP. These reported sales amount to half of industry estimates (Winter 1992). Based on the census data and information gathered by AAP from its members, the Book Industry Study Group has produced *Book Industry Trends* since 1977, annually covering recent years and projecting several years into the future. Publishers' data includes exports, wholesale prices, and the resulting domestic consumer expenditures. Library expenditure data and manufacturing expense data complete the picture.

The growth and diversification of book publishing serves demographic and economic developments in literacy, business, education, research, and professional activity. These patterns stimulate readership, authorship, and institutional markets for published materials. Several measures tripled during the twentieth century:

- The total U.S. population rose from 76 million to over 260 million today.
- Enrollment in public elementary and secondary schools rose from 15.5 million to 45 million.
- Numbers of high-school graduates climbed from 95 thousand to 2.7 million.
- Instructional staff climbed more sharply, from 423 thousand to 3.2 million (U.S. Department of Education. National Center for Education Statistics 1997a, pp. 50, 108).

Greater growth of postsecondary education also supports many aspects of publishing industry growth, ranging from publications for general readers to highly specialized materials aimed at elite niches populated by researchers and their organizations. In terms of the growth of publishing activity, the baby boom in the 1960s—perhaps an aftershock of the GI Bill—is reflected in the sharp growth after 1960. (See Figure3.)

Nearly 4,000 U.S. college and university libraries purchase books of academic interest. The database maintained by Blackwell's Book Services, which serves this market, provides near thirty years of title and price history for English language monographs and reference works, including imports (Wagner 1993; Blackwell's Book Services 1999–2000). The titles are identified by country origin (for example, the United States, United Kingdom) and sorted by Library of Congress Classification, leading to further analysis. For example, scientific, technical, and medical (STM) classes included about 26 percent of 16,271 new books in 1972. STM title output doubled in the following ten years, while the total number of new books took fifteen years to double. By 1999, STM titles constituted 31 percent of the total 31,474 titles recorded (the latter figure excludes popular and undergraduate texts that were found in earlier statistics, numbering 3,839 as late as 1996). Arts and humanities con-

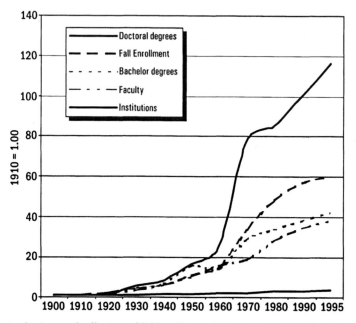

Figure 3. Academic growth affecting publishing. (*Source:* National Center for Education Statistics.)

tributed 35 percent of the 1999 total, while the social sciences accounted for 34 percent. Measuring the significance of foreign publishers, 39 percent were imported.

The increasing affluence of scientific research made a significant impact on the growth of book publishing, as it did on the publication of journals. At the turn of the twentieth century, government sponsorship of academic research and development was not even a wisp of smoke on the statistical horizon. Currently, the federal government stokes university research with $15 billion annually, and industry and other sources contribute another $10 billion. According to *The Bowker Annual of Library and Book Trade Information,* the number of new books of technical interest published per year increased from 3,379 in 1960 to 22,395 by 1997. As a percentage of the total, this broad category rose from 22.5 to 34. *Statistical Indicators of Scientific and Technical Communication* prepared for the National Science Foundation (1976; 1977) estimated that between 1960 and 1977, the number of scientists and engineers in the United States rose from 1.2 million to 2 million; the number of copies of books sold per scientist or engineer rose from 10 to 13.5. Today the National Science Board estimates 3.2 million people with a bachelor's degree or higher were employed as scientists and engineers in 1995 (1998).

Statistical History of the Growth of Book Publishing: Units and Dollars

The current approach to economic statistics divides and subdivides the industry into groups that reflect the views of publishers. The most visible is the "trade" category: books found in book stores, authored by celebrities, scholars, journalists, poets, and professional writers, hardcover and paperback, adult and juvenile, mass market, book clubs, and mail order. Book Industry Study Group (BISG) estimates total sales in this category climbed from $5,023 million to $6,149 million between 1993 and 1998. Unit sales climbed from 789.9 million to 860.3 million books (1999).

In contrast, the *Economic Census* reports sales by primary activity of each establishment: 220 adult trade publishers at $5,112 million, plus 80 religious publishers' $796 million, 10 mass market paperback publishers' $219 million, 34 mail-order publishers' $1,750 million. This totals nearly $7,900 million or 28 percent more than the BISG estimates. The difference is significant only when attempting to reconcile the irreconcilable. The 1997 census, which omits "units sold" data included in earlier tables, also reports:

- One hundred and eighty-two technical, scientific and professional book publishers shipped $2,820 million—about 10 percent—of a total $22,648 million for the total book publishing industry.
- One hundred and fifty-eight textbook publishers shipped $6,190 million.
- Three audio-book publishers shipped $19 million.
- Twenty-nine electronic book publishers (i.e., CD-ROM, diskette) shipped $1,688 million.

*Speculations About the Future of These Forms of
Information/Knowledge Transfer*

Population growth is expected to continue to drive many aspects of publishing. High-school graduations in the year 2000 set new records. As a percentage of the population of seventeen-year-olds, graduates rose from 6.4 percent to 69.7 percent during the twentieth century. The other major factor is technology, a topic subject to hyperbole. Reports of the death of print cite no evidence that this is indeed happening. In fact, when it comes to formal publications deserving archival preservation, the luster of computers' capacity to provide access is clouded by the fragility and perpetual obsolescence of digital media.

The variety of publishing formats provided by new communications media blurs many of the distinctions that were clearly apparent when the only option was mechanical presswork on paper. As an e-book guru employed by

Barnes & Noble remarked to me, he envisioned infinite new potentials for error in providing the correct format for customers' equipment. In addition to hard-cover books and paperbacks, new titles, reprints, and new editions, we can already see audio, microform, and CD-ROM in the statistics with a variety of e-book formats and the Internet waiting in the wings. In addition to books, newspapers, and periodicals, the 1997 economic census data recognize database, directory, software, and greeting card publishers as separate industry segments. Microform publishers are found in an "other" segment that also includes publishers specializing in calendars, maps, yearbooks, newsletters, shopping news, patterns, and the like. Except for acknowledging the value of materials used by publishers, the technology of printers and paper producers has been separated from publishers.

At the same time, the noisy sizzle of modern technology has discouraged investment by publishers and libraries in many of the noblest original works, the real meat of science and culture. Having lost sales to the photocopier and "fair use," publishers ranging from the physics publisher AIP Press to the largest trade houses simply abandoned "midlist" books. University presses, which cautiously offset expansions into trade publishing by demanding subventions for specialized academic manuscripts, may eventually demand subsidies for every title. Those who run university in the United States continue to believe that anything of value will be available from some other source, wherever it may be. They now must import hundreds of thousands of photocopies. They also deny the well-known inability of computers to store information indefinitely. Further erosion of copyright and adoption of new technology is sought now by universities—the very institutions that are charged with the long-term preservation and dissemination of knowledge.

Summary

Reflecting on the development of information science, José-Marie Griffiths recently enumerated some subdisciplines of the field as identified by Fritz Machlup and Una Mansfield about fifteen years ago (2000). Nowhere does Griffiths or her predecessors see any sign of an "information policy"—the reasoned allocation of resources to information. In 1975, the Congressional Research Service reported that a "policy vacuum" interfered with the dissemination of scientific and technical information (U.S. Congress. Senate. Special Subcommittee on the National Science Foundation of the Committee on Labor and Public Welfare, 1975). The following year, Congress passed the National Science and Technology Policy, Organization, and Priorities Act. Among other elements addressing information policy, it called for a President's Committee on Science and Technology (PCST) to be staffed with an expert in dissemination. The panel was to consider "the role to be played by the private sector in the dissemination of information." The U.S. Congress's now-defunct Office of Technology Assessment noted that this and related mandates of the act were never exercised (1989). Moreover, perhaps in passive-aggressive defiance of Congress, the National Science Foundation quietly abandoned its two decades-old program of research into communications behavior. "Dissemination" no longer appears in the policy vocabulary. I have evidence that the National Science Board has trouble spelling it. In fact, I found that the only official use of the word "library" to be in U.S. Office of Management and Budget Circular A-21 (governing reimbursement of $5 billion research overhead), with a formula that comes nowhere near to addressing the use of research collections by government-sponsored scientists (1995).

The confusion of statistics and the routine misrepresentation of facts by policy managers suggest that the policy vacuum is greater than ever. Congressman Newt Gingrich, while Speaker of the House, complained about the "incoherence" of science. He suggested that the problem was rooted in the preference of bureaucrats for process before results (1997). In the so-called "information age," it appears that "information" has little value and less respect, except as an adjective used to promote technology. As Michael Gorman has pointed out, "the *technovandals* want to use technology to break up the culture of learning and . . . to replace that world with a howling wilderness of unstructured, unrelated gobbets of 'information' and random images in which the hapless individual wanders without direction or sense of value" (1994). Thorstein Veblen might have added: "The last resort of the apologists for these more sordid endeavours is the plea that only by this means can the ulterior ends of a civilization of intelligence be served. The argument may fairly be paraphrased to the effect that in order to serve God in the end, we must all be ready to serve the Devil in the meantime" ([1918] 1993, pp. 8–9).

References

Advisory Panel for Scientific Publications. 1992. The cost effectiveness of science journals *Publishing Research Quarterly* 8,3: 72–91. Supplemented by Henderson (1992).

Andrew W. Mellon Foundation. 1993. *University Libraries and Scholarly Communication.* Washington, D.C.: Association of Research Libraries.

Association of Research Libraries. 1989. *Report of the ARL Serials Prices Project.* Washington, D.C.: Association of Research Libraries.

Axford, H. William. 1962. Rider revisited. *College and Research Libraries* 23: 345–347.

Bartle, Robert G. 1995. A brief history of the mathematical literature. *Publishing Research Quarterly* 11,2:3–13.

Barzun, Jacques. 1993. 2d ed. *The American University.* Chicago: University of Chicago Press, 1968.

Baumol, William J., and Sue Anne Batey Blackman. 1983. Electronics, the cost disease, and the operation of libraries. *Journal of the American Society for Information Science* 34,3:181–191.

Begg, C., M. Cho, S. Eastwood, et al. 1996. Improving the quality of reporting of randomonized controlled trials: the CONSORT statement. *JAMA* 276:637–639.

Bell, Daniel. 1971. *The Coming of Post-Industrial Society. A Venture in Social Forecasting.* New York: Basic Books.

Blackwell's Book Services. 1999–2000. North American Approval Program and Cost Study 1998/99. *Publishing Research Quarterly* 15,4:14–22.

Book Industry Study Group. 1999. *Book Industry Trends Covering the Years 1993–2003.* New York: Book Industry Study Group.

Borkowski, Casimir, and M.J.N. MacLeod. 1979. Report on the Kent study of library use: a University of Pittsburgh reply. *Library Acquisitions: Practice and Theory* 3:125–151.

Brodman, Estelle, and Seymour I. Taine. 1958. Current medical literature: A quantitative survey of articles and journals. *Proceedings of the International Conference on Scientific Information.* Washington, D.C. National Academy of Sciences–National Research Council 1959. 435–447.

Bush, Vannevar. 1990. *Science—The Endless Frontier. A Report to the President on a Program for Postwar Scientific Research.* 1945. Reprint, Washington, D.C.: National Science Foundation.

Corning, Mary E., and Martin M. Cummings. 1976. Biomedical communication. Vol. 2 of *Advances in American Medicine.,* Edited by John Z. Bowers and Elizabeth F. Purcell. New York: Josiah Macy Jr. Foundation.

Day, Edmund E., and Woodlief Thomas. 1928. *The Growth of Manufactures 1899 to 1923. A Study of Indexes of Increase in the Volume of Manufactured Products.* Washington, D.C.: U.S. Government Printing Office.

Deitz, L.L., and L.M. Osegueda. 1989. Effectiveness of bibliographic databases for retrieving entomological literature: a lesson based on the Membracoidea (Homoptera). *Bulletin of the Entomological Society of America* 35:33–39.

Dessauer, John P. 1993. The growing gap in book industry statistics. *Publishing Research Quarterly* 9,2:68–71.

Eisenhower, Dwight D. Jan. 17, 1961. Farewell Address.

Freedman, Bernadette. 1995. Growth and change in the world's biological literature as reflected in BIOSIS publication. *Publishing Research Quarterly* 11,3:61–79.

Fry, Bernard M., and Herbert S. White. 1975. *Economics and Interaction of the Publisher–Library Relationship in the Production and Use of Scholarly and Research Journals.* Washington, D.C.: National Science Foundation.

Garvey, William D. 1979. *Communication: The Essence of Science.* Oxford: Pergamon Press.

Gelfand, Julia M. Academic libraries and collection development. *Publishing Research Quarterly* 13,2:15–23.

Gibbs, W. Wayt. 1995. Lost science in the third world. *Scientific American* 273,2: 92–99.

Gingrich, Newt. Oct. 23, 1997. Statement to the House Committee on Science. [originally found at http://www.house.gov/science/gingrich_10_23.htm]

Goodstein, David L. 1995. The era of exponential expansion: implications of its end for student support. *AAAS Science and Technology Policy Yearbook 1995*. Edited by Albert H. Teich, Stephen D. Nelson, and Celia McEnaney. Washington, D.C.: American Association for the Advancement of Science.

Gorman, Michael. 1994. The treason of the learned. The real agenda of those who would destroy libraries and books. *Library Journal* 119,3:130–131.

Griffiths, José-Marie. 2000. Back to the future: information science for the new millennium. *Bulletin of the American Society for Information Science* 26,4:24–27.

Harris, Douglas H., ed. 1994. *Organizational Linkages: Understanding the Productivity Paradox*. Committee on Human Factors, Commission on Behavioral and Social Sciences and Education, National Research Council. Washington, D.C.: National Academy Press.

Henderson, Albert. 1992. Cost effectiveness of science journals. Supplement to the report published in *Publishing Research Quarterly*.

Henderson, Albert. 1999. Information science and information policy. The use of constant dollars and other indicators to manage research investments. *Journal of the American Society for Information Science* 50,4:366–379.

Herring, Conyers. 1968. Distill or drown: the need for reviews. *Physics Today* 21,9:27–33.

Huth, Edward J. 1989. The information explosion. *Bulletin of the New York Academy of Medicine* 65:647–661.

Ink, Gary. 1999. Book title output and average prices. *Bowker Annual 1999*.

Judson, Horace Freeland. 1994. Structural transformations of the science and the end of peer review. *International Congress on Biomedical Peer Review and Scientific Publication*. http://www.ama-assn.org/public/peer/7_13_94/pv3112x.htm

Kalfus, K. 1989. Scientists balk at soaring journal prices. *The Scientist* 3,15:1,16.

Kaser, Richard T. 1995. Secondary information services. Mirrors of scholarly communication. *Publishing Research Quarterly* 11,3:10–24.

King, Donald W., José-Marie Griffiths, Nancy K. Roderer, and Robert R. V. Wiederkehr. 1982. *Value of the Energy Data Base*. Oak Ridge, Tenn.: Technical Information Center, U.S. Department of Energy.

King, Donald W., Dennis D. McDonald, and Nancy K. Roderer. 1981. *Scientific Journals in the United States. Their Production, Use, and Economics*. Stroudsburg, Pa.: Hutchinson Ross Publishing.

Kingson, J.A. 1989. Where information is all, pleas arise for less of it. *The New York Times,* 9 July, E9.

Koshland, D. 1989. Combating high journal costs. *Science* 244:1125.

Machlup, Fritz. 1962. *The Production and Distribution of Knowledge in the United States*. Princeton, N.J.: Princeton University Press.

McClure, Charles R., and Peter Hernon. 1989. *U.S. Scientific and Technical Information (STI) Policies: Views and Perspectives*. Norwood N.J.: Ablex.

Molyneux, Robert. 1986. Patterns, processes of growth, and the projection of library size: a critical review of the literature on academic library growth. *Library and Information Service Research* 8:5–28.

National Enquiry into Scholarly Communication. 1979. *Scholarly Communication. The Report.* Baltimore: The Johns Hopkins University Press.

National Science Board. 1989. *Science & Engineering Indicators 1989.* Washington, D.C.: National Science Foundation.

National Science Board. 1998. *Science & Engineering Indicators 1998* Washington, D.C.: National Science Foundation.

National Science Foundation. 1976. *Statistical Indicators of Scientific and Technical Communication 1960-1980.* Vol. 1. Summary report prepared by D.W. King et al. Vol. 2. A Research Report. Vol. 3. Data Appendix to Vol. 2. Vol. 4. *The Status of Journal Publishing in the United States 1975.* Washington, D.C., Supt. of Documents.

National Science Foundation. 1977. *Statistical Indicators of Scientific and Technical Communication 1960-1980.* Prepared by D.W. King, D.D. McDonald, N.K. Roderer, and C.G. Schell.

Nichols, Rodney W. 1971. Mission-oriented R&D. *Science* 172:29-37.

Nisbet, Robert A. 1997. *Degradation of the Academic Dogma.* New York: Basic Books, 1971. Reprint, New Brunswick, N.J.: Transaction.

Okerson, Ann, and Kendon Stubbs. 1992. Remembrance of things past, present . . . and future? *Publishers Weekly* 27 July, 22-23.

Peters, Jean. 1992. Book industry statistics from the R.R. Bowker Company. *Publishing Research Quarterly* 8,3:12-23.

Piternick, George. 1963. Library growth and academic quality. *College and Research Libraries* 24,3:223-229.

President's Science Advisory Committee. 1963. *Science, Government, and Information. The Responsibilities of the Technical Community and the Government in the Transfer of Information.* Washington, D.C.: U.S. Government Printing Office.

Price, Derek J. de Solla. 1975. *Science since Babylon.* New Haven, Conn.: Yale University Press enl. Ed.

Price, Derek J. de Solla. 1986. *Little Science, Big Science—and Beyond.* New York: Columbia University Press. 1963. Enl. Ed.

Quandt, R.E. and R. Ekman. 1999. Introduction: Electronic publishing, digital libraries, and the scholarly environment. In *Technology and Scholarly Communication* edited by Richard Ekman and Richard E. Quandt. Berkeley: University of California Press.

Rider, Fremont. 1944. *The Scholar and the Future of the Research Library.* New York: Hadham Press.

Scherer, Roberta W., Kay Dickersin, and Elise Kaplan. 1994. The accessible biomedical literature represents a fraction of all studies in a field. In *Editing the Refereed Scientific Journal: Practical, Political, and Ethical Issues.* Edited by Robert A. Weeks and Donald L. Kinser. New York: IEEE Press.

Shera, Jesse H. 1958. Memorandum. *Science and Technology Act of 1958: Analysis and summary prepared by the staff.* Senate Committee on Government Operations. Senate Doc. 90. Washington, D.C: U.S. Government Printing Office.

Shils, Edward. 1975. The academic ethos under strain. *Minerva* 13:1-37.

Shulenburger, David E. 1998. Moving with dispatch to resolve the scholarly communication crisis: from here to NEAR. *Proceedings of the 133rd annual meeting of the Association of Research Libraries. October 14-16, 1998.*

Spitzer, Walter O., Mary Louise Skovron, L. Rachid Salmi, J. David Cassidy, Jacques Duranceau, Samy Suissa, and Ellen Zeiss. 1995. Scientific monograph of the Quebec task force on whiplash-associated disorders: redefining "whiplash" and its management. *Spine* 20, 8S (supplement):1S–73S.

Stahl, Leslie. 1995. Academia exposed! The 60 Minutes file. *Lingua Franca.* 5,3:70–73

Stephan, Paula E., and Sharon G. Levin. 1992. *Striking the Mother Lode in Science: The Importance of Age, Place and Time.* New York: Oxford University Press.

Talbot, Richard. 1984. Lean years and fat years: lessons to be learned. College and research libraries. *Bowker Annual.*

Tenopir, Carol, and Donald W. King 1996. Setting the record straight on journal publishing: Myth versus reality. *Library Journal* 121,5:32–35.

U. S. Congress. Office of Technology Assessment. 1989. *Federal Scientific and Technical Information [STI] in an Electronic Age: Opportunities and Challenges.* Staff paper.

U.S. Department of Education. National Center for Education Statistics. 1997a. *Digest of Education Statistics 1997.* Washington, D.C.: U.S. Government Printing Office.

U.S. Department of Education. National Center for Education Statistics. 1997b. *Status of Academic Libraries in the United States.* Washington, D.C.: U.S. Government Printing Office.

U.S. Executive Office of the President. Office of Management and Budget. 1995. *Principles for Determining Costs Applicable to Grants, Contracts, and Other Agreements with Educational Institutions.* Washington, D.C.: U.S. Government Printing Office.

U.S. Senate. Special Subcommittee on the National Science Foundation of the Committee on Labor and Public Welfare. 1975. *Federal Management of Scientific and Technical Information (STINFO) Activities: The Role of the National Science Foundation.* Washington, D.C.: U.S. Government Printing Office.

Veblen, Thorstein. [1918] 1993. *The Higher Learning in America.* New Brunswick, N.J.: Transaction. Reprint, with a new introduction by Ivar Berg.

Wagner, Celia Scher. 1993. STM monographs—twenty-year retrospective. *Against the Grain* (June): 20–21.

Weber, Ellen J. , Michael L. Callaham, Robert L. Wears, Christopher Barton, and Gary Young. 1998. Unpublished research from a medical specialty meeting. *JAMA* 280,3:257–259.

White, Herbert S. 1990. The 26-mile, 380-yard marathon. *Library Journal* 115,19:51–52.

Wilson, David L. 1994. A journal's big break. National Library of Medicine will index an electronic journal on MEDLINE. *Chronicle of Higher Education,* 26 July, A23–25.

Winter, Robert F. 1992. AAP-BISG book industry data. *Publishing Research Quarterly* 8,3:5–11.

·2·

Introduction

The Change of Book and Journal Infrastructure: Two Publishers, Consolidation, and Niche Publishers

Richard E. Abel

While publishers' offices and practices were undergoing radical technological and procedural change in the course of the twentieth century, an equally radical change was occurring in the business, product, and market objectives. The orientation and structuring was not simply that of the individual publishing houses, but of the entire publishing sector. It is probably most useful to trace the history of these respective developments in sequence.

At the beginning of the twentieth century, most publishers offered a broad general list aimed at appealing to a wide range of book-buying interests. There were, to be sure, a handful of specialist houses that published what we now call science, technology, and medicine (STM) or other books for the professions: law, engineering, and others. They were, however, almost a species unto themselves. As the century advanced, though, following World War I, a band of new publishers entered the lists. They had new ideas about how to attract and capitalize on an emerging mass audience. Horace Liveright and his protégés, Alfred A. Knopf and Bennett Cerf, and others were among this group. While these newcomers soon expanded their editorial interests beyond trade books, most notably into textbooks, their primary focus remained the fiction and nonfiction publications that would find a receptive audience in the increasingly literate, more affluent body of general readers enjoying increasing amounts of leisure, which, in some cases was devoted to reading.

Meanwhile, a few new names and faces entered the fields of specialist publishing, STM, professional, and textbook publishing. Their entry did not produce the electric effect that the new trade publishers had created, but their presence markedly advanced the slow but steady differentiation of subject matter uniquely published by each, and, ipso facto, the audiences served by each.

Roughly two decades after the end of World War II, the great movement of acquisitions and consolidation in the publishing sector was put in motion; it included both domestic and international companies. One of the notable consequences of these repeated domestic and international reshuffling of firms was the vastly faster process of differentiation of both subject matter offered and the market sector that was served by particular publishers. This process of subject matter and market differentiation is still going forward; as managers seek to focus their firms on "businesses," they know best or in which they have been most successful.

An unexpected consequence of these continuing corporate reshufflings of imprints and staff has been the phenomenal growth of small-niche publishers. Many of these have been founded by publishing personnel weary of the musical chairs to which they have been repeatedly subjected at the large publishing houses. Many of these houses, founded and directed by highly talented professionals, are publishing, by design, to highly selective and differentiated audiences. This proliferation of niche publishers has, of course, markedly segmented the total book audience, while at the same time equally markedly increasing the available specialist subject matter among the broad range of books now on offer.

While many of the niche publishers and staff moved to that publishing subsector out of discouragement with corporate reshuffling or to pursue their profession as entrepreneurs, their success depended overtly and critically upon the continuing rapid introduction of the radical technological improvements—in short-run production as described above. Niche audiences are typically limited and by definition are unable to take up that quantity of copies of a title economically demanded by the older long-run technologies. In the absence of the new short-run technologies, the vast percentage of today's niche publishers would be unthinkable.

The broad classes of book subject matter and the audiences being served can most usefully be distinguished as follows:

1. Perhaps the most visible, because the government agencies that subsidize them must generate ever-continuing streams of publicity to legitimize their expenditure of tax monies, are the "small presses." The latter

specialize in avant garde literary publishing and serve relatively small and uneconomic markets for experimental, esoteric, and similar literature.

2. "Special interest" publishers serving numerous and widely diverse groups typically oriented to advancing narrow and clearly defined sociopolitical agendas.

3. Almost countless hobbyist groups serving every imaginable can of "spare time" interest. Probably the publishers publishing to the numerous groups of collectors of every imaginable object are the most evident representatives of this class of niche publishers.

4. Another quite visible body of niche publishers is dedicated to the knowledge requirements of the numerous vocational groups that make up the modern economy. The publications here range from finance to management to craft skills.

5. Lastly, a large body of niche publishers publishes in scholarly subject areas. The audiences served by these publishers are composed exclusively of serious students, both academic and lay, of specialized bodies of knowledge.

Few of the books published by the various niche publishers share the kind of visibility associated with trade, paperback, and textbooks. This is so because niche publishers serve clear and well-defined needs and, hence, audiences, as distinguished from the mass popular or other large markets. Niche books must, therefore, be marketed and promoted in quite other ways than those employed by the general trade and textbook publishers. Niche book marketing is confined almost exclusively to direct-mail shots to previous customers and presumed potential future buyers based on purchases by the latter of related books or journals. It may be said then that niche publishers have, given the present structures of the retail maketplaces for books, resorted to the nineteenth-century marketing technologies of the large direct-mail firms such as Sears Roebuck and Montgomery Ward to reach their audiences. This marketing strategy may be yielding in some small measure to the appearance of the chain super-store and the Internet bookseller.

It seems entirely clear that in an increasingly complex world marked by growing numbers of specialized interests, undertakings, vocations, and bodies of knowledge that readers will be served by a parallel growth in the niche publishers serving such interests.

•2•

Part One

*Technology in Publishing:
A Century of Progress*

Peter Adams

1901–1930: As It Was

If you walked into a publishing house in 1901, you would find very few typewriters and no copiers. Authors submitted manuscripts in longhand, and editors processed them by hand and forwarded them, with production markup, to the composition house. Costly typewriters were available, but not all publishers could afford them. Correspondence was processed manually, although carbon paper helped in retaining an office copy of letters that went out. Home delivery of newspapers was carried out principally by children.

Copy Preparation

The term "typewriter" described both the machine and its operator. The person and the machine, plus loose carbon paper together constituted office automation. Manuscripts were retyped repeatedly, with carbons, well into the 1960s.

Composition

Outside specialists—compositors—set type and justified everything from menus to encyclopedias either by hand-setting foundry type or at the keyboard of the newly developed Linotype and Monotype machines, which had been available since 1890. Proof sheets that were the length of a printer's galley tray were returned to the editor for correction and later casting off into pages. Illustrations were engraved in wood or copper, or processed as halftones by a costly photographic method requiring yet another group of out-side specialists. Such an expensive effort, together with the aura of gravity and permanence associated with metal type and letterpress, made for meticulous design, layout, editing, and "correcting of the press," often lacking in today's era of instant solutions.

Printing and Binding

At the start of the twentieth century, the letterpress process—in which pages of metal type locked into a form were inked and pressed into a sheet of paper—was the only choice, regardless of the kind of material to be replicated.

High-quantity, high-speed methods, such as the use of stereotype plates for long press runs, had been developed to achieve some economies of scale. Colossal web-fed rotary presses worked well for newspapers but were not feasible for scholarly monographs and journals with their relatively limited circulation. Offset lithography, first developed in 1905, slowly began to present a challenge to letterpress printing. The virtues of offset included better print quality on unsurfaced papers, less ink consumption, faster throughput, reliable color processes, and easier make-ready through the use of lightweight zinc plates. A century-long transition from letterpress began and is still in progress.

Book papers of the period, alas, were "improved" with acid-rich processes, a practice that today threatens the survival of much printed matter of the era.

Short-Run Manufacturing

Book and journal printing in short-run quantities was unthinkable for all but the most exotic of limited collector's editions. Although printing costs were relatively low, economies of scale dictated that press runs should exceed 500 to 1,000 copies.

Marketing and Distributing

The chief marketing methods for books were reviews, book departments, advertising in periodicals, and the judicious use of serialization in magazines, still used today. Salesmen called on bookstores and wholesalers. Coupon ads, the precursors of today's direct mail, used catchy headlines and beguiling copy to attract buyers for products such productions as *Dr. Eliot's Five Foot Shelf of Books* or Doubleday's *Book of Etiquette*. In 1926 the Book-of-the-Month Club opened a new, direct channel for marketing books by mail; the Literary Guild followed a year later. Booksellers, at first disturbed by the potential threat to their business, eventually approved book clubs because of their ability to reach and develop new readers and customers.

Back Office

The publisher's back office was powered by good penmanship, a few manual typewriters, and carbon paper with some support from spirit duplicators from Gestetner and A.B. Dick. Specialist correspondents clarified orders and maintained accounts, transcribing orders onto shipping documents for the warehouse, and filing many copies with elaborate indexing systems by customer, date, or title. In 1912 the U.S. Postal Service began shipping parcel post, reducing the dependency of publishers on private freight forwarders.

1931–1960: Electric Publishing

By 1931 the publisher's office had come a long way from the turn of the century. Typewriters, now plentiful and cheap, were being used everywhere. Many facilities were air-conditioned The mass-market paperback book was everywhere (except in bookstores). New machines, for duplicating from stencils, copying, and platemaking were being tried. New media such as fax and microfilm, were the subjects of experiments. Punched-card equipment had invaded the back office, and printing companies were changing over to offset lithography as illustrations and color crept into publications.

Copy Preparation

Two devices were developed in the 1940s that enabled in-house copy preparation: the Varityper and the slightly later IBM Executive Electric Typewriter with proportional spacing. The Varityper used a fixed type element that was joggled (in the manner of the much-later IBM Selectric) to impress each character to the paper. The Varityper operator entered a line of text twice first to get the character count and second to produce the justified line. The IBM Executive with proportional spacing was able to produce acceptable but unjustified camera-ready copy. Some publishers were able to "set" acceptable copy using these devices (see "Short-Run Manufacturing" below).

Composition

Linotype and Monotype composition machines were joined by Ludlow and Intertype devices. In 1956, research into photomechanical methods produced the first Photon, based on a photographic type matrix, but the technology was not to spread until the 1960s.

Printing and Binding

Advances in perfect binding fostered the development of mass-market paper-back books in the 1930s. High-speed rotary magazine presses, dragooned into use for manufacturing huge quantities of Armed Services Editions in uniform format during World War II, provided valuable lessons in manufacturing. During the period, offset, whose advantages were understood first by consumer-magazine publishers, and during the 1940s by publishers of four-color school textbooks, continued to grow.

Practical microfilm cameras, readers, and printers were introduced in the 1940s, although the technology had been developed much earlier. The first major application of microfilm was the recording of 22 million pages of English literature for the British Museum, another wartime application. Microfilm quickly became accepted as a substitute for the publication of dissertations, and UMiI adroitly became a repository for abstracts. The university presses, liberated from this task, enlarged their editorial programs beyond the confines of their own campuses; the growth thus begun in wartime continues today. It was believed that microfilm would also foster the printing on demand of entire works, but the technology did not catch on for general distribution of print.

Short-Run Manufacturing

Fueled in part by mimeograph and spirit duplication, short-run techniques began to emerge out of need for alternatives to giant press runs and out of wartime necessity: the Japanese surrender documents were prepared by Varityper and printed by Multilith, the emerging small-scale offset press. After the war, the IBM Executive was combined with a new electrostatic ("xerographic") process to transfer camera copy of scientific articles from typed originals to Multilith plates for the short-run manufacture of journals at publishing houses such as Consultants Bureau an early instance of end-to-end in-house publishing. This technique avoided the use of an out-of-house photo studio to shoot the originals and transfer them photographically to offset plates—a costlier and slower process.

Marketing and Distribution

Armed Services Editions taught publishers that the appetite for books of all kinds was not limited to bookstore customers, and to an extent emboldened early paperback publishers such as Penguin, Pocket, Bantam, and Signet to broaden their lists considerably to offer Homer and Dr. Spock along with the usual popular fiction and how-to literature. These books were distributed to many more mass-market outlets—in drugstores, newsstands, railroad stations, bus terminals and airports—than is the practice today.

Facsimile transmission experiments were begun by newspapers such as the *St. Louis Post-Dispatch* offering "radio facsimile" copies of the paper to properly equipped customers in 1938. The development of microfilm also held forth the promise of printing on demand, but the technology did not catch on for general distribution of print.

Back Office

The hard-pressed clericals of the back office began to use punched-card equipment for gathering sales and inventory information from invoices. Many publishers adopted machines like the Friden Flexowriter or Computyper to prepare invoices and produce punched paper tape as a by-product for later processing. The quest for a way to connect devices and processes was under way, but it would take longer than anyone could have imagined to find reliable and usable solutions.

1961–1980: Early Electronic Solutions and Their Impact

By the mid 1970s the publisher's office had been transformed again. The principal goal of technologists was "machine-readable" text that could be edited and formatted without being keyboarded again. The spread of the plain-paper copier, begun by the Xerox 914, affected editorial and production units, as well as the back office. By the end of the 1980s futurists were predicting the "paperless office" based on networked word-processing machines. With copiers everywhere, however, publishers went the other way. The development of "what-you-see-is-what-you-get" (WYSIWYG) display and output technologies were to come later. Experiments with data communication were begun in the dark recesses of the DP department. Early providers of on-line data (OCLC, MEDLINE, Dialog) were launched but audiences were small.

Copy Preparation

Publishers and technology companies sought after "electronic publishing" without real success. The IBM Magnetic Tape Selectric Typewriter (MTST) was an improvement over devices such as the earlier pneumatic RoboTyper for copy preparation and promotional mailing. The later Magnetic Card Selectric was a step forward. The magnetic media were, of course, incompatible with the mainframe computers of the day, preventing the use of computers for sorting or indexing.

Various electronics companies such as Wang Laboratories diddled with word processors, text editors, and formatters to provide the functionality that IBM's Administrative Terminal System never could. Despite obstacles, Wang and Lanier in the late 1970s marketed successful minicomputer-based WP systems that publishers could use for copy management. These systems featured on-screen editing and formatting, but no WYSIWYG. They were encumbered by slow and cantankerous daisy-wheel printers. Some WP manufacturers, including Wang, offered a small and limited-font photocomposition system as an output device, elevating in-house composition to a new but problematic level. In-house facilities competed with traditional outside composition shops with four shortcomings: (1) no second or third shift, (2) no substantial experience, (3) no other customers, and (4) no budget for entertaining their one customer, and (5) no specialists in the special handling of customer input.

But the quest for high-end in-house composition would not end with the word processing systems of the 1970s, whose days were numbered.

Composition

Unmindful of the developments within their publisher-clients, the composition firms, from 1965 to 1980, perfected electronic photocomposition and rapidly displaced thousands of traditional Linotype and Monotype machines along with their highly skilled operators in many cases. Photon had started things in France in the 50s, but, spurred by machines such as RCA's heavy-duty VideoComp (1966), which used photo-matrices but was attached to a costly mainframe, other companies moved ahead to put on the market equipment based on cathode-ray etching of characters based on electronic fonts and later to laser imaging in just a few years. From 1970 to 1980, more 100 machines were marketed. These included Compugraphic, Harris' TXT, Mergenthaler's VIP, and the Photon 7000 which later became Autologic. The next wave of machines used laser engines to create output directly on paper.

Printing and Binding

From 1961 onward, printing and binding technologies became ever more refined, with photo-offset lithography, driven by the publishers' growing infatuation with color, continued to make gains over letterpress. Acid-free paper was introduced to correct the problems caused by earlier "improvements" in papermaking that occurred at the turn of the century. The big gains, however, were in the short-run arena.

Short-Run Manufacturing

The Xerox 914 plain-paper copier, and its offspring, dramatically increased the choices open to short-run customers. Copy shops proliferated to serve smaller firms while larger publishers spread copiers into every department. It was now possible to replicate small batches of paper originals that had a professional look if not always of the highest typographic quality.

Marketing and Distribution

New ways to distribute books were being studied. In the early 1960s the promise of the teaching machine (delivering instructional "software" in lieu of printed textbooks) seemed just around the corner. RCA, CBS, Westinghouse, Xerox, and other electronics companies purchased publishers only to divest them later when it became apparent that the machines were not soon going to be adopted in schools. Visionaries like Alan Kay experimented with handheld devices like the DynaBook (1975), but almost all the required computer components were still too big, and too slow, to enable personal readers. Late in the 1970s a few pioneering on-line services such as OCLC, MEDLINE, and Dialog were launched, mostly for professionals.

Back Office

Mainframe computers spread as the IBM 3601370 and its rivals became available at ever lower cost and with improved performance. The programs to run in-house order processing and similar activities were all hand-written by the publisher because off-the-shelf business systems for publishers were not developed until the minicomputer boom of the mid to late 1970s.

1981–1990: Things Come Together

By the very early 1980s computers were no longer confined to a glass-fronted ultracool showroom. Smaller machines began to proliferate in and around editorial and production offices. These machines, the remarkably expensive word processing systems of the era, proliferated and were frequently set up next to the desktop computers that eventually were to replace them. The use of facsimile transmission, originally the province of the legal department in the 1960s, became widespread among the publishers after the introduction of the digital Group III fax standard. Authors whose articles were "almost finished" found that they had no place to hide.

Copy Preparation

The migration of "word processing" software from minicomputer-based systems to the personal computer took place during this decade. The triggering event in this period was the confluence in 1984 of the graphical user interface (Apple Macintosh) with the Apple LaserWriter and Aldus PageMaker, leading to WYSIWYG at the display and on paper, joined with what became the PostScript page-description language. This combination allowed in-house editors and production persons to create and modify finished pages to be sent outside only for mastering in final form. Copy preparation and composition became the same process.

Composition

Composition houses reinvented themselves as service bureaus and output houses, providing services that continued to be impractical in house.

Printing and Binding

High-speed offset presses were now supplemented in special applications by computer-driven laser printers, of which an early example was the Xerox 9700, used to produce frequently-updated text, tables, and charts for *Value Line*.

Short-Run Manufacturing

Large-scale copiers such as the Xerox 5000 series, enabled short-run printing, collation, and primitive binding of some book-length material.

The Xerox DocuTech (1988) made possible the storage of sets of originals for reuse and practical printing on demand. The DocuTech's relatively high price prevented its wide use in publishing.

Marketing and Distribution

Pioneering on-line services continued to grow, but were hampered by prevailing data communications technology that required a slow and constant peer-to-peer "connection" in order to transfer information.

Chain bookstores such as Waldenbooks and B. Dalton grew to dominate trade book distribution.

Back Office

Minicomputers and their off-the-shelf publishing systems suffered as the wave of personal computers, started by the IBM PC in 1981, splashed through business offices and accounting departments. Nevertheless, it took a decade to transfer stable business software to the PC because of memory and speed limitations on early models.

Stacks of modems proliferated in the DP departments as data communications between back office, branch office, and warehouse became cost-effective for transmitting orders and similar applications.

1991–2000: Things Hang Together

Copy Preparation and Composition

Desktop machines with lots of memory and good network capabilities drove the spread of Mac-based copy preparation and design. Quark Xpress came to dominate the page-makeup field. Other electronic formats such as Adobe Acrobat emerged for other purposes. Feared incompatibility between the Mac and IBM PC was overcome or neutralized.

Printing and Binding

Mergenthaler-Hell and others developed new lower-cost presses for short-run in color. Research and development produced ways to produce plates direct from the publisher's final-form output.

"Printing-on-demand" devices proliferated, but were still somewhat hampered by lack of a compact binding feature to produce a professional finish. Endless experiments with hand-held reading appliances, or "e-books," as a substitute for print, sputtered—starting with the Sony ReadMan of 1991 and ending with the Franidin eBookman of 2000. In the words of the futurist Paul Saffo, "Like a comet in some giant, loopy orbit, the electronic book comes around every 8 or 10 years, not quite hitting the Earth but coming closer each time."

Short Run Manufacturing

IBM introduced a high-speed web-fed laser-print device that became the basis of Lightning Print in 1997. Other, smaller machines have entered the market. Printing on demand has now been joined by "delivery on demand" via the World Wide Web to desktops, the above-mentioned reading appliances, and hand-held personal information managers such as the Palm Pilot. Serious questions about print-on-demand remain, especially marketing and where ideally to situate the machines.

Marketing and Distribution

The confluence of lower-cost telecommunication, ease of use of client-server architecture (no more connection problems), and the attractive visual idiom of the World Wide Web brought an audience of millions to an immense global network. This is changing marketing, with easy-to-find websites helping customers find books, journals, and articles for sale. Some even say that authors will no longer need publishers in order to reach the public.

Back Office

Networking continually tightened the links between publishers, wholesalers, booksellers, and consumers. Large publishers with many imprints and business units engaged in large-scale rebuilding of in-house systems at large-scale cost. Rather than rely on intermediaries, many—journals publishers in particular—have now built e-commerce hubs of their own.

Retrospective

The Impact on People and Professions

- *Authors and editors,* in the opinion of many, still have difficult tasks not much improved by twentieth-century technology. Authors must create. Editors must find new sources of talent and nurture them.
- *Production persons* within the publishing house have changed greatly. Originally designing and marking up manuscript, these folk have now brought new tools to bear in the entire graphic-arts process—working with images, tables, and all forms of matter to be disseminated—all in house.
- *Typesetters, compositors, and printers* have to a large extent disappeared as more and more of the prepress process moved back to the publisher. Printers, now almost entirely pressmen on large photo-offset facilities, continue their craft with skill and precision. The lower-end job printer has been replaced by copy shops and chains of copy shops.
- *Marketing and distribution* personnel have better tools than in earlier times. But the mission—to reach as many in an audience as possible—remains daunting.
- *Back-office staff* have found that the "paperless office" has not quite yet arrived. New tools for record-keeping and reporting have not simplified the business side of publishing, as authors and agents create ever-increasing numbers of royalty payments arrangements on which reports must be rendered.

In other words, automation has impacted publishing persons quite selectively. It has ended the careers of many craftsmen in the graphic arts while creating opportunities for everybody with a computer to be an artist.

The Impact on Processes

The process of writing *is* easier for some and will become easier still when the obstacle of the keyboard is removed by reliable voice-to-computer systems for creating text and by improved methods for editing text and images on screen.

The publishing process—the mean time from manuscript to printed copy—has improved, on average. Modern tools make it easier and cheaper to take a simple text through the process of publication. However, rapid publication is nothing new: in 1953, given limited access to the Yalta papers, the *New York Times,* in a single day, managed to transmit the full text of 383,000 words from Washington, D.C. to the composing room in New York, producing a fifty-page supplement to the morning paper. It would be easier to do this today, since the combination of ThermoFax copiers and teleLinotype has been replaced with better scanners and faster transmission; but how much faster? And our newspapers are still delivered by children.

◆2◆

Part Two

Differentiation of Publishing by Class of Publication

Richard Zeldin

Trade Books

Description

Trade books are books that are published for the general reader. This publishing area covers a wide range of subject matter, including fiction, nonfiction, biography, travel, art, sports, cooking, "how-to" books, and other specialized categories. Most trade books are issued in hard cover, but a good number are published in soft cover as quality paperbacks at a higher price than mass-market paperback titles. Some books have short lives; others stay in print for years and are called backlist titles.

Manuscript Considerations

Trade-book authors are almost always represented by a literary agent. The agent's job is to place the prospective manuscript with the appropriate publisher. Today, agents do most of the screening of newly submitted manuscripts, a job that individual publishers used to do. Very few unsolicited manuscripts are accepted for publication "over the transom"—that is, not submitted by an agent—by the major publishers.

Distribution

These books can be easily purchased in large bookstores (Barnes & Noble, Borders, Walden Books), independent bookstores, the Internet, and nontrade outlets such as price clubs and other specialized outlets. Obviously, libraries of all kinds are a market for trade books. The book jobber, or distributor, plays a key role in serving the various book outlets. Important markets for trade books include foreign markets, as well as translation by foreign publishers. Sale of reprint rights and subsidiary sales are also important income sources.

Mass-Market Paperbacks

Description

Mass-market paperback books are usually books of broad interest designed to be sold to a general market at a lower price than a hard cover trade book. Subject matter covers a wide spectrum that includes westerns, mysteries, romance, science fiction, and other genres. Many titles are reprints of hard-cover trade books, but some are first published as paperbacks.

Manuscript Considerations

As in trade books, manuscripts for mass-market paperback books are directed by a literary agent to the proper publisher. However, it should be remembered that the majority of mass-market paperbacks are reprints of hard-cover titles.

Distribution

Paperback books can be found in many different places. Popular outlets include general bookstores, college bookstores, news stands, drug stores, and supermarkets. Specialty outlets such as garden and hardware stores sell related paperbacks. Generally, the independent news wholesaler services the various markets.

Juvenile Literature

Description

As the name implies, juvenile books are books developed for children. They have relatively few pages, are heavily illustrated, and are published in a wide variety of sizes and formats.

Manuscript Considerations

Most juvenile manuscripts come to the publisher unsolicited, that is, over the transom. Some are already illustrated; others require the work of an illustrator. Few are handled by an agent. In most cases, the publisher's editor engages the proper illustrator, who works independently of the author.

Distribution

The institutional market, libraries of all types, are the chief buyers of juvenile books. The secondary market is similar to trade-book distribution.

Elementary and Secondary School Texts

Description

Elementary and secondary school books and programs are developed for elementary and secondary school students. In this publishing area, supplementary materials are very important. These include computer programs, tapes, audiovisual materials, project and workbooks, kits, lab manuals, tests, teacher guides, and other materials.

Manuscript Considerations

Texts in this area mainly originate with the publisher. The publishing company evaluates a particular subject area as to the number of pupils enrolled, competitive titles, curriculum trends, and other factors. The publisher next assembles a team to develop the manuscript and related materials. The team includes a subject-matter specialist (generally a teacher), an illustrator, a curriculum expert, and the publisher's editor, who oversees the project. Frequently, the editor actively participates in the writing and choice of illustrative material. Other experts are called on if the "package" includes supplementary materials, such as tapes, audiovisual materials, tests, kits, and the like.

Distribution

Texts are promoted and sold by the publisher's representatives. who call on individual schools, textbook adoption committees, and attend meetings of education professionals. Direct mail promotion and journal advertising also play a role. Telemarketing proves valuable in those areas where it is too expensive or remote to support a sales representative. In some cases, texts are pretested in selected schools.

College Textbooks

Description

This area includes texts, anthologies, workbooks, lab manuals, teaching aids, computer materials, and study guides for the undergraduate and graduate student. This includes basic texts, as well as related supplementary material in both print and other formats.

Manuscript Considerations

In the main, college texts are written by college professors who write to reflect the course that they teach. Manuscripts are reviewed by the publisher's advisors as to accuracy, relevance, scope, and any other element that reflects the use of a text. The publisher may also suggest supplementary material to make the text more useful and competitive with existing works. Because modern areas of interest change rapidly, the book must be planned carefully so that it will be saleable for several years.

Distribution

Publishers' representatives do the bulk of promoting texts to college professors. Direct mail, educational meetings, and advertising in professional journals are also used. A major problem is the used-book market, which recirculates used books into the market, making it extremely difficult for publishers to estimate sales and make economical printing decisions.

Professional Books

Description

This category includes fundamental material for the professional in the areas of science, engineering, business, and technology. The level of interest ranges from the introductory level to the advanced scientific or professional level. Publishing mirrors the growth of the various professional categories on every level. These books are practical tools for those already working in a given field.

Manuscript Considerations

The most successful books in this category are written by professionals practicing in a particular field. Sometimes the books are an expansion of an article written for a professional journal. This field is famous for the "branching" or "twigging" phenomenon in which major areas are subdivided and in time further subdivided into practical publishing areas. Major handbooks with sections written by experts that cover a broad engineering, scientific, or business area are prominent in this publishing category. A publisher is able to estimate the market for a specific title by examining the number of individuals active in the field.

Distribution

It is unfortunate that there are relatively few stores with a good representative selection of professional books. Major college bookstores are a good source, as are various Internet sites. The major outlets such as Barnes & Noble, Borders, and Walden Books generally have good selections. Direct mail, journal advertising, card packs, and attendance at professional meetings are ways publishers promote their books. The overseas market is also a fertile avenue for the professional book publisher.

Scholarly Books

Description

These are generally specialized books, many with regional themes, appealing to relatively limited markets. Books of this type are the bread and butter of university presses. Because of the small printings, publication is usually subsidized in some form, by either the university, a professional society, or an association.

Manuscript Considerations

The specialized nature of many of the titles makes it difficult for the publisher to evaluate manuscripts, and reviewers are frequently used prior to arriving at a publishing decision.

Distribution

Most scholarly books reach readers through academic and special libraries. Scholarly publishers also use direct mail in limited mailings to their specialized audience.

Legal and Medical Books

Description

As the name implies, these are books aimed at the specialized areas of law and medicine. They include titles for students as well as practitioners.

Manuscript Considerations

These books are written by professionals in the fields and are given a thorough peer review before publication. The books can be broad-based and cover entire area more limited in scope, reviewing a narrow range of subject matter.

Distribution

Direct mail is the primary method of reaching potential buyers; mailing lists are easily available.

•3•

Growth and Change in Trade Publishing: What I Learned at the Library

Sam Vaughan

It was about the size of our living and dining rooms combined. This library occupied part of a settlement house. Settlement houses were community facilities, set up to help immigrants newly arrived in the United States, to find their feet and eventually their futures. To me, a boy under ten, a fairly new arrival in the world of the 1930s myself (and newly literate), this place was a piece of paradise. Lined floor to ceiling with shelves of books, it seemed immense.

I had heard about St. Martha's House. But the carving in the stone lintel over the front door read *St. Martha's Hovse.* Puzzled by the misspelling—no one I knew spoke Gothic—but willing to mispronounce it if they insisted, I stood in that one seemingly vast room and, like millions of kids before and since, resolved to start with the first book on the upper left, high in the A's, and read through all the rest.

I begin this essay with a memory of a personal moment because reliable data about books and reading are hard to come by, and I don't propose to spread more misinformation. My essay will be merely typical, anecdotal—a few experiences of a person who stumbled into the community of the book through a glass door marked *LIBRARY* and never left.

Later, in the South Philadelphia High School for Boys, scouting that library's shelves, I pulled down a novel called, I think, *Tap Root,* by a then-popular Southern writer named James Street. The story could have been catalogued under "steamy." Thumbing through the pages, I came upon a passage describing two people in love. Or at least in bed.

It stirred me strangely. Soon, because my body as well as mind was beginning to be affected, I sat down. The moment was eye opening. Mine eyes had seen the glory. . . .

> *Lesson 1 for the day:* Libraries could move one deeply. Leave it
> to others to learn the laws of gravity, magnetism, or astronomy.
> My specialty had become the evolution of species; I had
> evolved right on the spot.

> *Lesson 2:* Books, words on paper, had power.

My next major experience of books was at a place where many were produced. After college, I began work at Doubleday, publishers of what were called, archaically, "trade books." (They issued books to be sold primarily through the book trade, that is, book retailers and wholesalers.) Other kinds of publishers, I'd learn, put out textbooks, technical or scientific works, or were university presses or academic publishers, or trafficked in mail-order books. Some houses were known as "library publishers" because their principal customers were librarians; many of their books were highly specialized, even arcane.

It was 1952. I came to the vocation largely unprepared, except for a love of books—which everyone would soon assure me was not enough—from *Treasure Island* through Thomas Wolfe to *The Catcher in the Rye*. Oh, yes—I also had a little practical experience in editing a college humor magazine and in founding a literary magazine that lasted several issues before it foundered. At Doubleday, my job was to sell serial rights or excerpts to magazines and to syndicate certain books to newspapers. Ours was a two-man department— thus, I was the "assistant manager," an early example of title inflation or social promotion. One of the first books that I saw published and even had a very minor hand in, was a "small" book, thought to be rather "special." The first printing was set initially at under 5,000 copies. I thought it a doubtful prospect, too fragile a candidate for newspaper syndication, but my boss liked the book and wanted to try. We sold it to a half-dozen or so papers, most of them major ones, and they helped contribute to the starburst and fireworks the little book caused. This journal of a young girl named Anne Frank remains special to this day, although hardly small.

> *Lesson Learned:* Trust your own opinions but don't confuse
> them with the truth. Or with prophesy.

> *Additional lesson:* With a phenomenal book, all bets are off, as
> is conventional wisdom.

Doubleday was then one of the largest, uniquely organized, and best-known of the general publishers, with its fabled mail-order address in Garden City, New York. Although the house's marketing tilt was toward booksellers (as well as book clubs), there were said to be no more than three or four hundred good bookstores in the entire country. Most were said to be in a dozen big cities. Some said that the country could not support many more. That "information" was flawed and prejudiced, like many of the "facts" still circulated about the book world. Still, the general idea was probably correct. There were too few first-rate bookshops, just as there were said to be too many books. ("Too many books!" was a cry heard in Florence during the fifteenth century and very likely earlier. Someone must have muttered it immediately prior to the destruction of the great library at Alexandria.)

Such a sad condition in our country was blamed on the "Americans," a group of persons as disparate and elusive as "The American People," for whom every political candidate has the presumption to speak. The Americans just were not readers.[1]

Or the blame was ascribed to publishers themselves for not setting up bookshops, or further subsidizing the ones that existed with higher discounts. At times, blame for the eternal "decline" in reading was assigned to the "schools," despite clear evidence that every year, now as then, millions of modestly literate graduates are loosed upon the nation. The *Harry Potter,* or the *Roots* sort of phenomenon always confounds. Anyone who has watched the sales of good children's books to libraries and the best bookstores in the latter part of the twentieth century should find it difficult to swallow whole the libels committed upon our children and their influences, including parents, librarians, teachers, television, radio, movies, their peers, computers, and acne.

Even then, I saw the conundrum: How could Doubleday, a publisher aspiring to "vertical integration," and to become the "General Motors of Publishing," with its book clubs, printing plants, bookstores, and other parts, be doing so well if (1) there were so few good booksellers and (2) if Americans didn't read?

Here again, evidence was everywhere. For example: even the lesser bookstores sold books. Also, many of the most dynamic or "personal" booksellers in those days were not in bookstores but in department stores—John Wanamaker, Miller & Rhoads, Marshall Field, Rich's of Atlanta, and others, some clusters of which would later give birth to the modern "chain" store. Stores other than bookstores sold books: stationery and certain drug or general stores, the more elaborate or ambitious newspaper and magazine stands

---

1 A charge I've since heard levied against the pleasure-loving, lazy Italians by pleasure-loving, lazy Italian publishers; against the Filipinos, a hard-working, self-improving group if I ever saw one; even against the notoriously literate British, by their publishers.

and shops. No one read except when a *Gone with the Wind* or a *Caine Mutiny* came along, and then everyone appeared to be reading.

But I had begun to bump into the splendid contradictions and complexities, eccentricities and anomalies, of the community of the book.

A fresher example: Today, with corporate capitalism's love of numbers, all sorts of bean-counters as well as cultural watchdogs peer intently at (or genuflect before) the bestseller lists. But what do such listings tell us? The whole story? Not quite. They omit the part of the story that libraries could tell. There is no widely recognized count of which books are the most circulated, or, in effect, the best read, if not the most frequently bought. Library circulations go untabulated by the book publishing world, thus missing what in the magazine world they speak of "pass along" readership. A magazine's secondary life, its unpaid circulation, can be useful in attracting advertisers. How does one library's copy of a book, or two, or three, circulating freely (for years) compare in readership to how many copies sold at your local Book Nook?

With all their talk, one wonders how many of today's marketing-minded publishers know that there are, for instance, some 41,000 elementary and secondary school and library media specialists. Or 24,000 academic and professional library folks. And at least 65,000 librarians throughout the nation.

They are a small city of book buyers and readers in themselves and they are not on the usual maps. I know only because I read those numbers in *Library Journal.*

Doubleday was different in other ways at that time. Its respect for middle-brow authors and readers of popular fiction and history was consistent. In addition, as publishers, they believed the United States to be more than the vision in cartoonist Saul Steinberg's well-known myopic map of the United States. Most trade publishers had fewer than a dozen salesmen "covering" the country. It was not uncommon for a book traveler to have three or five states as his territory. The publishing nation was seen by many as composed largely of New York (Manhattan, ignoring, for the most part, the "outer" boroughs, cities in themselves), Philadelphia, Boston (a sort of suburb of London), and, just beyond the Hudson, a bump in the horizon called Chicago. San Francisco was a book town, but Los Angeles was not. If a traveler had time, there were a few frontier outposts like Cleveland, maybe Miami, and just for laughs, you could stop in and take an order or two in Dallas, Detroit, or Washington (D.C., not state).

Doubleday was unique in that it fielded a second sales force to call on public and school libraries. It took some time before I learned that the S&L men's main markets were not the big city, big budget systems that everyone else coveted but smaller, even rural institutions. Puzzling.

The demeanor and demands of these S&L reps were different from those of the trade sales force—they seemed less literary and less oriented toward blockbusters. They welcomed "clean" books and wanted advance warnings of controversial content to protect their customers. They approved of well-bred, bloodless English mysteries; sexless, cozy romances by female authors with three names (this was the pre-Harlequin Age); and almost all children's books except those that—trafficked in rough reality. These travelers didn't worry overmuch about retail prices, while the trade men always argued for lower pricing. S&L books were often re-bound by outside binderies. Such re-clothing in a forerunner of ballistic nylon made the books apparently bullet-proof. It made them more expensive as well. Why re-bind? First, books were expected to last. Second, publisher's bindings were getting flimsier. Third, children could not be trusted to forego eating them. (One could envision the movie to be made out of the havoc wrought upon children's books: "SWARM!! Attack of the Killer Kids!")

Anyone with even a minimal grasp of publishing economics—such as mine—could see that you couldn't afford a sales force that sold books in the boondocks in ones and twos. Many of our competitors didn't understand either. The secret turned out to be The Junior Literary Guild (JLG)—and other book club-style memberships made available to libraries. The JLG, an off-shoot of Doubleday's best-known book club, made it possible to offer librarians packages of carefully chosen books, new or previously published, most with official approvals, at bargain prices. They were selling subscriptions in other words, dispensing books to a market that needed help in both the selection process and the cost.

Many big city librarians wouldn't think of relinquishing their claim to professionalism and power, that is, in selection and purchasing, but here and there in the smaller towns were librarians, some well-trained, some not, who welcomed the vetting and the pricing.

Rising through the ranks, each move one small step for mankind, I attended more and more S&L sales conferences and librarians' conventions. I learned that librarians liked indexes in books. They also liked books by authors who were authorities, not just writers; they wanted books that were well researched and fact-checked—reliable, responsible, fair. (Some publishers had the same standards.) They also enjoyed backstage, background information, you might even say gossip, about authors. At national conventions and regional gatherings, I found that librarians were thoroughly professional, hard-working, in issue-oriented meeting after meeting.[2] Not a few were hard-drink-

---

2 Decades later, in a report for the Association of American Publishers, *The Accidental Profession*, I wrote that most people in publishing were not professionals, as the term is classically defined. Many had backed into the field, had some education but little at the graduate level; the industry had no accepted standards or rules of ethical conduct, etc. The same was true of most booksellers, who were not systematically trained, as they were in, say, Germany. I concluded that the only people who could be called true professionals in the community of the book were teachers, publishers' lawyers, and CPAs—and librarians.

ing, as well, as we nearly all were in those days of the martini, the Bloody Mary, the late highball. Even then, they were fighting the stereotype of the little old woman with her hair in a bun, flat shoes, and spectacles, saying "Shhhhhh!"

Latest lesson: Librarians were human.

M., a friend from college, went to work as a librarian in Marysville, Ohio. The small town was home to the Scott Seed Company. (I always imagined Marysville as one large lawn.) Once I asked M. what she did when confronted with the acquisition of a controversial, for example, explicitly sexy book. She said that if she thought it worthwhile, hot or not, she'd buy the book, but think twice before displaying it on the open shelves where little children could get at it. (Those Killer Kids again.) But any adult who asked could obtain the book—from the shelf underneath her desk.

I chewed on this for a time. Eventually, I got a view of the complex roles of the public librarian: as public servant, responsible to the community, concerned about the welfare of children, and yet desirous of upholding the First Amendment.

One more interesting insight came to me: not only publishers and booksellers had the difficult task of estimating demand.

In succeeding decades, all sorts of changes continued to happen in the book world, as elsewhere. Bigger bookstore chains were evolving, the offspring at first of the old department store networks, in which clusters of stores would attempt to buy as a group, combining their purchases for larger discounts. Offset printing was making possible the more liberal use of artwork in books than the old, expensive—although frequently better—engravings. (Eventually it would help to make text composition easier to revise and thus a less costly factor in the economic makeup of the book.) Color printing was shifting, although not entirely, from Germany, Italy, and Switzerland to Japan, Spain, and then to South America and the Southeast Asia. The Xerox machine was new and novel, making the copying of manuscripts (and everything else) much easier—and adding to the flood of paper everywhere.

At Doubleday, also in full flood, we were doing many more books. We had discovered that the first line of sales for mysteries, science fiction, western or "cowboy" novels, and poetry were the libraries. If you could control your costs, it was possible to publish many more of these at a modest profit. The burgeoning mass-market paperback reprints of the first three categories made them even more valuable. In fact, the rise of the paperback market soon saw Bantam, Pocket Books, and others becoming important customers for reprint rights, for which they paid increasingly impressive sums. For the popular and especially for the phenomenal book—*Jaws* and *Roots* and Stephen King from Doubleday alone—we were talking millions. Paperback revenues shared with the authors so much added to our profits that the once-lowly paperback houses were becoming the dominant financiers of many new books, and our good paperback customers were soon threatening our existence as competitors.

So there were new generalizations and doomsday predictions: many in both kinds of publishing were saying that the hardcover book was a dodo, doomed to extinction. For those of us who did not subscribe to that theory, the same four-letter word was applied. Our eyesight was failing; we could not see the inevitable future.

In the meantime, hard-cover publishing continued to rise on the seas of demographics. Experimental writing and publishing were coupled with continuing delivery of time-tested varieties of reading matter. In the 1950s we had on one list such books as the Truman Memoirs; Andre Malraux's monumental *The Voices of Silence;* Robert Ruark's novel of Africa, *Something of Value;* and the massive, marvelous *Columbia Historical Portrait of New York.* In addition to the traditional regulars, Daphne du Maurier, Somerset Maugham, Kenneth Roberts, Taylor Caldwell, and others of equal stature, we were adding Arthur Hailey, Leon Uris, Allen Drury's *Advise and Consent.* The company began trying out a line of large-formatted, trade paperbacks. They were called "trade" in this case because not only were they aimed at booksellers but also, unlike previous paperbacks, they were to be sold by the publishers at higher prices, at more generous trade discounts, and were fully returnable to the publisher. Paperbacks had not been welcomed previously in most bookstores, where they were regarded as too cheap, competitive, or inferior.

We shortly found that we were republishing with miraculous success such books of university press quality such as *The Lonely Crowd, The Idea of a Theatre,* and other substantial works, including *The Organization Man* (which many of us were). Eventually, we described them as perfect "for the permanent personal library of the serious reader." Elements of the much-derided "nonreading" American public were somehow snapping up Anchor Books, as were institutions of higher learning. They were perfect for the burgeoning college populations, too, and the government-underwritten book purchases made possible by the G.I. Bill. Soon we were, almost by accident, in the college textbook-like business of supplying reading for the long lists prescribed by professors.

In addition, the company had been building big reference books to order: *Amy Vanderbilt's Etiquette* and *The Parents Encyclopedia,* both successful, and *The Doubleday Dictionary,* a quick-use desk edition for spelling and ready reference, and *The Doubleday Cookbook,* a superb competitor for *Fannie Farmer* and *The Joy of Cooking;* neither was successful enough to continue.

We began sending more men and—breakthrough!—women into the field. We bought a textbook company, a book export company, a group of radio stations, built new printing plants, and continued our vertical climb. With acquired companies, as with acquired books, not everything worked out. But we went on seeking not only new books and authors but new ways of selling, packaging, pricing, and we were enjoying a quiet boom. Following the end of World War II, those aforementioned demographics were almost entirely in our favor: a vastly increasing college-educated population and rising income for many (the two most usual clues that we looked at every time we tried to find out who America's readers were); phenomenal growth in family formation and size and in home ownership—in short the creation of a new middle class, as well as new technological, scientific, and cultural elites. At the end of the 1950s, the Soviets threw a small metal object into the air (or as some said, space), and its transmitter sent back signals during its ninety-two-day life that shocked the American government to throw money after it by armloads. Washington was convinced that the Russians were out-teaching, out-learning, out-researching, and outdistancing us The resultant gusher of federal aid to education was a boon (and in part a boondoggle) for schools and libraries and any publisher with a good backlist of books.

We bought a series called Tutor Texts (TT), modeled on a new teaching "machine." The books' pages, after the first few, were not to be read consecutively. The TT would pose a question, offer multiple-choice answers, and then refer you to other pages further along. There, the reader would confront pages that said, in effect, either: Good choice! Nice reasoning or No Good, Dumbo! Here's why. Try again.

These new machines were part of an immense enthusiasm for "audiovisual" teaching aids, the wave of the future. Some were destined to fail, while others would be overtaken in a few years by infinitely more complex and powerful machines called computers. Meanwhile, much of the expensive audiovisual stuff, purchased in the post-Sputnik frenzy, languished in school and library closets. This was in part because no one had taught the teachers to use the new gear comfortably or how to integrate it with traditional teaching techniques. The equipment went unused, too, partly because many educators thought the best audible and visual aid was a live human being at the front of the classroom.

The computer, which came to us through a variety of sources, including the World War II cryptography, the attic-sized ENIAC, the University of Pennsylvania, and the postwar Defense Department, was—although not intended specifically for the book—ideal. As the computer would later be for the Internet, where the first notable business turned out to be the sale of those ancient rectangular objects pioneered by Gutenberg.

The International Standard Book Number (ISBN) helped bring machine-readable order to a situation where forty or fifty thousand new books were appearing annually in the United States alone, hundreds of thousands were in print, and millions out of print.

New demands began to descend upon the librarian, who was asked to train or retrain to become an "information technologist," or whatever the term of the moment. All had been dispensing information with whatever technology was at hand for a long time.

Most of the major changes came not from publishers but from outside forces or innovators: the computer, as suggested; xerography; lithography; television; reprogrammed radio; movies; the growth of bookstore chains and the disappearance of nearly all but the hardiest, most adaptable, and creative independent bookstores. Now, the Newest New Things, the e(lectronic)-book, a clunky but evolving device, and the iBook, or instant book on demand, if I have the alphabetic terminology correct, promise to transform us once again. Maybe they will. Or maybe they, and later, better versions, will simply take their place beside traditional techniques. Among other genuine wonders, I hope it will give new voices out of the silence of books long presumed dead.

And a good thing, too. In my experience, the vaunted backlist, books previously published live on because they sell a viable number of copies every year,[3] is, like the library, spoken of with respect but otherwise is given little attention, except sporadically. (And, in the case of the library, except for the usually small department devoted to library promotion.)

No matter. As someone wrote of our political system, *somehow it works*. "Benign neglect" didn't succeed as a popular social and economic strategy, though coined by a statesman-scholar, Senator Daniel P. Moynihan, but it carries the day much of the time. Some books sell whether we will them to or not; some die a premature death only to be recollected and revived. Caught up in the new, we manage to sideline for long periods other issues like deep-dyed illiteracy, or author and publisher responsibilities, or the vexing questions of how to head off censorship and antibook vigilantism while respecting the rights and opinions of others we see as the enemy, but who may simply be less enlightened. But we endure.

The absorbing or merging or melting down of book publishing companies is currently much remarked on, as if it had not happened before. Publishers have long bought up other publishers. Some observers think that ownership by "nonbook people" will squeeze the life out of them, even if in a number of

3 My favorite example, among the top books on the Doubleday backlist of some 5,000-plus titles, was the venerable *Ashley Book of Knots*, which Annie Proulx used as epigraphs for chapters of her chilly, but warm-hearted novel, *The Shipping News*.

cases it proved life-sustaining, at least at first. At midcentury, the oilman Clint Murchison thought it might be a pretty good idea to own a book publishing company and bought himself one, Henry Holt. Murchison was in fact vision-ary because he foresaw that with all the surviving postwar soldiers coming home for an education and a career, they'd need books. Later, General Elec-tric thought so, too, as did IT&T, CBS, and others. Some of those big fish fairly promptly disgorged what was left of the publishing firms they had swal-lowed. Imprints were revived, some were melted down, some continued in their mystifying ways as if they had never been bought. The surprised survi-vors were of two kinds: the publishers, the book people, who sold and yet somehow thought they could go on running things, with "autonomy" (trendy, utopian, gibberish like "synergy"), and those executives from other fields who bought in, without any real reason to believe that books could yield as satisfying a return on investment, profit, as a percentage of sales, rate of cash flow, and productivity per employee (the key people are authors, who are not employees at all), as other businesses.

There is a process before a company-buying-company deal goes through called "due diligence," in which both sides are supposed to investigate and/or produce facts. Too often, the mystery is: who's diligent? And who stands a chance of getting anything like what he thinks of as his due?

Lately, the big conglomerates have come from abroad: Germany, Austra-lia, England, France, and Japan. For the most part, these *are* book people, less likely to be surprised by the antic economics of publishing. They are not lack-ing in ambition, despite the mountain of evidence that, although there might be gold in them thar hills, it can be extracted, much of the time, only slowly. At least they are publishers at heart, although most draw criticism as if they had none.

My own recent lesson-learning was done in a dynamic place that grew out of a little up-and-at-'em firm called Random House, founded in the late 1920s by Bennett Cerf and Donald Klopfer. Over time, they would buy up the snobby but classy house of Alfred A. Knopf, the always-interesting imprint called Pantheon. Random would one day also add Crown, Ballantine, Fawcett, Schocken, and others.

This group was bought in turn by General Electric, then sold off to Si and Donald Newhouse, prominent magazine and newspaper publishers, who, amused for a while, sold in due course to Bertlesmann of Germany.

The publisher of Farrar, Straus and Giroux, an impressive imprint, inveighed against all bigness for years, and then sold out to Holtzbrinck, a very substantial German publishing empire. (He also carried on about big commercial bestsellers until one of his newer editors bought Scott Turow's novel, *Presumed Innocent*.) Meanwhile, Simon & Schuster, whose founders were feisty and clever, became its own sort of conglomerate, until taken over by Viacom, an American company.

At a meeting to receive a major announcement one day, a much-admired editor turned to me. She said softly, with a sigh, "I'm getting tired of breaking in new publishers."

I've kept learning throughout. Sometimes it's the obvious: things change. But though encouraged by the editors of this journal to speak to change, I think that some of the news is in what doesn't change. Not all things change as quickly as some say—or some would like. And some intangible or invisible changes are among the most significant.

Though the surface roils, and big noises blow in from Winnetka, or from corporate America, announcing The New Economy, or from cultural observers and literary watchdogs, predicting new forms of doom for the book and its producers, partners and purveyors, underneath the waves and the wind, a certain amount of fine writing, editing, publishing, teaching, library services, parenting, bookselling, and reviewing goes on. The people of the book not only endure, they persist.

For example, despite frequent declarations otherwise, there are more excellent editors at work today than ever before. (And this may be true of the number of reckless or lazy editors. You have to be able to comprehend two seemingly contradictory and simultaneous truths at once.) The number of free-standing houses seems to shrink or to be drawn deeper under capacious corporate umbrellas, yet smaller publishers proliferate. The big waves create chaos or conformity, but they also generate interesting niches and tide pools of opportunity. Publishing is like the theater, a hardy invalid, with patience and wily survival skills. If this is true of book people, it is also true of the book. The bicycle was thought to be one of the first threats to leisure time and book reading, as was the automobile, the camera, the stereoscope, radio, movies, television, and the *Reader's Digest*. Though into the conference rooms men and women go, seldom speaking of Michelangelo, but more often of discounts, TV spots, marketing innovations, formats, and websites full of electronic wonders, some of what we do is what we have been doing-looking for books and authors, helping to produce and promote them. Though scores of Mom & Pop bookshops—good *and* bad; let's not oversentimentalize—have gone, there are more places for the reader to find books than ever before.

Entranced as much as enhanced by "technology"—the very word rolls off the tongue as if it were prophesy in itself—the new men and women of virtual books, surfing the e and the i worlds, soaring into the virtual space of unlimited marketing possibilities, seeing books as so many "titles," or lately "content" (formerly, among the climbing classes, it was "product"). They need their own kind of settlement house. The smartest will find their footing.

There is nothing wrong with imagined possibilities, but a solid grounding in certain fundamentals might help to realize them.

In thinking of what is really changing and what is less mutable, perhaps, I don't want to deny change or cry, "The sky is still in place!" I'm speaking for a closer look at what has changed. One of the most profound differences in the last half of the last century was the gradual disappearance of family names from the houses that bear their names. Though Doubleday, Scribner, Simon, Farrar, Harper, and other names are still printed on the backs of books, there are no such persons in the great houses.

This is not a minor erosion. Such names were not merely decorative. They represented the persons who bought the books for publication (or refused them), and they each had a kind of culture—rigid, loose, flexible, sniffish, democratic, capricious, or demanding as they might have been—but a culture nevertheless, and the symbols on their books stood for something. Today, the name on the spine seldom stands for anything. The lists of the big houses are undifferentiated, and in some cases undistinguished; we all chase the same books. Or nearly all.

That's a change and a major one, though not one that was reflected immediately on the New York Stock Exchange. Such disappearances aren't as newsy, perhaps, as the latest model of an electronic "personal assistant" or electronic reading device (trying to become, without admitting it, as ingenious, portable, and comfortable as the traditional book) but they are pertinent. The long-term effect on a publishing company's value will eventually reveal itself.

Those who succeed in the new century will be able to court the future while learning from the past. The best of them will understand, as did the old movie moguls, in the words of one historian, the "equation" of the entire business—writers, editors, story, subject, and the work of those involved in design, production, pricing, sales, distribution, accounting, financing—these are not listed in order of importance—and more. (Perhaps instant books printed on demand will solve the problem of publishing's most underrated difficult decision, the mystery of how many copies to print. I doubt it.)

With luck, if they last, they may learn, too, sooner or later what those Americans, among others, have shown through the centuries: that the book, and its companions and competitors, the play, motion picture, concert, painting, ballet, and other arts represent a fundamental need, a basic hunger. This is a need not merely for diversion, or a pleasant recreation, but an elementary human appetite for stories and for information. No passing fancy, no small matter. This is as fundamental as the desire for bread, love, or sleep.

The book is a hardy survivor. It does not lack for competition and will not run out of it, but it is sustained by the same force that first caused "primitive peoples" to lean in closer around the campfire when someone began to speak, saying, "Listen, my best beloved. . . ."

Meanwhile, there are new ideas in the air, some exciting, some nutty and passé as the fruitcake. Critics say publishers put too much emphasis upon popular showbiz people, athletes, businessmen, preachers, and pop-psych teachers as "authors." They deplore book tie-ins and "product placements" with Pepsi Cola, the Generals—Foods and Mills and Electric—and with Sony and Disney. These are not literature, they argue. And they are not—great literature, that is. Very little is. They see it as a very contemporary misuse of publishing time and money. The romantic French movie hit of thirty years ago, *A Man and a Woman,* was a stunning example of "product placement"; it was called one long Ford commercial. I own a Big Little Book (remember those chunky, almost square, fat forerunners to the paperback?) titled *Little Big Shot* a Warner Brothers and Vitaphone film, with "Read the Book—See the Picture" on the cover. Date? 1935.

There is much hand wringing and head shaking about the seeming growth of the "star" system among authors. That's true of Hollywood, too, where once the studios held sway, as publishers did, to an extent.

But the star phenomenon has been swaying for much of the century. It didn't begin with Hemingway. Publishers, like movie men, pay more than they would like for "brand name" authors whose work consistently attracts devoted audiences. (Not nearly enough has been studied or written about the loyalty of readers to authors, at times long after the author has delivered his or her best work.) This is a "system" that takes some of the guesswork out of publishing's gamble, or at least tends to improve the odds. But more than half the time we pay much more than the work is worth. Less-known authors with smaller followings feel threatened by the stars. But the question of whether the stars get too much of the money is offset by the possibility that the sales and publishing profits earned by the star, even on her worst day, helps to pay for, partly subsidize, the publishing of many writers without an audience of any size.

A publishing house, like a studio, that cannot survive does not have the luxury of being a good company or a bad one.

Some experienced publishing hands have written recently that the sheer diversion of funds, publishing energies, and facilities, and the greed of a few authors and publishers will cause the whole edifice to come crashing down. This may be so and well-known imprints in our time have disappeared because of a few too many bets poorly placed. The only offsetting fact is that much the same grim pronouncements have been made of aggressive practices for at least fifty years.

This worry is compounded by the persistence of rumors of the "gradual neglect of mid-list writers." Those who should know better, inside and outside publishing, have said that the larger houses are leaving mid-list and serious publishing to small or academic publishers. First, mid-list and serious are not synonymous terms. Second, many if not most "small publishers" are not essentially "serious," in the sense of literary, avant garde, or philosophically inclined. Most are determinedly commercial and would be willing to shed their size like a skin they've outgrown if they could just strike it right.

Third, even a cursory look at the lists of the larger houses show that the charge is unfounded. True, much of poetry publishing is in the hand of university presses. True, books that might once have been published by the big guns are being issued by the not inconsiderable guns of the university presses. But that is as much a reflection of the recent impelling need for university presses to pay their own way as it is of the policies of the Random Houses or the Holtzbrinck houses. And the overlap between kinds of publishing has become one great, intellectually fervent blur since, say, Anchor Books were invented in the 1950s.

The chairman of one well-known house was speaking to me one day with concern about the burden and the losses of mid-list books. I observed that the mid-list book would always be with us. If we published 300 books per year, at least 200 of them would be bound to be mid-list—or lesser list. If we published ten books, six or eight would be mid-list. And, I observed, when a mid-list book connects, takes off, goes in a swift rising arc toward the left field fence, it's apt to throw off profits at a greater rate than the much-vaunted blockbuster. You probably haven't paid too much for it in the first place, or too much in promotion to get it airborne in the second. Also, it hasn't tied up a great deal of your capital (at a significant rate of interest) for very long.

The chairman seemed impressed that I had pointed this out, as he pointed the way out, with a firm finger, toward the door.

The vitalizing effect of online bookselling, like online libraries and online publishing, has been electric. Or perhaps electronic, electric being the Old Technology, except when you want to turn on the lights. The Amazons and other online outlets are providing marvelously convenient search engines for a large fraction of the populace and a convenient way to order. Yet they have had to learn how to do less dazzling things, like how to warehouse, package, deliver, and fuss with annoying stuff like accounting, bad credit, cash flow, paying their bills, shopping for suppliers, and hiring managers who know how and whom to manage.

I like a lot about the dotcoms. I just wish they and their cheerleaders weren't so dotty. The fusty view of those of us who still use a pencil on occasion is that the initial public offering is followed by a period called The Long Haul.

*   *   *

Since I started learning about libraries,[4] their people out front and, importantly, too, those behind the stacks, I've been involved with the Library of Congress as a speaker, author, and planner of symposia; with the Mercantile Library in New York; and the Morgan Library as a gift-shop customer and gallerygoer. I've also seen with pride the latter day Jeffersons, Morgans, and Carnegies. In my hometown, the Tenafly (N.J.) public library is being redone with a donation made by one woman. The libraries at Penn State where I went to college are the beneficiaries of the football coach and his wife, Joe and Sue Paterno. They have led the fundraising and also given millions personally for a new library, which has just been built.

Some years back, at an ALA meeting in Los Angeles, speaking as one of a number of "Friends of the Libraries," I followed moviemaker Sir David Attenborough; Wally Amos, "one smart cookie" and a one-man literacy effort; and Samuel Goldwyn Jr. Not long before, Mr. Goldwyn saw a fire destroy the Hollywood branch of the Los Angeles public library. The cause was arson. Not everybody is a Friend of the Libraries, apparently. He called the library line and offered to help with a gift. The person on the other end of the phone, agitated, perhaps understandably, said No, no, we don't need any more books at the moment. We've just had a fire. To which Goldwyn replied: You don't understand. I'm offering to give you a new library."

And did. The resulting grant from the Samuel Goldwyn Foundation for a new building designed by architect Frank O. Gehry was, at $3.24 million, at the time the largest single gift ever in the United States for the construction of one library.

Through my fellow townswomen, the Paternos, the Goldwyns, and others, I've learned a final lesson. Certain people know and feel a great deal about the importance of libraries in our culture, our commerce, and our hearts.

One night, after a day at a sales conference in Arizona, I went for a walk. We had been filling the rooms with adjectives about books-to-come, and I sought fresh air and a moment's silence in honor of the slaughter of our dear departed language. Outside, a superb Arizona dusk was in progress, with the mountains and the fading but still vibrant colors and the perfume of wood smoke. A few blocks further on, I saw an oasis of light.

Nightlife in Scottsdale not being one of its grandest attractions, that beacon beckoned. Was there a movie theater or a supermarket opening? Approaching, I could see that it turned out to be the glow of a library.

4 Especially through Carole Nemeyer, Daniel Boorstin, John Cole, Jack Frantz, Charles Mann, and Margie McNamara.

To my pleasure, I found it full—not only of books and stacks and racks, computers and magazines and newspapers and journals, but people. There were the dreaded kids, looking for all the world as if they were civilized beings. Despite their reputed illiteracy, they seemed to be soaking up words on paper or off a screen. There, too, were middle-aged adults, pursuing their special interests, including some answers, one guessed, to the questions of how to get through middle age. And there were the gray-haired like myself, what my kids called once the Q-Tips, actively mixing in, reading, occasionally looking up, some in search of answers to crossword puzzles, others to puzzles about the meaning of life. It was, as the poet wrote, in the best sense, "a clean, well-lighted place."

The poet, of course, was speaking of the grave (adding, the spoilsport, "But none I think do there embrace"), but this was far from the graveyard. Just the reverse. Here were people of all ages and sorts embracing all the life the library had to offer. People, I learned anew, still turned to such places for information and inspiration, corroboration or stimulation, for enlightenment, entertainment, and excitement; to escape in reading, or to find themselves in words.

I had a sudden urge to stay.

And to start on the left, high up in the A's and read every book in the place.

◆4◆

Growth and Change in Trade Book Publishing: What I Learned from the Numbers

Stephanie Oda

Increase in the Number of Publishers

The U.S. trade book publishing market is the largest in the world, with 1999 revenues reaching $6.51 billion. Trade publishing is here defined as hardcover and paperback, adult and juvenile, sold in bookstores. As in all areas of the publishing business, a dearth of hard statistical information exists on the exact number of trade publishing houses in the United States. The Census Bureau puts it at about 3,500, but publishers counted by the bureau must have at least one paid employee and an employer identification number.

Below the top tier, thousands of smaller players exist, and more join the business every year. Estimates of their number also vary wildly—ranging from 8,000 to 50,000. A 1999 study, conducted jointly by Book Industry Study Group (BISG) and Publishers Marketing Association, of presses with revenues ranging between $100,000 and $10 million, estimated the market at $14 billion. These players are not included in the overall publishing market estimate of $24 billion by the Association of American Publishers (AAP).

In the years between 1997 and 1999, the number of new publishers increased dramatically. According to R.R. Bowker, 9,982 new ISBN prefixes were assigned in 1999, up 43 percent from 6,981 in 1997. Of course, many of these small startups go out of business quickly. New technology is driving this boom in publishing entrepreneurs. With the advent of Internet bookselling, small, niche publishers are reaching new readers as they never could before. In the past, these publishers had to seek out and target their audiences mainly through mailing lists.

Also contributing strongly to the proliferation of smaller players is print-on-demand technology. In the past, small publishers used traditional offset printing, which, in runs of fewer than 1,000 were not cost-effective. Publishers forced to print more copies than they could sell in order to bring down the unit price often ended up with the operating expense of books that did not sell, yet had to be shipped, warehoused, shelved, and eventually remaindered or destroyed.

A number of companies, including Xerox and Ingram, are offering short-run printing services to publishers. Ingram launched its Lightning Source in November 1997. By digitizing and "warehousing" books, printing can be done in short runs or on an "as-needed" basis, decreasing costs of inventory, handling, and print set-up. On-demand printing also allows out-of-print books to be brought back into print inexpensively. With this process, books can be produced in print runs of fewer than 1,000 for about $4 a copy.

Electronic publishing, although in its nascent stages, promises to add to the explosion of new independent publishers. The e-books allow publishers to cut costs even further, since they do not require the expense of creating the physical book. Industry analysts are predicting an explosion of new small players with the advent of e-publishing. The "e-revolution," however, still has to gain the interest of the consumer.

Growth in the Number of Titles and Dollar Sales

There are more than 1.5 million distinct titles in print, according to R.R. Bowker's *Books in Print.* In a separate report—*Book Industry Statistics*—from the R.R. Bowker Company, the company revealed that between 1880 and 1989, 1.8 million new titles were issued (Table 1). The decade between 1980 and 1989 was the most prolific in terms of the number of books published, accounting for 510,286 new titles or an average of 51,000 each year. In the 1990s, title output decreased to an average of about of about 45,000 each year. This number includes all categories of books because no breakout exists for trade only. However, since the majority of frontlist or new titles are published in the trade segment, it is reasonable to estimate that trade accounts for some 70 percent to 80 percent of new titles published every year.

In 1999, U.S. trade publishers' domestic dollar sales, as compiled by the AAP and the BIRG, reached $6.51 billion (Table 2). Between 1987, when revenues were $2.71 billion, and 1999, the U.S. trade market increased 140 percent. With total revenues of $6.51 billion, trade publishing is the largest category, accounting for 27 percent of the $24 billion U.S. book market. Within trade, adult hardcover is the largest category, with sales of $2.82 billion, representing 43 percent of trade; adult trade paperbacks accounted for

TABLE 1
Total U.S. New Books Published by Decade: 1880–1989

Decade	Total Title Output	Percent Change
1880–1889	37,896	
1890–1899	50,011	31.97%
1900–1909	83,512	66.99%
1910–1919	107,906	29.21%
1920–1929	79,006	−26.78%
1930–1939	98,480	24.65%
1940–1949	91,514	−7.07%
1950–1959	124,675	36.24%
1960–1969	256,584	105.80%
1970–1979	402,911	57.03%
1980–1989	510,286	26.65%
Total 1880–1990:	1,842,781	

Sources: Jean Peters, Book Industry Statistics from the R. R. Bowker Company, Publishing Research Quarterly (Fall 1992), and The Book Publishing Industry, Albert N. Greco, Allyn & Bacon

just under $2 billion; juvenile hardcover about $1.0 billion, and juvenile paperbacks $661 million.

Foreign Invasion of the U.S. Book Business

Foreign-based publishers entered the U.S. market in force in the final decade of the twentieth century, increasing their share of book-publishing sales in the U.S. market. Globalization has remained a potent force in book publishing, crossing all segments—trade, professional, and educational. The U.S. market is attractive to foreign investors for a number of reasons, the most obvious being that a U.S. property affords immediate access to the largest book market in the world. Unlike Canada and many other countries, the United States government imposes no restrictions on foreign-owned businesses in this country.

As Table 3 shows, the three largest U.S. trade publishers, Random House, Penguin Putnam, and HarperCollins, are owned by overseas conglomerates.

TABLE 2
Book Publishing Net Trade Sales, 1987, 1992, 1997–1999 ($ in millions)

	1987	1992	1997	1998	1999
AdultHB	$1,350.60	$2,222.50	$2,663.60	$2,751.50	$2,823.90
Adult PB	$ 727.10	$1,261.70	$1,731.70	$1,908.30	$1,969.10
Juvenile HB	$ 478.50	$ 850.80	$ 908.50	$ 953.90	$1,060.10
Juvenile PB	$ 156.60	$ 326.60	$ 470.30	$v535.20	$ 660.80
Trade (Total)	$2,712.80	$4,661.60	$5,774.10	$6,148.90	$6,513.90

Growth		
1998–1999	1987–1999	1992–1999
2.60%	109.10%	27.10%
3.20%	170.80%	56.10%
11.10%	121.50%	24.60%
23.50%	322.00%	102.30%
5.90%	140.10%	39.70%

Source: Book Industry Study Group

TABLE 3
Market Share of Three Largest Foreign-Owned Trade Publishers in the United States (Estimated $ in millions)

Publisher	U.S. Revenues 1999	Parent	Country
Random House	$1,410	Bertelsmann	Germany
Penguin Putnam	$ 900	Pearson	U.K.
HarperCollins	$ 800	News Corp.	Australia
Total	$3,110		
Total U.S. Domestic Trade Publishing 1999:	$6,514		
Combined Sales of 3 Major Foreign Players:	$3,110		
Percentage of U.S. Trade Market:	48%		

Source: The Subtext 2000–2001 Perspective on Book Publishing: Numbers, Issues & Trends, Open Book Publishing, Inc., 2001

Revenues of the three alone account for an estimated at $3.1 billion, or 48 percent of the $6.5 billion domestic trade market. Germany-based conglomerate Bertelsmann, which already owned Bantam Doubleday Dell, stunned the industry in 1998 by acquiring Random House, the largest trade publisher, bringing its share of the American trade market to just under 22 percent.

Pearson, based in the United Kingdom and parent company of Penguin Putnam, bought Simon & Schuster's educational business in the same year. Pearson did not acquire the publisher's trade properties, having bought Putnam in the mid 1990s. Penguin's trade sales topped the $1 billion mark in 2000. Sales in the United States are estimated at about $900 million, giving it a solid 14 percent share of the domestic market. HarperCollins, formed from two venerable houses—Harper & Row and Collins Publishers—and acquired by News Corp.'s Rupert Murdoch in the 1980s, scooped up Hearst book imprints Morrow and Avon in 1999 to bring its share to just over 12 percent.

The German conglomerate Bertelsmann owns 23.2 percent of the entire market, while American top players Simon & Schuster, Time Warner Trade (Warner Books, Little Brown), and Houghton Muffin account for 15 percent of the market. In total, these three account for $979 million. The largest foreign investor country in the U.S. trade market is Germany, accounting for 26.3 percent.

Trade Top Heavy as Mergers Continue

For 1999, the combined domestic sales of the ten largest trade publishing companies amounted to $4.6 billion, representing 70.7 percent of the entire $6.5 billion U.S. trade business, as estimated by the AAP. Including their overseas subsidiaries, combined revenues of the top ten were $5.4 billion.Swelled by acquisitions, Random House and HarperCollins dominated the trade sector in 1999. The latter, having acquired Hearst's book business in mid 1999, crossed the $1 billion mark to occupy second spot, with fiscal 2000 revenue growth at 36 percent. In April, Pearson acquired Dorling Kindersley, whose 1999 revenues were $325 million. Added to Pearson's 1999 revenues of $909 million, the acquisition will push Pearson's trade business well over the $1 billion mark.

The 1999 standings serve as a dramatic illustration of the whirlwind of mergers that has occurred in trade over the past three years. Combined, the global sales of the top three, at $3.7 billion account for 67 percent of the ten largest players combined. Below the top three, the gap widens by more than 30 percent, with Simon & Schuster's $611 million. Nearly two years after Pearson acquired the education business of Simon & Schuster, the trade segment remains a subsidiary of Viacom. However, persistent speculation that

TABLE 4
Estimated Market Share of Major Trade Publishers in the United States
($ in millions; sales estimated)

Country	U.S. Revenues ($ millions)	Percent of U.S. Trade Market
U.S.	979	15.00
Simon & Schuster	590	9.10
Time Warner Trade	300	4.60
Houghton Mifflin	89	1.40
Germany	1,710	26.30
Random House Inc.	1,410	21.60
Holtzbrinck (St. Martin's Press, FSG, Henry Holt)	300	4.60
UK	909	13.80
Pearson (Penguin/Putnam, Macmillan Computer, DK, USA)		
Australia	800	12.30
HarperCollins		
Total U.S. Domestic Sales 100. 0%		$6. 51 billion
Total U.S.-Owned Large Publishers' Share of Trade Market: 15.0%		$979 million
Total Foreign Owned Large Publishers Share of Trade: 52.3 %		$3.41 billion

Source: The Subtext 2000–2001 Perspective on Book Publishing: Numbers, Issues & Trends, Open Book Publishing, Inc., Open Book Publishing, Inc. 2001.

the company has been considering alliances as a means of competing with its mammoth competitors may become a reality.

Time Warner's trade imprints, Little Brown and Warner Books, in the fifth slot with estimated revenues of $320 million, could also be in for some changes following the merger of America Online and Time Warner. The company has indicated that the linkup will be a positive development for its book businesses. Although a small piece of Time Warner properties, their content could be of large importance in the marriage.

The "other" German media conglomerate, Verlagsgruppe George von Holtzbrinck, has become a player in the U.S. trade market as the owner of three houses, St. Martin's Press, Farrar Straus & Giroux, and Henry Holt.

TABLE 5
The Ten Largest U.S. Trade Publishers, 1999, Share of Domestic Market
(Estimated $ in millions)

Rank	Publisher	World 1999 Revenues	Est. U.S. 1999 Revenues	Percent of Total U.S. Market*
1	Random House[1]	1,710	1,410	21.60
2	Harper Collins[2]	1,040	780	12.00
3	Penguin Putnam	909	705	10.80
4	Simon & Schuster	611	590	9.00
5	Warner/Little Brown[1]	320	298	4.60
6	St. Martin's/Holt/FSG[1]	300	300	4.60
7	Thomas Nelson[3]	183	183	2.80
8	IDG Books Worldwide	180	165	2.50
9	Houghton Mifflin	91	89	1.40
10	Andrews McMeel[4]	85	85	1.30
Total:		5,429	4,605	
Total Domestic Trade Sales:			$6,514*	
Ten Largest Publishers' Combined Share:			$4,605	71%

*As tablulated by the Association of American Publishers and Book Industry Study Group
1: Estimated.
2: Estimated, FY ending 6/30/00. Includes Avon & Morrow, Acquired July 1999.
3: Book and Bible sales only, does not include gift business.
4: Estimated, books only.

Source: The Subtext 2000–2001 Perspective on Book Publishing: Numbers, Issues & Trends, Open Book Publishing, Inc., 2001.

Below the Holtzbrinck Group, only Houghton Mifflin remains a purely trade house in that it publishes general fiction and nonfiction books.

Nelson, IDG Books Worldwide, and Andrews McMeel are included in the ranking because, although they could best be described as niche publishers, they are sold in trade outlets. Their presence indicates that branded, niche publishers are about the only trade category that can attain even the lower end of the ranking in today's climate.

Taylor & Francis of the United Kingdom continued growing its U.S. base with the purchase of Routledge, building on its 1997 acquisitions of Garland

and Brunner/Mazel. Batsford, also of the United Kingdom, acquired Brassey's Inc., a publisher of military books.

Religion Publishing

The Resurgence of Religion Publishing

The religion segment showed the slowest growth in the past five years. Despite greater expectations—based on repenting baby boomers and the dawn of a new millennium—the segment gained only 3.3 percent to $1.2 billion in 1999. In 2000, sales hovered at the $1.2 billion mark, growing 2.5 percent (Table 6). Still, religion books continue to sell, and they range from nondenominational inspirational titles to Bibles to Christian romance to books on theology. At least one book on dieting with God graced the 1999 bestsellers for the second consecutive year—*The Weight Down Diet,* published by Doubleday.

Although the most recent wave of seekers has come from a wide range of traditions, they tend to favor nondenominational books with spiritual and religious themes. To meet this trend, many of the traditional religious houses have honed their offerings to capture their faithful through the mainstream market. In addition to stores specializing in religious books, all the major

TABLE 6
Religion Book Sales, 1990–2000 ($ in millions)

Year	Sales	Change
1990	$ 788.00	
1991	854.70	8.50%
1992	907.10	6.10%
1993	931.50	2.70%
1994	979.40	5.10%
1995	1,036.90	5.90%
1996	1,093.40	5.40%
1997	1,132.70	3.60%
1998	1,178.00	4.00%
1999	1,216.90	3.30%
2000	1,246.90	2.50%

Source: Book Industry Study Group

chains and independents carry a religious/inspirational section. The "soft-core" side of religion—spirituality, meditation, inspiration—appears to be growing, based on publishers' expanding lists.

Women buy a majority of these types of books, and a number of titles directed to the female audience made the best-seller list in 1999, including *The Power of a Praying Wife* (Harvest House), *Daily Wisdom for Women* (Barbour), and *Touchpoints for Women* (Tyndale).

Although the Protestant Evangelical Christians have the most visible presence as drivers of the American religion market, other religions are also responding to the quest for the spiritual that is rooted in their traditions. Jewish Lights Publishing, based in Woodstock, Vermont, publishes books that skillfully package old traditions for a new generation of seekers. On the company's fall 2000 list were titles *The Way into Jewish Prayer* and the *Jewish Lights Spirituality Handbook*.

Samuel Weiser, Inc., a small Maine religion publisher, is truly ecumenical. Titles appearing in its fall 2000 catalogue had something for all tastes, ranging from *Barefoot Zen* to *The Heart of Wicca* to *The Mysteries of the Quabalah*. Most of the large trade houses have religious or Christian imprints. Harper San Francisco publishes on just about every religion, while its Zondervan imprint is mostly Bible and evangelical works. In July 2000, Warner Books hired Rolf Zettersten from Nelson to form a new Christian imprint.

Christian Retailing: a Mix of Mission and Business

The Evangelical Christian book retail business is well established and strongly entrenched in the "bible belt" geographic areas of the United States. Once family-owned by believers who viewed their stores as a ministry as much as a business, over the past two decades these independents have gone the way of the secular independents.

Many of the small stores have been acquired by Christian chains, apparently without the competitive rancor that still brews among their secular counterparts. It may be that the sense of mission and focus on a single segment of the market contributes to this unity. In addition, the segment has its own organization, The Christian Booksellers Association (CBA). No longer simple mom-and-pop operations, Christian booksellers have become as sophisticated as their secular brothers, adopting many of their business practices and technology.

Formerly a unit of Zondervan (HarperCollins) publishing, Family Christian Stores (FCS) was acquired by management in 1994. Family Christian Stores has continued to expand by acquisitions, buying up more than sixty independents. Having acquired the fifty-six-store Joshua chain for $11 million in 1998, FCS sold a majority equity stake to Madison Dearborn Partners. FCS's revenues increased by 31.8 percent to $290 million in 1999, making it the fifth largest in the United States.

The Christian retailing business, including books, music, and gifts, is estimated at $4 billion. About 40 percent of this accounts for books and an estimated 75 percent of all religion books sold in the United States. The remaining 25 percent are sold through mainstream trade bookstores or stores specializing in non-Christian religions.

For independents, Parable Group has formed a marketing consortium of more than 300 Christian member stores. Combined member revenues are estimated at $350 million for 1999. Started eleven years ago by the independent Christian bookseller Steve Potraz, Parable is located in San Luis Obispo, California. Run by Jim Seybert, Parable has fifty employees. Participating stores have an average of $1.2 million in revenues. The group provides four-color catalogs customized with the store's name. Parable collects point-of-sale data from stores on a monthly basis. It also provides such services as inventory analysis, just-in-time inventory services, and store security systems.

Book Distribution

The Backdrop: Supersizing and Resistance

Bookselling in the decade of the 1990s went a long way to becoming "supersized," lagging as an industry in the tracks of other retail businesses, such as food, hardware, and prescription drugs. The 1970s and 1980s had seen a significant expansion for independent booksellers, a period of growth and maturation for existing players, a bountiful and flourishing crop of new stores, and a downturn of fortunes for mall retailing and traditional chains.

The early 1990s marked a change in the bookselling landscape, a new bias toward the principle, tried and true for other businesses, that selling through large chains was a more efficient and profitable way for companies to operate. The shadow on independent bookselling started to darken when the New York bookseller Barnes & Noble acquired BookStop, a discount book chain in Texas with a history of competing against regional independent bookstores. Barnes & Noble then acquired the mall chain B. Dalton and became the largest retail book business.

On separate but parallel tracks, Borders of Ann Arbor, Michigan, a formidable chain in its own right, was acquired by Kmart, which subsequently bought the other major mall chain Waldenbooks. Thus, the two major superstore giants were poised for an expansion that altered the face of retail bookselling in America. In their wake came Crown Books, an aggressive discounter based in Washington, D.C. and destined for bankruptcy in the latter years of the decade, and Books-A-Million of Birmingham, Alabama, which built its presence in the Southeast.

Superstores and warehouse stores (also called price clubs) proliferated, draining business from the independents with the huge discounts they offered consumers. Some regarded their advance as an improvement in book distribution. These new "supermarketers" enable consumers to better locate titles that they couldn't track down in their local bookstores. It was argued that they offered more options with respect to titles, store types (with cappuccino and other new amenities), store locations, spacious parking, and the like. They made more titles available, they made more new readers, and they made more readers read more, thereby helping book sales and the book business as a whole.

But others saw the demise of hundreds of independents, with a precipitous drop in membership for the Association of American Booksellers (ABA) from 5,200 to 4,400 in 1991–1992, the first year of the superstores. Describing the mood of the independents at this time, the former ABA presi-

TABLE 7
Consumer Adult Book Purchasing by Outlet, 1996–1999
(Outlet Shares by Percent of Units Purchased)

Stores	1999	1998	1997	1996
Large Chains	24.6%	25.3%	25%	25%
Book Clubs	17.7	18.0	20	18
Indep/Small Chains	15.2	16.6	17	18
Other-Specialized	9.6	10.1	9	10
Warehouse/Price Clubs	6.5	6.4	6	6
Mass Merchandisers	6.2	5.9	6	NA
E-Commerce	5.4	1.9	NA	NA
Mail Order	4.4	4.9	6	5
Food/Drug	3.5	3.6	4	5
Discount	3.0	3.3	3	9
Used Book	3.0	3.0	3	4
Multimedia	0.9	1.0	1	NA
Total	100%	100%	100%	100%

Source: BISG Consumer Research Study on Book Purchasing.

TABLE 8
The Nine Largest North American Bookstore Chains, FY 2000 ($ in millions)

	Company Revenues			Number of Stores		
	FY2000	FY1999	Change	2000	1999	Change
Barnes & Noble[1]	3,262.0	3,006.0	8.50%	942	1,009	−6.60%
Borders Group[2]	2,992.2	2,595.0	15.60%	1,195	1,150	3.90%
Chapters*	445.2	370.5	20.20%	310	326	−4.90%
Books-a-Million[1]	404.1	347.9	16.20%	180	175	2.90%
Family Christian*	290.0	220.0	31.80%	350	290	20.70%
Musicland*[3]	200.0	130.0	53.80%	69	73	−5.40%
Crown Books*[4]	189.0	189.0	0	92	92	0
Hastings*[5]	100.0	96.0	4.20%	150	129	16.30%
Tower*[6]	40.0	35.0	14.30%	120	121	−0.80%
Totals	7,929.5	6,989.4	13.50%	3,408	3,365	1.30%

*Estimates
1: FY ended Jan. 31, 2000.
2: FY ended Jan. 25, 2000.
3: Store numbers represent Media Play only. Musicland's 180 On Que Stores also sell a small
   number of books. Revenueincludes these.
4: Having emerged from bankruptcy, Crown Books has not resumed trading.
Source: The Subtext 2000–2001 Perspective on Book Publishing: Numbers, Issues, & Trends, Open
Book Publishing Inc, 2001.

dent Richard Howorth wrote in his book *Independent Bookselling & True Market Expansion*: "Many independent booksellers saw the writing on the wall, believing that what had happened to small pharmacies and family farms was now visiting its inevitability on them. The dominant chain superstores immediately showed their predatory teeth . . . opening their outlets strategically to drive independents out of business."

The long-range impact of the superstores cannot yet be known. Will the superstores prevail and the independents wilt away like their corner store counterparts in the food industry, struggling to compete with the supermarket? "The book industry is destined to go through exactly this type of confrontation, with only the strongest and smartest independents surviving," said Albert Greco in his 1997 study, *The Book Publishing Industry*.

At this writing in 2001, the smart and strong independents are surviving. Judging by the spirit evident at their latest annual convention in Chicago, their resilience and resourcefulness has fueled their optimism. Their feelings are of having "turned the corner," even if the superstore is still just down the block.

It has been argued that "supermarketing" may lend itself to food, hardware, and prescription drugs in a way that it doesn't to bookselling, particularly as handled by independents. The level of knowledge, approachability, and personal touch that independent booksellers claim are endemic to their success as retailers just doesn't fit the supermarket mold.

The surviving independents have proved themselves to be remarkably resilient. A majority took hits from superstores, but a surprising number claim to be recovering. Some long-term customers stayed loyal, and some who defected came back. Booksellers have attributed service, creative special events, and sheer grit as aids to their survival. If anything was remarkable at the 1999 BookExpo America convention, it was the ABA's comeback and the general sense of optimism among the booksellers attending. Ever the underdog in today's publishing climate, independent booksellers use any means they can to hold their ground.

Contrary to the view that superstores were good for the book business, the ABA and its hard-bitten constituency contended that the superstores were to blame for the glut of returns in 1996. The ABA's Howorth contended that book demand fell short of supply. He drew a sharp contrast between the ascendancy of the independents and decline of the mall stores in the 1980s and the growing dominance of the superstores in the 1990s: While the growth of the independents was gradual, natural, and appropriate to many distinct markets," he said, "the chain superstores expansion was forced, hurried, ubiquitous, careless. The publishers, who took part in subsidizing the expansion, paid dearly."

For the independents, the struggle to survive, which involved considerable litigation in the course of the 1990s, goes on and gets tougher as competition escalates, not only from the chains, but from nonbookstore retailers such as the warehouse club outlets, epitomized by Costco. And then there is the Internet, where Barnes & Noble and Borders are staking out a piece of the action alongside of Amazon.com. In addition to the supersizing that has occurred in bookselling, the number of distribution channels has increased, not only on land, but in cyberspace as well.

Differentiation of Channels: New Player Fastest Growing

Although online bookselling has yet to be profitable, the number of books bought through the Internet more than doubled in 1999 from the previous year. *The 1999 Consumer Research Study on Book Purchasing*, published in May 2000 by the BISG, indicates that the percentage of books bought online rose from 1.9 percent in 1998 to 5.4 percent in 1999.

TABLE 9
Revenues of Publicly Held Online Bookstores, 1998–1999

Company	1998	1999	Percent Change
Amazon.com*	610.00	1,640.00	168.90
Barnesandnoble.com	61.80	203.00	228.50
Fatbrain.com†	10.70	28.80	169.20
Borders.com	4.60	17.90	289.10
Total	687.10	1, 889.70	175.00

*Book sales are estimated at $1.2 billion. B&N.com and Borders also sell nonbook merchandise
†In September 2000, Barnes & Noble.com acquired Fatbrain.com for $64 million.
Source: The Subtext 2000-2001 Perspective on Book Publishing: Numbers, Issues, & Trends, Open Book Publishing Inc, 2001.

Although this percentage is small, the outlet was the fastest growing of the twelve tracked by the study. This 5.4 percent translates to nearly 50 million adult book units bought by customers over the Internet, compared to 20 million in 1998 and 4 million in 1997.

Meanwhile, the land-bound independents continued to lose turf in 1999, with their percentage of the market sliding from 16.6 percent to 15.2 percent. Marking a change from past years, superstores shed some market share in 1999, with their slice shrinking from 25.3 percent in 1998 to 24.6 percent in 1999. The chains are evidently not picking up business lost by the independents, as they historically did.

Book clubs and mail order lost ground with book buyers, with their market shares slipping to 17.7 percent from 18.0 percent and 4.4 percent from 4.9 percent, respectively. Warehouses and price clubs, which typically sell heavily discounted frontlist titles, remained relatively flat, enjoying only a 0.1 percent gain from 6.4 percent of the market in 1998 to 6.5 percent in 1999. Mass merchandisers' share of units sold increased to 6.2 percent from 5.9 percent in 1998.

The BISG tracks the smaller chains with the independents. These chains, such as Crown Books and Lauriat's, had a rough couple of years. Both filed for bankruptcy in 1998, with only Crown emerging to carry on with a decidedly scaled-down business. In 2001, Crown again went into bankruptcy. At this writing, it is believed that the long-beleaguered chain will close all its stores.

Sales of Top Nine Chains Gain 13.5 Percent in 1999

The departure of Lauriat's from the bookselling scene in 1999 had no impact on the ever-widening bite that megaretailers are taking from the market. Indeed, despite Lauriat's closing, combined sales of the nine largest bookstore chains in North America increased by 13.5 percent to $7.9 billion in 1999, according to *The 2000–2001 Subtext Perspective on Book Publishing: Numbers, Issues & Trends,* published by Open Book Publishing.

Increasingly dominating the picture are Barnes & Noble and Borders, in first and second slot, with sales up by 8.5 percent and 15.6 percent, respectively. Combined, the revenues of these two giants amounted to $6.3 billion, more than 50 percent of the some $12 billion U.S. bookselling market. Although a distant third in 1999, the Canadian chain Chapters saw its sales rise by a robust 20.2 percent to $445 million (U.S.), as it opened additional superstores and shuttered smaller outlets.

At this writing, Chapters, after a bitter struggle to stave off a hostile take-over, was acquired by Trilogy, parent of its long-standing rival Indigo Books & More, brainchild of entrepreneur Heather Reisman. She became chief executive officer (CEO) of Chapters in 2001.

Books-A-Million, albeit dwarfed by Barnes & Noble and Borders, remained the third-largest U.S. bookstore chain in 1999. In sales, Books-A-Million held its own with a handsome 16.2 percent hike to $404.1 million.

Family Christian Stores, which has expanded by buying up Christian independents, moved into fifth place in North America and fourth in the United States. The president and CEO, Leslie Dietzman, said in early 2000 that the company acquired more than sixty independents. Having absorbed the fifty-six-store Joshua chain for $11 million in 1998, FCS sold a majority equity stake to Madison Dearborn Partners. Family Christian's revenues increased by 31.8 percent to $290 million in 1999.

Combined, sales of the four largest of these top nine book chains increased by *12.5 percent* to more than $7 billion in 1999, compared to $6.3 billion for the previous year. Notable is the fact that Barnes & Noble's $3.3 billion in revenues accounts for nearly 46 percent of the number. Borders and Barnes & Noble sales together amount to $7.1 billion, or almost 90 percent of the total for the top four.

Mall Stores, Small Chains Linger in Superstore Shadows

Smaller chains, or mall stores, such as Barnes & Noble's B. Dalton, have not delivered results comparable to the superstores. In 1999, Barnes & Noble closed eighty-nine B. Dalton Stores. Although it also closed sixteen superstores, it opened thirty-eight new ones, giving Barnes & Noble a net of twenty-six new superstores, down from fifty in 1998. This indicates the superstores may be reaching saturation point after a decade of rapid growth. B. Dalton stores registered sales of $426 million in 1999, down nearly 10 percent from $468.4 million for the previous year. At $2.82 billion, superstore revenue accounted for 86 percent of Barnes & Noble's 2000 revenues.

Borders' Waldenbooks stores also have consistently performed below its superstores. With revenues of $981 million in 1999, they gained only 4.2 percent over the previous year, while superstore sales rose 22.4 percent. Borders' superstore revenues were $1.91 billion, or 64 percent of overall sales. Both Barnes & Noble and Borders have been steadily closing their mall stores as their leases have expired.

Although there is no doubt that the independent bookstores have suffered most from the superstore boom, smaller chains have also been hurt. The lackluster performance of Waldenbooks and B. Dalton mirrors the troubles of small store chains such as Lauriat's and Crown Books.

Lacking the Wall Street cushion enfolding Walden and Dalton, privately held Lauriat's, the sixth-largest chain in the United States in 1997, fell victim to too much expansion and too little cash in 1998. After a three-year struggle, including a failed attempt to find a buyer, Lauriat's was forced to file for Chapter 11 protection. It managed to stay operational until spring 1999, when the long-established New England chain was forced to close its doors. As indicated, Crown Books also went into bankruptcy and is soon to be gone from the bookselling landscape.

Independents: A New Spirit, but Still Litigious

Even as ABA's litigation of chains has continued, and many independents have been shuttered, a more optimistic outlook has taken hold among the survivors and was pervasive at an upbeat BookExpo America 2000. Although BookExpo made much of its metamorphosis from a booksellers' convention to one encompassing all quarters of the book business, independents still regard it as their event.

This upbeat mood also surrounded Book Sense, the national marketing program for independents initiated by the ABA in 1999 and aimed at helping members boost sales. The program collects and publishes independent bestseller lists and offers a gift certificate program, a newsletter whereby independents can review and recommend books, and a website, BookSense.com, through which independents can set up their own Web storefronts to sell on a 24/7 basis. BookSense.com went into operation in November 2000.

Online Bookselling: Catching on, Profits Still Elusive

The number of books bought through the Internet more than doubled in 1999 from the previous year. According to the BISG's 1999 *Consumer Research Study on Book Purchasing,* the percentage of books bought online rose from 1.9 percent in 1998 to 5.4 percent in 1999.

Although the numbers may be small compared to those of other outlets, Internet bookselling is the fastest growing among the twelve tracked in the study. These percentages translate to nearly 50 million adult book units bought by customers over the Internet, compared to 20 million in 1998 and 4 million in 1997. The four largest public online bookselling companies reported combined revenues of $1.89 billion, more than 2.5 times the sales of $687 million in 1998.

While some disagree about the exact size of the online bookselling market, there is no doubt that it is growing rapidly. Spurred by the success of Amazon.com, traditional booksellers and entrepreneurs of every stripe have entered online bookselling, and publishers have placed great hope in this venue.

Online retailers range from the bricks-and-mortar stores that have added an online component to mass merchandisers (Wal-Mart) to multimedia stores (Hastings) to used and out-of-print booksellers such as Alibris.com. Also joining the fray are the independents, many setting up their own sites, such as Powell's, and others entering through BookSense.com.

In 1999, Amazon.com remained by far the largest online bookselling company, with revenues tipping over the $1.6 billion mark. Its sales grew 168.9 percent in 1999. The Barnes & Noble online store, bn.com, was the second largest, with revenues of $203 million increasing 228.5 percent from $61.8 million in 1998. The German media conglomerate Bertelsmann. owns 40 percent of bn.com. Fatbrain, in third place, registered a revenue hike of 169.2 percent to $28.8 million from $10.7 million the prior year. Borders.com saw the largest revenue gain, up 289 percent to $17.9 million from $4.1 million in 1999.

In the face of such expanded online bookselling activity, the independents and small chains continued to lose share in 1999, down from 16.6 percent to 15.2 percent. In a departure from past years, however, the large chains also suffered some shrinkage, with their share slipping from 25.3 percent of the market to 24.6 percent. Online bookselling may not have expanded the bookselling pie, but it seems to have carved it up into different sized slices.

STILL PLUMBING FOR PROFITS

While Amazon.com chief Jeff Bezos predicted profits from the company's book business in 2000, none have materialized. In fact, while the company's sales for the year rose to $2.76 billion, its net loss doubled to $1.4 billion from $719.0 million in 1999.

Amazon bit hard on the bullet. The six-year-old company announced its most extensive layoffs to date, 15 percent of its employees or 1,300, and the closure of its warehouse in McDonough, Georgia, which affected 450 employees. In hometown Seattle, the company planned to shutter a customer service center, an additional 400 layoffs. Following the dismal results, Amazon lowered its 2001 sales estimated from $4 billion to between $3.3 billion and $3.6 billion.

Like the book chains, Amazon scaled back its discounts on books in the last year. Over the past five years, Amazon.com has lost $2.28 billion on sales of *$5.17* billion. The company has some $1.1 billion cash in its coffers, which is expected to shrink about 30 percent after it pays its 2000 bills. Still, Amazon said that it will not need to seek out additional financing in 2001.

In June 2000, Amazon.com had covered another base by partnering with Lightning Source, Ingram's print-on-demand division. It has also diversified into other product areas in order to parlay its well-known name into a one-stop site, selling a wide variety of merchandise and services, ranging from power tools to video games to health and beauty aids.

Amazon.com has also expanded overseas and continues to outdo rivals such as Bol.com in Europe. It made forays into Asia in 2000, and in September acquired a 10 percent interest in Dakas.com, an Internet startup based in New Delhi, India. In November 2000 Amazon moved aggressively into Japan, which beckons with an Internet book sales potential of nearly $2 billion.

In addition to the four public online booksellers, other sites having meaningful sales include Books.com, BuyBooks.com, and walmart.com. The total number of sites selling books is difficult to pin down. Prudential Securities estimated about 600 sites selling books in early 1998, a figure that likely doubled by 2000.

SPEED, EFFICIENCY ALL

Although there has been an explosion in online bookstores because of ease of entry, it is also true that the costs to remain a major player in the market keep going up. When it first launched its site, Amazon.com bragged that it was the largest bookstore on earth, stocking 2.5 million titles. The fact of the matter was that Amazon kept a relatively small number of titles in stock and depended on wholesalers, primarily the Ingram Book Company, to fulfill the majority of its orders. Amazon.com executives stressed that being a cyberbusiness with little physical infrastructure held down costs and gave the company an edge in competing with traditional bookstores.

Although Amazon.com does not own any physical bookstores, it has a huge land-based distribution network. The company has decided that it could drive down costs by fulfilling orders itself, rather than relying on third parties. As a result, Amazon.com had about 3.5 million square feet of warehouse space by the end of 1999. The distribution network is designed to speed delivery of books (and music and videos) to consumers.

Speedier, more efficient delivery of products by bn.com was the driving force behind Barnes & Noble's failed effort to acquire Ingram. When the Federal Trade Commission blocked the deal, Barnes & Noble immediately said it would open new distribution centers in Reno, Nevada, and Memphis, Tennessee, adding to an existing one million square-foot warehouse in New Jersey.

Timely delivery of books is becoming increasingly important to the major e-retailers, as some of the other areas of competition have become blurred. For example, the large online retailers have access to nearly all the same mainstream books through their own stocks or through wholesalers, making selection less critical for e-retailers who are trying to differentiate themselves from one another. Also, price has become less of a factor since all major online stores offer discounts on bestsellers.

Trade Distribution

Retailers in the United States buy directly from publishers as well as wholesalers. Frontlist titles are often bought direct, especially if the order is large enough to qualify for the maximum discount. Replenishments come from wholesalers, whom publishers regard as competitors vying for sales to the same outlets.

According to the BISG's analysis of the split between the direct and wholesale distribution channels used by publishers, their direct trade sales, for adult and juvenile combined, have averaged about 79 percent for the years 1994 to 1996. From 1996 on, direct sales rose to an average of 81 percent, a significant gain from the long-time average of 77 percent.

The share distributed by wholesalers, which averaged 21 percent for the three years (1994–1996), saw a dramatic decrease to 18.7 percent, a clear indication that retailers are increasingly bypassing wholesalers to buy direct from publishers. This trend is the result of ABA litigation that forced publishers to give higher discounts to all retail accounts—in some cases, as much as 48 percent. With such high discounts available from publishers, wholesalers like Ingram are under mounting pressure to compete for the retailer's business. In addition, Amazon and the chains—including Barnes & Noble—are buying more of their books direct.

TABLE 10
Direct Sales* versus Sales to Wholesalers/Jobbers, 1994–1999 ($ in millions)

	1994	1995	1996	1997	1998	1999
Total Trade	5,540.6	5,560.8	5,643.0	5,453.2	5,597.6	5,803.6
Direct	4,533.2	4,533.0	4,586.6	4,443.5	4,555.1	4,716.1
Wholesale	1,007.4	1,027.8	1,056.4	1,009.7	1,042.5	1,087.5
Share						
Direct	81.8%	81.5%	81.3%	81.5%	81.4%	81.3%
Wholesale	18.2%	18.5%	18.7%	18.5%	18.6%	18.7%
Adult Trade	4.324.2	4,234.1	4,195.4	4,095.2	4,160.0	4,279.8
Direct	3,708.0	3,633.3	3,604.4	3,521.6	3,578.6	3,681.2
Wholesale	616.2	600.8	591.0	573.6	581.4	598.6
Share						
Direct	85.7%	85.8%	85.9%	86.0%	86.0%	86.0%
Wholesale	14.3%	14.2%	14.1%	14.0%	14.0%	14.0%
Juvenile Trade	1,216.4	1,326.7	1,447.6	1,358.0	1,437.6	1,523.8
Direct	825.2	899.7	982.2	921.9	976.5	1,034.9
Wholesale	391.2	427.0	465.4	436.1	561.1	488.9
Share						
Direct	67.8%	67.8%	67.9%	67.9%	68.0%	68.0%
Wholesale	32.2%	32.2%	32.1%	32.1%	32.0%	32.0%

*Publishers' sales to retailer/consumer.
Source: BISG Book Industry Trends 2000.

Improved inventory and ordering technology at most publishing houses as well as better customer service are also encouraging direct buying. Many publishers use highly skilled telemarketers and invest in training and educating them about the needs of booksellers. They know, for instance, what sells in a given region. This type of selling, along with computerized order placement and fulfillment systems, is making it more feasible for publishers to self-distribute.

When separated into adult and juvenile segments, the ratio of direct-to-wholesale changes dramatically. Only 14 percent of adult books are sold through wholesalers with nearly 86 percent being sold direct. Notable again is the increase in direct buying by retailers starting in 1995.

Juvenile books, up until the early 1990s, had the highest ratio of wholesaler buying to direct. The BISG's projections said that ratio was likely to hold, but when its actual numbers were tabulated, a very different picture emerged. Like their adult counterparts, juvenile books are increasingly being bought directly from the publishers.

Ingram Leader in Distribution Chain

Based in Nashville, Tennessee, the Ingram Book Company is the world's largest book distributor. The company carries nearly 300,000 titles from 3,000 publishers in the United States. In addition to independent bookstores, Ingram services large chains such as Barnes & Noble, Borders, and Crown Books, and commands a 55 percent share of the wholesale market in the United States. With the percentage of books being bought through wholesalers dramatically decreasing, 55 percent of the market is not what it used to be. This, along with Ingram's ill-fated plan to merge with Barnes & Noble, has moved the company into new areas.

In 1999, Ingram Books founded Lightning Print, a print-on-demand unit. Renamed Lightning Source in 2000, it opened an expanded headquarters at La Vergne, Tennessee, to reflect its increased e-book capabilities and digital fulfillment services.

Baker & Taylor, the second-largest wholesaler, has also extended its reach. In mid 1999, Baker & Taylor acquired Yankee Book Peddler, a family-owned academic library distributor based in New Hampshire. About a month later the company filed for an initial public offering to raise $75 million to increase business with Internet retailers and superstores.

Ingram operates as both a wholesaler and a distributor. Although the terms are frequently used interchangeably, they represent two distinct functions. Publishers Resources Inc. is Ingram's distribution arm for medium-size and large publishers. It contracts with publishers for a fee to distribute books.

Wholesalers buy books from publishers in anticipation of demand. They employ buyers, ideally with publishing or bookselling backgrounds. In assessing customers' needs, buyers utilize computer data—as well as personal knowledge of the market—to track customers' (booksellers) buying habits. Wholesalers use other tools to help booksellers. Ingram, for example, also utilizes its Booksellers' First Choice program. This involves a sheet sent to booksellers listing categories.

Participants can indicate on the sheet which books they want reserved in each given category and when they want them. In addition, booksellers use

Ingram's buying judgment as a barometer. If the bookseller is current with his account with Ingram, he can order any publisher's books. If booksellers deal with individual publishers, however, they must keep each separate account current. But once the wholesaler is paid up, in essence, everyone is.

INGRAM'S "JUST IN TIME" SERVICE

Among wholesale benefits is Ingram's "Just in Time" ordering system. Booksellers can get maximum discounts, and where shelf space equals dollars, do not have to keep the stock on hand. The Just In Time program, in effect, offers warehousing to bookstores. By searching on Ingram's own book database, the bookseller can find a book requested by a customer, order it, and have it delivered within twenty-four hours. Next-day delivery is possible to 85 percent of booksellers in the United States.

The advantage of this program is that the booksellers need not tie up their money and space in multiple copies of one book. Rather, they can have one copy of many titles and, therefore, a better chance of meeting the needs of more customers. If a book is not in stock, the bookseller can tell the customer that he has it in his warehouse (actually at Ingram) and can get it in one day. Baker & Taylor also has a similar system.

Fewer Distributors

As in retailing and publishing, consolidation has also proved to be a shaping trend in distribution. The two largest distributors, Ingram and Baker & Taylor, still command the lion's share of trade distribution. In the past five years, a number of small distributors have disappeared from the scene, including Atrium, Inland, Pacific Pipeline, and Southern Publishers Group.

The diminishing numbers of small national distributors hurts the small independent publishers. With about a dozen such operations left, it is increasingly difficult for smaller publishers, who are most in need of distributors, to find one. And the number of small publishers is expanding rapidly, while that of distributors is waning. As the business changes, new distributors serving special outlets have emerged. Such players include Advanced Marketing Services (AMS), a San Diego distributor, which serves only price clubs, warehouse clubs, and large stores such as Kmart.

Apart from the large players and the specialists, one independent distributor thrives, perhaps because it has diversified into other areas. National Book Network (NBN), based in Lanham, Maryland, is a distributor specializing in independent book publishers and has acquired a total of seventeen small independent publishers over the past three years. Through its various imprints, the company now publishes 1,000 original titles across the academic, reference, and general trade markets.

Book Clubs

Shaped by Consolidation and Community

Book clubs made their appearance in the pre-Wal-Mart days when there were few bookstores selling books and when publishers mostly released hardcover editions. As malls and chain stores gained in prominence with their discounts, book clubs started to lose their force in the marketplace. The segment was further affected by the rise of superstores, online selling, and even home shopping television networks. Superstores have been generally blamed for the downturn in book clubs in the early 1990s, according to *The Book Publishing Industry* by Albert N. Greco.

Two trends have shaped the book club segment: targeting to niche and special interest communities and consolidation. With respect to the first, book clubs resemble online shopping in that they are private, used at-home, and particularly adept at reaching niches. Given Doubleday Direct (DD) and its expertise at targeted marketing, Bertelsmann's entry into the online fray in 1998 through its partnership with bn.com seemed a natural step.

In the evolution of book clubs, the general interest clubs that began in their heyday by selling high-quality first editions of fiction, nonfiction, reference

TABLE 11
Book Club Sales, 1990-2000 ($ in millions)

Year	Sales	Change
1990	725.1	
1991	749.8	3.4%
1992	742.3	–1.0%
1993	804.7	8.4%
1994	873.9	8.6%
1995	976.1	11.7%
1996	1,091.8	11.9%
1997	1,143.1	4.7%
1998	1,209.4	5.8%
1999	1,254.4	3.7%
2000	1,291.6	3.0%

Source: Book Industry Study Group; Association of American Publishers.

titles, and other categories were eventually joined by clubs that were organized around more specialized interests. These clubs segmented the market, addressing the needs of highly targeted interest communities as business, mystery, health, and other areas.

A sense of community built around such enclaves can give book clubs a strong attraction, as can those built around a strong brand. Leveraging the *Prevention* magazine brand, for example, Rodale Press's health-based book club business has flourished. But the smattering of small, independent clubs that have continued to exist are besieged by competitors from numerous fronts—the superstores, the Internet and the mammoth Bookspan, the epitome of the second trend, consolidation. Bookspan dominates the segment. Formed in March 2000, it is a partnership between Bertelsmann's DD and Time Warner's Book-of-the-Month Club (BOMC).

Even before this union, consolidation activity had been a considerable force in the book club segment. The three main players were DD, BOMC, and Rodale Press. Doubleday Direct had bought Newbridge from K-Ill (Primedia) in late 1997, adding nearly a million members to its fold. (K-Ill had sold its children's book club in 1995 to Geografico De Agnosti in 1995). Time Warner's BOMC had twelve clubs, including three acquired from Meredith's book clubs in 1995. Although the BOMC line had concentrated on general hardcover titles, the Meredith acquisition allowed it to build on its home service franchise.

The Bookspan combine now accounts for more than $900 million, or 69 percent, of the annual revenues of $1.3 billion for the book clubs. Bookspan has 10 million members and employs some 3,000, located in New York, Pennsylvania, and Indiana. Bookspan represents a virtual monopoly of the book club segment. The terms of the agreement between Time Warner and Bertelsmann were not made public, but Bookspan is represented as a single entity, with back office functions combined for profitability.

Bookspan has clubs in four categories: general interest, specialty, lifestyle, and professional. The general interest category includes BOMC, The Literary Guild, Quality Paperback Club, Doubleday Book Club. Lifestyles includes Crossings, Children's Book-of-the-Month Club, and One Spirit. Specialty clubs include Mystery Guild, Science Fiction Book Club, The Good Cook, and Crafter's Choice. In the professional category are: Computer Books Direct, Telecommunications Book Club, Library of Computer and Information Sciences, and Behavioral Science Book Service.

Crossings and One Spirit are the religion clubs of DD and BOMC, respectively. Crossings, launched a decade ago by Doubleday, boasted more than a million members at the time of the merger and was DD's fastest growing club. One Spirit, its BOMC counterpart, was launched in 1995 and was also BOMC's fastest growing club. Combined, the two Christian clubs have an estimated 1.6 million members. The online division of Bookspan, booksonline.com, will feature many of the book clubs at a single website. "It combines the time-tested advantages of the traditional book club with the convenience, ease of use, and interactivity of the Internet," Bookspan said. According to PC Data Online, booksonline.com ranks third among online book destinations.

Although Bookspan is the most dramatic instance of the consolidation that has driven the book club segment, it also fuses this trend with the first, given its plans to expand by launching new book clubs focusing on niche markets.

Electronic Books

The e-book Evolution

Only two years have elapsed since NuvoMedia, a small California startup, introduced the Rocket eBook, a "dedicated handheld device" for reading books off a screen. All but ignored by traditional print publishers at first, the books were subject to media hype and soon were touted as the greatest innovation in publishing since the Gutenberg printing press. In the spring of 2000, Stephen King became the first high-profile author to publish a novel electronically. Jammed websites ensued as more than 500,000 copies were downloaded. That momentous event sparked a frenzy of deal making by publishers eager to join on the e-book parade.

Clearly, the e-book had arrived. Hastily arranged conferences were packing publishers to the doors as they came to listen to the evangelists. A tangle of alliances and cross-alliances ensued as the giants of print publishing rushed to stake out their chunk of e-territory. Prognosticators, Barnes & Noble vice-chairman Steve Riggio among them, believe the e-book business will grow to anywhere between $1 billion and $3 billion in five years. And more than a few industry analysts are saying e-books will make up "about 10 percent of the book publishing market in as little as five years." Dick Brass, Microsoft's vice-president of technology development, expects e-book sales to reach $1 billion in four years, and he believes that by 2020, 50 percent of everything that is read will be in electronic form.

These predictions could be overly optimistic. Despite some encouraging developments, one element of the e-book business appears slow to pick up on their creators' enthusiasm—the buying public. Thus far, it appears more likely that consumer acceptance of e-books will be less of a revolution than an evolution. However, a new generation of digital readers is rising, and the

Internet is here to stay. Whether the demand for e-books materializes in the near or long term, there is little doubt that it will happen.

Book publishers, software and hardware producers, online booksellers, and digital research suppliers are betting on this and investing dollars and energy in the digital future. But even at this early stage, players are pondering a vexing array of problems. Issues range from developing standards for hardware and software to ways to ensure copyright protection, fairly compensate authors, sort out pricing, and, above all, survive in a business on the cusp of radical change.

Enter the Software Giants

Within a short time, dominant software players Adobe Systems and Microsoft started major e-book efforts built on their systems for formatting and reading e-books on desktops or personal digital assistant screens. Microsoft made a splashy entry into the digital publishing arena when it unveiled its Microsoft Reader with Clear Type software in January 2000 at the International CES. A month later, Adobe Systems and e-book publisher Glassbook said that they had joined in an agreement to integrate the Glassbook Reader and the Adobe Acrobat Reader into so-called Portable Document Files (PDFs) for electronic documents. With these and other major developments, the dawn of the new millennium seemed to hold out great promise as an auspicious time for e-books. Both the Adobe and Microsoft systems claim to read most like a paper book, and both boast case of use and hacker-proof security.

In January 2000, Gemstar International acquired both NuvoMedia and SoftBook, putting the company in a key position to "technologically enhance" the reading experience, according to Gemstar's chief executive officer and chairman Henry C. Yuen. In the fall, Gemstar and Thomson Multimedia, its manufacturing partner, introduced two new models, the black-and-white REB 1100, priced at $299, and the color REB 1200 ($699).

Stephen King: An Epiphany for Publishers

A watershed event occurred on March 14, 2000, when Stephen King became the first high-profile author to publish electronically, igniting widespread consumer—and publisher—interest in e-books. In an arrangement between Simon & Schuster and his own Philtrum Press, King released *Riding the Bullet,* a 16,000-word novella that could be downloaded from the Internet and read on computers or handheld devices. The cost was $2.50, and some websites offered it for free. Demand was overwhelming, sites jammed, and over one-half million copies were downloaded.

The unprecedented public response confirmed that there was indeed an audience for e-books and triggered a stampede of deal-making by publishers and others eager to grab a piece of the electronic book business. As a result, many new, and in some cases, seemingly unlikely, alliances were formed, as the lure of e-book riches blurred traditional lines in the publishing industry.

Amid all the deal-making hoopla, one of the most powerful unions is between Barnes & Noble and Microsoft. In April 2000, Barnes & Noble announced it would begin distributing books formatted for Microsoft's Clear Type software on its website, for downloading to Windows desktops or personal digital assistants made by Casio, Compaq, and Hewlett Packard.

Microsoft, a relative latecomer to the e-publishing fray, moved quickly to sign up the major publishers. May was a busy month for the software giant. In quick succession it partnered with Simon & Schuster, Random House, and Time Warner Trade Publishing.

Wrapping up its sweep of the publishing business, Microsoft closed an agreement with Lightning Source, Ingram's print-on-demand and digital fulfillment unit, to make its e-books compatible with the Microsoft Reader software. The deal gave Microsoft significantly more e-book titles to offer via its Reader, and made Lightning's digital library more accessible to publishers, retailers, and consumers.

Publishers Set up E-imprints

In May 2000, Time Warner Trade Publishing unveiled the company's new e-book publishing business, iPublish.com. Slated to debut in early 2001, iPublish.com, will produce, distribute and sell fiction and nonfiction specifically for the Internet. It has a dedicated marketing and editorial staff of fifteen. Its mission is to brand Time Warner authors, brand iPublish authors, and attract new authors. iPublish.com also forged relationships with Microsoft, Gcmstar, bn.com, and Amazon.com, among others.

Random House announced plans in August 2000 to launch AtRandom, an imprint offering original e-books by prominent authors, including Henry Alford, Donald Katz, Lewis Latham, and Elizabeth Wurtzel. Titles will be available in digital format and as print-on-demand paperbacks.

Barnes & Noble: Publisher, Printer, Distributor, Bookseller . . .

Barnes & Noble, with a finger in virtually every section of the e-publishing pie, is making traditional publishers jumpy. The company has no qualms about prospecting in areas once considered their exclusive domain. Already quietly entrenched in print publishing to the tune of $150 million annually, the giant chain has made no secret of its intent to become a leading e-publisher as well as distributor.

In 2000, it opened an online e-book superstore, acquired a large stake in vanity publisher iUniverse.com, and launched its own e-books list. Its acquisition of Fatbrain brought with it nearly half of Internet publisher Mighty Words. The company also owns a stake in Gemstar's eBook unit, acquired when the Rocket eBook was owned by NuvoMedia.

Barnes & Noble also plans to take advantage of new print-on-demand technology. The company has installed digital printers at its warehouses in order to print books from publishers' digital files. In October 2000, bn.com published its first e-books list through agreements with both traditional and c-book publishers.

How Soon? How Serious?

All these developments were occurring in an environment where, according to a recent survey by Book Expo America and *Publisher's Weekly,* 63 percent of book buyers are aware of the existence of e-books, but 70 percent are "not at all likely" to buy one in the next six months. Moreover, an October 2, 2000 *Wall Street Journal* story quoted online publisher Xlibris Corporation's founder and CEO John Feldcamp as saying, "Let's be frank: with the exception of phenomena related to Stephen King, nothing is selling."

Indeed, some industry pundits have even questioned the commitment of the publishers who arc the loudest trumpeters of their e-book initiatives. At Penton Media's eBook World conference in New York in November 2000, chairman Michael Wolff confronted a panel of e-publishing representatives from the major houses with the question: "How serious are you about this?"

For now, it seems probable that many of the publishing deals discussed between technology players and print publishers do not involve large cash investments. Instead, they are benefiting from competition among the three major technology players, Microsoft, Adobe, and Gemstar. As these companies vie for dominance, they are courting publishers for their content, and publishers are only too happy to barter their (usually backlist) titles in exchange for exposure in e-format. Digital publication of their content may put it before a new readership, and if publishers happen to collect some revenues by actually selling e-books, that's icing on the cake.

If publishers are reluctant to throw real money at the nascent e-book business, they can hardly be blamed. They were badly burned in the early to mid 1990s when the new media hype drove them disastrously into new media. All the major houses—and some smaller ones—set up expensive new media divisions to publish CD-ROMs. The products turned out to be a huge flop, and publishers bled millions. Even though the Internet changes the picture, publishers have learned a bitter lesson and are not apt to believe what the new media shills told them less than a decade ago—that print was dead, and the technology train was leaving without them.

Standardization of Formats Crucial

Industry standards and standardization are a major concern to all e-book players. The two current formats for e-book content, PDF and a variation of HTML and XML, are supported by different e-book reading software. But e-book developers are working to unify the industry with the *Open eBook 1.0 Publication Structure Specification,* a public-domain offering outlining in a common file format for e-book content based on XML and HTML.

Initiated by the National Institute of Standards and Technology (NIST) in 1998, the Open eBook forum (OEBF) is devoted to developing a standard for electronic content, as well as pushing for content interoperability between the many interfaces in the e-chain needed to get digital content securely from content provider to end-user.

The first annual spring meeting of the OEBF convened in New York City in May 2000. The two sessions that were open to publishers free of charge were filled to standing room only with about 200 attending each session, including a "Town Hall" meeting on digital rights management. Of the eighty-three principal (annual dues $5,000) and associate ($1,000) members listed, only six were traditional print publishers, and these were large players, such as Houghton Mifflin, Random House, and Simon & Schuster. Thus far, the membership list remains top-heavy with technology players, including Microsoft, Gemstar, and OverDrive.

Fear of Being "Napstered"

Digital rights management firms and websites such as Rightsworld.com and Rightscenter.com have emerged to offer publishers encryption and other systems to protect their content from piracy and to assure proper payment of fees. In May 2000, the Copyright Clearance Center (CCC) developed a new digital rights management system for Internet copyrighted materials. The program is intended to minimize copyright infringement of digital content delivered over the Internet by providing instantaneous permissions.

Also in the content protection business is Reciprocal, a digital content service provider that outsources a Digital Rights Management (DRM) solution for secure e-books and digital text for Palm Pilot devices. The solution, intended to protect and control access to digital content so that it can be distributed to end-users without a risk of losing copyright control for the content owner, is set for launch in early 2001.

Horror stories of hackers in the music world have flooded the industry in 1999 and 2000, and publishers' greatest nightmare is that Napster-types may spring up, rendering content valueless. Speaking at a recent NIST conference, Dick Brass, vice-president of technology development at Microsoft, warned that widespread piracy could derail the e-book industry. "The irony is that the more sophisticated [the e-book industry] becomes, the more tempting it will be for pirates," Brass told attendees. Moreover, if e-books were to become as easy to copy and distribute as MP3 music files, Brass said, "the whole tradition of fee-based content publishing could collapse."

The fear is not unwarranted. In his book, *Future Consumer.com; The Webolution of Shopping to 2010* (published by Warwick, based in Toronto), global business futurist Frank Feather writes: "Providers of any and every kind of content face an inescapable law of the Internet: anything that can be digitized will be digitized and downloadable. After the first copy is digitized, the cost of electronic distribution is next to zero." That chilling view was echoed in a Forrester Research report published in September 2000. The report, *Content out of Control,* "predicts the book industry will lose $1.5 billion by 2005 to rip-off websites similar to Napster." Forrester analyst Eric Schierer said that neither digital security nor lawsuits will stop the pirates.

Balance of Power Shifting

On the creative front, the Internet could upset the already uneasy symbiosis that exists between author and publisher. Authors resent the power publishers have to call the shots on just about everything from advances to print runs to marketing plans. Publishers have seen authors as prima donnas with no interest in or knowledge of the hard realities of the business of publishing. The Internet, bolstered the plethora of vanity e-publishers such as iUniverse and Xlibris, has made it easy for authors to self-publish.

Stephen King followed up his digital publishing success with *Riding the Bullet* by serializing a novel, *The Plant,* on his website, asking those who downloaded it to pay $1 per chapter. No traditional publisher or bookseller was needed. Thousands of other, less well-known writers are getting their literary efforts directly to the reader via the Internet. If more well-known authors were to go the same route, both publisher and booksellers could become obsolete. In another scenario, authors could opt to hold onto electronic rights to their works and sell them elsewhere. Publishers may have felt relieved when Stephen King had to discontinue the serialized publication of *The Plant* because of too few downloads and dollars. However, King's experiment is hardly the last word on self-publishing via the Internet.

In recent years, more and more battles have been fought between authors, publishers, and agents over who owns electronic rights. The Author's Guild believes all parties will lose if publishers don't agree to compensate authors fairly and takes the position that: "the author's rate should be increased commensurate with the publisher's increase in profits from electronic sales."

Some accommodations have been made, if one judges by the growing number of works by best-selling authors available in electronic formats. Random House recently said that it would pay authors 50 percent of the net it receives on e-books. This percentage will apply to both its frontlist and backlist books. Previously, Random House set royalty payments for e-books at 15 percent of the retail price. With the new rate, a $20 dollar e-book, which in round numbers would net the publisher about $10, gives the author $5, which is 60 percent more than he would get at 15 percent of list retail. Random House has historically been adamant in its demand of electronic rights from its authors, and this new royalty rate certainly sweetens the pot.

So much content is available for free on the Web, however, that publishers also have been fretting over just how much consumers are willing to pay for e-books. Current prices range from free to the same price as print books, which some publishers justify, saying e-books are not less expensive to produce, and profit margins are smaller. Others contend that prices should fluctuate based on consumer demand, costing more, for instance, when a new title is released.

Ultimately, the consumer will set the price, choose the format, and adopt or reject handheld reading gizmos. Thus far, little has been heard from the key player in the entire e-publishing enterprise, the consumer. And while the loudest buzz is coming from the trade segment of publishing, it appears logical that trade—certainly fiction—will not be e-books' first or best application.

For those who read for pleasure, e-books must improve on the print book, and that is hard to do. Daniel O'Brien, a Forrester Research analyst tracking e-books, says that consumers have shown very little interest in reading on a screen. O'Brien doesn't see e-books as tempting the reader away from print books anytime soon, pointing out that "books are pretty elegant."

But for students, professionals, and researchers, the e-book is an invaluable invention. Dozens of works can be downloaded onto a laptop, an electronic personal planner, or a dedicated handheld device such as Gemstar's eBooks. Digitized content can be stored, highlighted, bookmarked, annotated, and carried. Customized digital libraries can be easily created for consumer, academic, and business use. Study will be easier and more efficient, and as e-books make their way into education, the hunched-over backs of middle and high-school students under their crushing backpacks of books will disappear from the landscape. The first serious adoption of the e-book, we believe, will be for practical purposes such as research and education. These users, as time goes on and technology improves, will eventually buy e-books for their pleasure reading.

Bibliography

Book Industry Study Group. *Book Industry Trends, 2000.,* New York, 2000.

Book Industry Study Group. *Consumer Research Study On Book Purchasing.* New York, 2000.

Book Industry Study Group. *The Rest of Us.* New York, 1999.

Greco, Albert N. *The Book Publishing Industry.* Needham Heights, Mass:, Allyn & Bacon, 1997.

Open Book Publishing, Inc. The Subtext 2000–2001 Perspective on Book Publishing Numbers, *Issues & Trends,* Darien, Conn., 2001.

Peters, Jean. 1992. "Book Industry Statistics from the R. R. Bowkcr Company," *Publishing Research Quarterly* 8 (fall): 18.

◆5◆

Textbook Publishing

Robert J. R. Follett

Fifty years ago, I had just graduated from college and was teaching in an elementary school on the edge of Harlem in New York City. I am amazed at how little has changed in the lecture halls or classrooms in the intervening fifty years. Teaching still goes on as it has for the past one hundred or two hundred years.

To understand textbook publishing, it is important to start with an understanding of the markets that this industry serves.

This essay will begin with some general observations about the marketplace for textbooks. Next, it will focus on publishing for elementary and secondary schools, and then on publishing for colleges and universities. It will include brief references to other kinds of textbook markets. Finally, I will speculate on where the industry may be headed.

The General Characteristics of the Textbook Market

Schools and colleges, teachers and professors—all resist change. Several factors help explain this tendency. In part, it is a desire to conserve the practices that have worked for fifty years and for centuries before. At the same time, it is inertia—the reluctance of human beings to leave familiar ways to leap into the unknown. Finally, this resistance to change is related to the incentives affecting the education establishment. Professors do not achieve status and increased income by finding more effective ways of teaching. Classroom teachers, despite the current emphasis on assessing students' performance, gain little benefit from changing the way they teach. There are few incentives for experimentation in education.

We know some things about learning. Often, however, what we know has little impact on actual classroom practices.

We know that students have different learning styles. Not everyone is best taught through the written word or by lecture. Nevertheless, these remain the predominant modes of presentation.

We know that learning, especially among those who are not focused adults, occurs more effectively in groups than it does in individuals. Most work in society is done by teams, and despite the emphasis within educational establishments on individual performance, a great deal of learning occurs when members of a team, group, or class help one another.

We know that high teacher expectations result in higher student performance. In many situations, teachers expect poor performance, and they get it. The content of textbooks has been made easier over the years—"dumbed down"—to reflect low expectations.

It is also clear that there is only a tenuous connection between the amount of money spent per student and student performance. There is little correlation between the quantity and quality of published materials used by students and students' performances. I am not aware of any valid studies that demonstrate that the use of a particular textbook or a particular type of course material results in significantly improved learning. Perhaps textbooks don't really matter. Or perhaps textbooks that would make a real difference have not been successful in gaining acceptance.

For these and other reasons, it should not surprise us that textbook publishing has none of the dynamic, innovative drive of, for example, the software industry.

There are some other very important characteristics of the textbook marketplace. In most kinds of publishing, the person who selects the publication, the person who pays for it, and the person who uses it are the same person. This is not true in textbook publishing.

The person who selects the textbook does not have to pay for it. The students who use the textbook have no say in the decision to select it.

In colleges, the professors select textbooks. The college bookstore purchases them and then sells them to the students. In elementary and secondary schools, it is usually a committee of administrators and teachers (with the administrators generally dominating the process) that choose the textbook. In most school districts, tax funds are used to purchase the textbook. Needless to say, students have no input.

This separation of the selection from the purchase and also from the user has many implications. One is that those who make the selection have different criteria for their choice than would those who use the selection. For example, to those who select textbooks, that a book has clearly written text is usually less important than are flashy illustrations and graphics. This is because it is easy to differentiate among a variety of possible textbook choices by how well the graphics attract. It is difficult and much more time-consuming to evaluate the organization and presentation of written text.

Another implication is that those who decide which textbook to choose care little about cost. They don't have to dig into their own pockets to pay. In contrast, those who must pay are very conscious of the cost, but care little about the content, especially because they had no part in making the selection. The reasons for choosing a specific textbook are obscure to them; the cost is very clear.

Finally, the users—students—have no commitment to the selection and often find textbooks unsuited to their capabilities and needs. The textbook does not have a high value to them.

Keeping these general characteristics in mind, let's explore more deeply the specific textbook markets.

Elementary and Secondary School Textbook Publishing

In 1999, publishers of elementary and secondary school textbooks had sales of $3.4 billion, according to the Association of American Publishers. These sales were almost all generated by only four large companies. In the U.S. economy, $3.4 billion is small change. This amount is dwarfed by the sales of many individual companies in other industries.

Elementary and secondary school textbooks are almost always selected by a committee. However, the choices available to committees are limited by the peculiarities of the textbook adoption system.

In my youth, some states selected a single textbook for use by every student in the state who was in that course and grade. The decision on which textbook to adopt was made at the state level. Because of the high stakes involved, unsavory practices were common. I was often solicited for payoffs—to get the textbooks I published selected, payments would need to be made to a politician.

In time, this practice of adopting a single textbook came to an end, as payoff scandals made headlines and even sent prominent state and big city educators to prison, and as teachers and principals became more vocal in wanting a say in choosing the textbooks that they would use in their local classrooms.

Nevertheless, many of the pernicious effects of this system are still with us. A handful of very large states—California, Texas, and Florida among them—still establish statewide curriculum standards and courses of study. At the state level, a group of textbooks is selected from which local districts may choose. Of course, all of the textbooks chosen at the state level conform to the state requirements. Unsurprisingly, the publishers endeavor to publish textbooks that conform as closely as possible to these requirements, and there is hardly any substantial difference among the various textbooks that are submitted for adoption and finally chosen for purchase.

The importance of these large state adoptions and the economic advantage of publishing a single series for the entire country is that almost all textbooks offered to schools anywhere in the United States conform to the requirements of these few large states. Schools have little real choice. Even if school administrators had a choice between radically different approaches, there is little likelihood that they would choose unconventional course materials.

On what basis do educators choose among very similar textbooks? Educational efficacy ought to be the criteria. Seldom, however, is there the time or know-how to exhaustively investigate the educational efficacy of the materials offered; other criteria are more important. The graphic attraction of the textbooks counts a lot. The promised convenience and ease of use for teachers is very important. This has put a premium on teacher's guides and other ancillary materials that add to publishers' costs but produce little or no revenue.

And salesmanship counts for a lot. A salesperson who has been in the territory for a long time and has established personal relationships with those who select the textbooks will sell many more than a brand-new salesperson, regardless of the quality of the textbooks. A company that can afford to have a salesperson in frequent contact with those who select textbooks will be much more successful than a company that has its sales force spread thin, allowing only infrequent contact with customers.

For publishers of elementary and secondary school textbooks, the cost of the sales effort is very significant. Much of the consolidation of the textbook-publishing industry has been driven by the push to have each salesperson sell more textbooks in a smaller territory, providing both intensive contact with customers and sufficient sales potential to reduce the impact of selling costs on profits.

Elementary and secondary school textbooks are selected, perhaps first at the state level, then at the school-district level by a committee of administrators and teachers. Few classroom teachers have much say in selecting the textbooks that they will use. The textbooks delivered to their classrooms may or may not be appropriate to their students, to their teaching styles, or even to the educational outcomes that the administrators have in mind.

The order for the textbooks comes from the school-district business office. Shipments often go from the publisher to the district warehouse, which then handles distribution to individual schools. Payment, usually slow, comes from the district business office. School taxes provide the funds for the purchase.

The cost of textbooks is usually of most concern to the district business officer. This person is far removed from the classroom and from the learning outcomes that occur there. Textbooks represent a very small portion of the total school budget. They are, however, among the easiest items to cut in the budget. The salaries and fringe benefits of teachers and other school personnel can almost never be reduced. They usually increase each year. Building maintenance can only be deferred for so long. Parents demand new band uniforms. And so on. The constituency pushing for textbook expenditures has little power to affect budget decisions.

In many American schools, it now costs $9,000 or more per year to educate a student. Of that $9,000, usually less than $100 goes for the purchase of textbooks. District administrators keep even this small cost down by delaying the purchase of new texts to replace the old. On average, a textbook is used for seven years in a classroom. In contrast, we typically keep our cars for three or four years.

The costs of providing graphically attractive textbooks, accompanied by a raft of nonrevenue-producing ancillary materials, presented by a large and expensive sales force, yet only purchased every seventh year, means that textbook prices are high. The high prices only encourage school districts to delay replacement purchases longer.

What changes can be expected in the situation that has been described?

There was an era when change seemed likely. Baby boom children flooded the schools, and a new corps of young, idealistic teachers came into the classrooms. Politicians, galvanized by Sputnik and fear of falling behind the Soviet Union, poured funds into educational experiments and into the development and purchase of educational materials. As a young publisher in those heady times, I launched a number of innovative products. All of our publications sold well, and I thought myself a publisher of uncommon wisdom and skill.

The teachers became older; the Sputnik scare passed; the funding went away. I found that my wisdom and skill were not as great as I thought they were. Innovative products began to lose sales, and it became much more difficult to sell even conventional textbooks. The number of publishers of elementary and secondary school textbooks—two dozen or more—began to shrink.

Conditions that will generate a push for change now do not seem to be present. Many of the young, idealistic teachers have become old and cynical and are retiring. Their replacements are still idealistic, but they have much lower expectations about changing the system or dramatically increasing learning outcomes for students. In the current economy, the best and brightest of our young people seldom go into teaching.

There are many experiments going on with computers and the Internet. There is little evidence that the use of these digital devices makes any meaningful change in learning. And why should it, given the persistence of long-established modes of classroom activity? Much of the focus of computer-based experimentation is upon individual learning and does not consider that group learning is both ubiquitous and effective. Computers are often used for drill and practice—substitute workbooks. The Internet is usually used as a reference source. Neither affects basic learning to any degree.

Many classroom teachers have difficulty operating the film projector or VCR. To train them to use computer-based learning tools effectively will be a time-consuming and costly endeavor.

Textbook publishers are lured by the appeal of new technology, but as long as major adoption states and large school districts select and primarily purchase textbooks, the publishers are unlikely to stray far from the products that produce the profits.

New technology seems to require much higher levels of expenditure than do conventional textbooks. Perhaps that will change, but in the near future, there does not seem to be much chance that most schools will come up with the funds to replace textbooks with computer-based learning tools.

In my view, the textbook will remain the primary instructional tool used in school classrooms for a long time to come. Financial pressures will keep textbook expenditures at a tiny percentage of overall spending. These factors will make it difficult for textbook publishers succeed and will increase the push for further consolidation of the industry.

College Textbook Publishing

The college textbook industry had sales of $3.1 billion in 1999, according to the Association of American Publishers. Most of these sales were made by only a few publishers. College textbook publishers face a daunting challenge to maintain even this sales level. Fewer than half the students enrolled in a course, on average, buy a new textbook. This percentage has been declining for years.

Why do so few students actually buy a textbook?

College professors receive boxes of textbook samples. They have little time and few objective criteria by which to make their selection. The choice may be made because the professor knows the author of a particular book. Colorful graphics may make one book stand out from all of the others. The relationship between the professor and a company's campus sales representative may be the deciding factor. Sometimes, the relationship between the professor's course structure and the textbook's organization determines the selection.

Cost almost never influences the professor's decision. Some professors are not selecting textbooks at all. Finding nothing that exactly meets their requirements, they assemble a selection of textbook chapters and articles from journals, magazines, and newspapers. This collection is then turned over to the bookstore, a copy shop, or some other supplier to reproduce in quantity for sale to students. Copyright permission may or may not be obtained from the publishers. It is estimated that some 10 percent of the course materials now offered are made up of such materials.

The price of a typical new textbook now approaches or has reached $70 a copy. The student who is expected to purchase this textbook has already spent a very large amount on tuition and room and board. There are many more appealing discretionary purchases competing for the limited funds available to the student from parents, part-time jobs, loans, and other sources.

The student has no say in selecting the textbook; the professor on the first day of class often says that exams will primarily be based on class presentations; and anyway, several chapters of the textbook are not going to be used. Older students confirm that the textbook plays only a small role in getting a good grade in that course. So the student's first inclination is to not buy a textbook. The next alternative is to band together with a group of students to buy one textbook to be shared among them. This is very common. Of course, if a textbook is to be purchased, the student (or group of students) will seek out a used book that can be bought at a lower price. Only as a last resort do most students buy a new textbook.

With customers like this, it is no wonder that the college textbook industry is feeling pressured.

In upper-level courses, there is greater emphasis on the use of library and Internet resources, with no textbook being used.

When professors select the textbook, they notify the bookstore of their selection. The bookstore places an order with the publisher for those books it needs beyond the number of used copies it has available. The professor is often insistent that the bookstore obtain one book for each student expected to enroll in the course. Even though most college bookstore text managers know that far fewer than 100 percent of those enrolled will actually purchase a book, they often feel constrained to order enough books for 100 percent of the students. Some professors come into the store and count the books on the shelf, so concerned are they that books will run out before all students have a chance to purchase copies.

On a campus with more than one bookstore, the total orders from the several bookstores will surely exceed 100 percent of the expected enrollment for the course.

Returns of unsold books are inevitable. This is a huge problem for college textbook publishers (as well as for the wholesalers of used textbooks). If they send out enough books for 100 percent of the enrollment, and only 50 percent are sold, this generates very large costs. The publishers must manufacture, ship, then handle returns of these textbooks, and often they must also junk them if a newer edition or a stronger competitor makes the returned copies obsolete.

Of course, most businesses try to recover increased costs by raising prices. In college textbook publishing, this has led to constantly escalating prices. The high prices lead students to make greater efforts to find ways not to buy a new book from the publisher. This vicious circle then leads to higher prices, fewer sales, more returns, still higher prices, and so on.

College professors have even less incentive to care about student learning outcomes than do teachers at the elementary and secondary levels. The status and pay of college professors bear almost no relation to his or her effectiveness as a teacher. That a textbook might make a significant difference in student learning is not a major consideration in selection. Professors care about their students, of course, but their incentives do not encourage careful selection of course materials for educational efficacy.

College professors usually receive little or no training in teaching. They usually teach in the same way that they were taught. The ways in which the material in college courses is presented have not changed all that much from the methods used in medieval European universities.

Computers are now everywhere on college campuses. No campus of any size is without its fiber-optic network and Internet connections. Yet these technologies have little impact upon instruction in the lower-level courses with large enrollments. They are used for information gathering, communication, as a substitute for the quill pen of old and the typewriter of more recent times. Certainly, statistical calculations are far easier with computers than they were with the hand-cranked calculators of my youth. Elegant graphs plot across the screen in eye-opening ways.

But the older technologies of film and television have had little impact on college instruction, and the newer digital technologies have had little direct impact upon textbook use. It seems likely that the textbook will continue to be the course material chosen by most professors for most courses. It also seems likely that the percentage of students actually buying a new textbook will continue to shrink as prices rise.

College textbook publishers have consolidated to reduce competition, to eliminate costs, and to try to cope with a shrinking percentage of purchasers and an increasing burden of returns. There continue to be small publishers on the fringes, but this stagnant market is likely to be dominated by a few large companies. These companies may be profitable for years to come, but it is not a business I would encourage young people to enter.

Other Markets for Textbooks

There are other markets for instructional materials produced by publishers. One very large market consists of companies and organizations that provide their employees with training. Another market is among individuals looking to upgrade their skills, to learn new skills, or to develop new avocations or hobbies.

Unlike the school and college markets, these markets are driven by results. Learning outcomes must be visible, and learning must occur quickly. Buyers and users want materials that work. Neither inertia nor a conservative stance has wedded them to a specific type of instructional material.

An organization's training director selects the materials, uses funds in his or her training budget to make the purchase, oversees the use of the materials, and is evaluated on whether or not the users of the materials found them productive and helpful. The feedback is usually quick and can be brutal if the course (and its materials) do not produce results.

An individual seeking a specific career or avocational outcome also expects results quickly. If something isn't working, the user will abandon it or drop the course. The loss of students tells the organization providing the training that the course is not succeeding. There will be rapid efforts to find the fix, and there is no commitment to retain a specific textbook or other kind of course material.

It is in these markets that technological innovation is most likely to find its place. Technology can deliver instructional materials to individual learners or organizational training sites in scattered locations. Technology provides for more rapid feedback from learners to instructors. Technology can be tailored more rapidly to specific learning environments and learner requirements. Technology allows rapid revision. There are many reasons why new technologies are being much more rapidly adopted for organizational and individual training.

The merits of technology notwithstanding, textbooks still have a strong position in these markets. But they have to produce visible results and suit the user, or they won't sell.

Many of the companies serving these markets are not book publishers. They are technology companies. Many of the companies serving these markets are small and nimble.

I have had little experience in these markets. It was my good fortune to publish some materials that were used in them, but this occurred more by happenstance than by plan. I do not want to say more than I know, so I will conclude this section by emphasizing again how different these markets are from the school and college markets that have been discussed at greater length above.

I should add that few colleges and almost no schools have been successful in capturing a significant portion of the organizational and individual training markets. Those colleges that have succeeded usually have a different structure, different personnel, and different incentives for this market than they have for their traditional student group. Thus, there is little overlap of customers who buy textbooks and other course materials for these different markets.

Conclusions

We have examined some of the characteristics of the major textbook markets and some important aspects of the purchasing of textbooks in these markets. One key factor is the disjuncture between selection, purchase, and use. Another is the ease of deferring or cutting textbook purchases compared with the difficulty of reducing other educational costs. Still another is the tenuous connection between the textbook and student learning outcomes, as well as the equally tenuous connection between learning outcomes and incentives for educators. New technologies are expensive, require substantial changes in classroom practice, succeed only with extensive training, and have yet to demonstrate significant and lasting changes in learning outcomes.

I have concluded that both the markets for school textbooks and for college textbooks are likely to be stagnant. Despite the hype for new technologies, I do not see that these will play a major role in classroom learning in either schools or colleges for the foreseeable future. Textbooks are likely to be the major instructional tool for years to come, even though spending on textbooks will probably be a smaller and smaller percentage of students' total spending on school or college education.

The textbook industry will continue to consolidate. Most stagnant industries eventually end up with no more than two or three significant competitors. Not more than two are usually able to generate acceptable levels of profits.

As markets for organizational and individual training continue to grow, new technologies and new companies may come to dominate these markets.

After a long career as a textbook publisher and as an operator of college bookstores, I retired to turn my attention to the publishing of books (and other materials) aimed to help very specific audiences meet their specific needs and concerns. The individuals who use my publications also select them and pay for them. These users provide quick and often vociferous feedback that guides revisions and new publications in a closely connected relationship between reader and publisher. My business is small, as befits an old-timer who wants to ski and hike in the mountains some part of every week. But it is also satisfying, and were I younger, it would be a business with the potential for substantial growth and one in which new technologies would play a significant part. It is a far different business than the textbook publishing and sales in which I worked for many years.

The publishing of materials that make a difference in the lives of people by providing education, information, inspiration, or entertainment is a noble profession. It deserves the best people giving their best efforts. This endeavor will continue forever, even though the means of transmitting and absorbing its content may change.

But as long as the current structure of the organized educational establishment remains the same, as long as the incentives that propel educators remain unchanged, and as long as the finances available for education remain at the same levels, it is unlikely that textbook publishing will be a dynamic, innovative, growing business. It is also unlikely that new technologies will rapidly displace Gutenberg's technology in this arena. A very few companies will dominate this stagnant business.

The best kind of publishing involves a close and intimate relationship between the author and the reader, with the publisher providing the essential bridge between them. This is not the case in most textbook publishing. That this is so is unfortunate for authors, publishers, educators, and most of all, students.

◆6◆

University Press Publishing in the United States

Peter Givler

Universities have been publishers for at least as long as there has been move-able type. In 1455 Gutenberg and Fust finished printing their Bible; twenty-three years later, in 1478, a commentary on the Apostle's Creed was printed at Oxford University. Cambridge University followed and set up a press in 1521. In the United States, Harvard College was founded in 1636; in 1640 the Cambridge Press (operating out of the president of Harvard College's house and no relation to Cambridge University Press) issued the *Bay Psalm Book,* the common hymnal of the Massachusetts Bay Colony. For the next fifty years, the Cambridge Press published books of laws and a translation of the Bible into the language of the local Native Americans, as well as almanacs, catechisms, and sermons.[1]

At the same time, it must be said that the relationship between universities and their presses has not always been easy. The capital requirements and financial ebbs and flows of the publishing business may seem unruly and unpredictable within the context of the more stable and settled financial structure of a university budget; mutual understanding and good communi-cations are essential. The presses at Oxford and Cambridge operated inter-mittently in their early years; it wasn't until the late sixteenth century that the presses at both universities were established that have published continuously ever since. Harvard's Cambridge Press closed in 1692; today's Harvard Uni-versity Press was founded in 1913.

In 1869, the president of Cornell University, Andrew D. White, opened the first American university press to operate in the name of the university itself. Cornell University Press combined a printing plant with a program that provided jobs to journalism students, and its list included two books of North

American ethnology and a French reader. The university closed its journalism program in 1878, however, and by 1884 the press was also shut down; the imprint remained inactive until today's Cornell University Press began operations in 1930. Other presses also began by fits and starts. The University of Minnesota and Stanford University each started presses to publish research in the late nineteenth century and then had to close them. The University of Pennsylvania Press has been in business continuously since 1927, but it was first incorporated in 1890, then closed, reopened in 1920, and closed again before it reopened for good.

The palm for oldest, continuously operating university press in the United States goes to Johns Hopkins University Press, founded by Daniel Coit Gilman in 1878, only two years after he had opened the university itself. Gilman's famous dictum, "It is one of the noblest duties of a university to advance knowledge, and to diffuse it not merely among those who can attend the daily lectures—but far and wide," articulated a clear, specific role for university presses. It is still valid today as one of the central responsibilities of a modern research university and the purpose of its press.

This new research university, as visualized by men like Gilman, William Rainey Harper, and Nicholas Butler (the first presidents of the University of Chicago and Columbia University, respectively), was to be more than an institution for molding the character of society's next generation of leaders and transmitting a knowledge of history and cultural traditions. It was also to be a center for the discovery of new knowledge. This new knowledge would be the product of research carried out in university libraries and laboratories by scholars—and research, if the discovery of knowledge was to progress, had to be shared through some formal system of dissemination. Gilman's injunction that scholarly knowledge should be spread more widely than only among those who could acquire it first-hand by attending university lectures sounds commonplace today, but it was a new idea in its time. University presses began to rise and flourish in the United States because they were an indispensable component of the modern research university itself.

Why, one might ask, did university presses have to be created to fill this role? Commercial publishing in the United States in the late nineteenth century was an active industry; why not leave the publication of scholarship to commercial publishers? Commercial publishing then, as it is today, was a highly competitive business. Gilman and others rightly understood that costs were too high and markets too small to attract a publisher hoping for financial profit. To leave the publication of scholarly, highly specialized research to the workings of a commercial marketplace would be, in effect, to condemn it to languish unseen.[2] If the aspiration of the university was to create new knowledge, the university would also have to assume the responsibility for disseminating it.

Gilman proposed, therefore, that the university take on the job of publication itself—and Johns Hopkins University Press was born: a publishing house relieved from the obligation to generate profits for owners and shareholders by operating under the nonprofit charter of the university and charged with publishing the results of postdoctoral research. Two of its first publications were the *American Journal of Mathematics* and the *American Chemical Journal*, and in 1887 it published its first book.

Other universities soon began to follow suit. In 1891, only one year after the university itself had opened, William Rainey Harper founded the University of Chicago Press. The University of California and Columbia University both opened presses in 1893. In 1896, Oxford University Press opened an office in New York to publish American editions of books originally published in England, but it soon began to develop an independent list of publications for the American market. Presses that still publish today were founded at the University of Toronto in 1901, Princeton in 1905, Fordham in 1907, Yale in 1908, Washington in 1909, Harvard in 1913, New York in 1916, Stanford in 1917, and Illinois in 1918.

By 1920, press managers started gathering informally to discuss their own concerns at the conclusion of the annual meeting of the National Association of Book Publishers. By then new university presses were being formed at a rate of about one per year.[3] In 1937 the group elected its first chairman, Donald P. Bean of the University of Chicago Press, and began to keep formal minutes and plan meetings of its own. In 1946 this group adopted bylaws and completed the formal organization of the Association of American University Presses.

By 1957 the association had thirty-eight members, and that year an event took place that was to have an enormous impact on scholarly publishing—and much else—in the United States: the Soviet Union launched the first artificial satellite, Sputnik, into space. Public opinion was galvanized. The race for space had started, and the United States was losing it. Within a year the United States had launched a satellite of its own, and President Dwight Eisenhower had declared the improvement of education an urgent national priority. The Cold War had a new battleground, and the new warriors would not come out of boot camps and military academies, but schools and universities. It wasn't enough to out-shoot the Russians; now we had to out-think them. The National Defense Education Act (NDEA) was born.

The NDEA provided substantial financial aid to education at all levels and to both public and private institutions. Its primary aim was to improve American education in science, mathematics, and technology, but it also provided support for programs in foreign languages, English as a second language, geography, area studies, educational media and instructional technology, librarianship—and libraries. Money poured into higher education as never before: money for teaching, for research and publication, and for building library collections. NDEA and programs like it created a golden age for publishers of scholarly research in the 1960s. The institutional market boomed, and university presses boomed along with it.

And then the boom ended. In 1969, Neil Armstrong took his famous giant leap for mankind, and the race for space—at least symbolically—was over. We had put two men on the moon, but we also had 550,000 troops on the ground in Vietnam, fighting a real war with no end in sight. Education no longer seemed an urgent national priority, and universities had become unpopular centers of political and social dissent. Congress began redirecting the money almost immediately.

Not surprisingly, the end of the Cold War boom in funding for higher education coincided with the leveling off of the population of university presses. From 1920 to 1970, new university presses continued to open at a rate of about one a year. Between 1970 and 1974, ten more new presses were founded, but only five more were started between 1975 and 2000. The year 1970 also marked the beginning of a slow decline in purchases by libraries of scholarly monographs, particularly in the humanities and social sciences, a decline that continues to this day and that has had a profound impact on university presses. Understanding why and how this change has had such far-reaching effects requires a brief explanation of the economics of scholarly publishing.

Daniel Coit Gilman's linking of the mission of university presses to the purpose of universities themselves helped lay an important legal cornerstone for a large part of today's system of formal scholarly communications. As nonprofit enterprises,[4] university presses seek to fulfill the university's mission of serving the public good through education, rather than of maximizing profits, increasing owners' equity, and paying out shareholders' dividends. Nonprofit status has also, over the years, provided an important measure of financial relief for university presses, who are eligible for noncommercial mailing rates and are not required to pay tax on their inventories. Even as nonprofits, though, university presses still face the same problems all publishers do in gaining access to capital and managing cash flow.

Publishing is a hybrid business. It is a vital cultural enterprise that nourishes the creative use of language and the growth of new ideas, and at the same time, it is an ordinary business with payrolls to meet and bills to pay. From a business point of view, publishing is a manufacturing enterprise. To publish a book a publisher first invests money in searching for, reviewing, acquiring, and editing a manuscript—the research and development phase of publishing, if you will. Then the book itself must be manufactured, requiring the purchase of raw material, the services of printers and binders, and so forth. Only when finished books can be shipped to bookstores and jobbers can readers and libraries purchase them and, finally, cash from sales can begin to flow back to the publisher.

From start to finish this process ordinarily takes two to three years; it can take as long as the publisher has patience for, but it is rarely less than a year. Each book is unique, so the entire process has to be repeated from start to finish for every book. Starting a publishing business requires, as does any other manufacturing business, enough capital to operate for those first years when sales are low. Once successfully started, keeping a publishing firm dynamic and healthy demands careful management of a business in which access to new capital is limited and the supply of cash is nearly always out of phase with demand. Scholarly publishing in particular has an additional difficulty. Publishing for small markets means that all costs have to be recovered from the sale of a small number of copies, creating razor-thin margins for error. The sale of as few as fifty copies can spell the difference between financial success and failure.

The difficulty of keeping the right financial balance has plagued university presses from the beginning. Shortly after it opened, the University of Chicago Press published a twenty-eight-volume series to celebrate its first ten years, a project that incurred heavy initial costs and almost bankrupted the press.[5] Harper, the university's president, defended the project, declaring its value to the university "inestimable," and the press survived, although some lean years followed. In 1998, the University of Chicago Press published 46 journals, 272 books, and had 4,600 of its titles in print, an extraordinary list that includes the canonical *Chicago Manual of Style,* now in its fourteenth edition.[6] Yet without Harper's vigorous support in its early years, this splendid press would have drowned in its own red ink before it had fairly begun.

If Chicago is not unique in having run into financial difficulties, neither is it alone in having overcome them. Every university press has at one time or another found itself running out of money, and virtually all have recovered, battered but wiser.[7] University presses have proven themselves skilled at survival in their quixotic mission of being simultaneously academic idealists and market realists.

Survival, though, requires adaptation. The shift in Congressional priorities that started in 1970 marked the beginning of a gradual reduction in federal funding to higher education. This, in turn, caused library acquisitions budgets to begin to shrink, leaving less money for the purchase of scholarly publications. The cuts in library acquisitions, however, were not distributed equally. Money for the purchase of new materials began to be reallocated internally. University-based scientific research had been increasingly funded by the federal government after World War II, and heavily so during the 1960s; in response, research universities had invested in the laboratories and scientists to carry out government-funded research, and in the process become increasingly dependent on federal funding to maintain this new infrastructure.[8]

To support the work of research scientists and their ability to attract new grants, many research libraries began to shift money within their acquisitions budgets, allocating more money for the purchase of serials, the primary medium for publishing in science and technology, and less to the purchase of books in the humanities and social sciences.[9] The cuts in the funds available for book purchases were deepened even further by the rapid increases in serials prices that began at about the same time. Not only was money being cut, but the money that was left was also losing purchasing power at an alarming rate.[10]

For university presses, the effect of this softening in a core market has been to reduce the amount of cash directly available from the sale of scholarly monographs to support the publication of new monographs, a development that occurred at the same time that universities were also reducing their direct funding to presses in the form of operating subsidies. In order to continue to fulfill their scholarly mission, university presses were forced to seek new sources of funding. Those sources were basically of two kinds: those that provided direct support for publishing scholarly books, and those that provided indirect support by creating new sources of publishing revenue that could then be used to cover the losses from scholarly publishing. Presses employed two strategies. They sought support from foundations, government agencies, and private donors, and they sought new—or at least more lucrative—markets. Most presses have employed some combination of both, which have been critical in shaping university press publishing today.

Outside support is a vital piece of the scholarly publishing financial puzzle. Support from the National Endowments of the Humanities and the Arts (NEH and NEA, respectively) has been especially important. For example, from 1977 to 1995, the NEH through its Publication Subvention Program supported the publication of 1,050 scholarly books in the humanities—books selected through a rigorous screening by expert judges that took place only after the books had already survived the submitting press's normal system of peer review and been accepted for publication by its editorial board. The program ended when the NEH's budget was cut by 37 percent in 1996, and funding for it has not yet been restored.[11]

The Andrew W. Mellon Foundation was also an important source of title subsidies in the 1970s and 1980s and supported the publication of many important scholarly books in the humanities through a series of block grants awarded to university presses. The Mellon Foundation is still the largest foundation in the country with a program interest in scholarly publishing in the humanities, and it continues to support many programs of great importance to university presses, primarily by funding research in scholarly communication and pilot and demonstration projects in electronic publishing.

Some presses have established endowments to support the publication of scholarly books, and fundraising has become a main order of business for many press directors.[12] The NEH offers a Challenge Grant Program through which it will provide $1 for every $4 in new money raised by the press. Some presses have been successful in getting the support of their university foundation for an NEH Challenge Grant or for raising funds through a university campaign.

Nevertheless, as important as outside funding is, it still remains a relatively small source of revenue overall. Data collected from AAUP members shows that from 1988 through 1998, outside gifts and grants (which lumps title subsidies and endowment income together) increased from 2 percent of net sales to only 3.6 percent.[13] It is also sobering to note that during the same period the total amount of nonpublishing income—basically, the sum of university support in the form of general operating subsidies, plus individual title subsidies and endowment income—has declined as a percentage of net sales. In other words, title subsidies and endowment income have gone up, but university support has gone down even faster.[14]

Publishing for other than scholarly markets is something university presses have always done. Research universities have a broader mandate than doing nothing but specialized research; they also teach, both through regular classroom instruction and through various educational outreach programs. For many state universities, an important component of that outreach was agricultural extension programs, through which universities offered information and advice about soil, crops, and animal husbandry to local farmers. University presses provided an important new avenue for expanding that outreach mission by publishing books in which the intellectual resources of the university were focused on topics of local or regional interest: state and community histories, area guidebooks, books about local wildflowers, birds, cooking, architecture, folklore and music, and biographies of statesmen and political leaders.

Some presses have also taken on the important role of keeping prominent local authors in print, ready to be rediscovered after their initial popularity has faded—writers like Zora Neale Hurston, Carl Sandburg, Jane Addams, and James T. Farrell. University presses have played an important role in the discovery of new writers: novelists like John Kennedy Toole (Louisiana University Press), Norman Maclean (University of Chicago Press), and Helen Hooven Santmyer (Ohio State University Press). Poetry series such as the University of Pittsburgh Press's Pitt Poets and Yale University Press's Yale Younger Poets have published poets such poets as Alicia Suskin Ostriker and Robert Hass. In addition to their contributions to national culture, these and similar books play a vital role in building both a sense of local community and pride in regional achievement—and they have also proved invaluable in helping to build essential public support for the university and its press.

Universities also teach, and textbook sales are an important source of revenue for university presses. Textbook publishing as practiced by commercial publishers is a highly competitive business, and developing course materials for large-population introductory courses requires a capital investment well beyond the reach of most university presses. But many books of scholarly research published by university presses become important enough in their fields to be used as textbooks in upper division and graduate courses, and some university presses have been successful at publishing anthologies of original essays for course use, especially in new or rapidly developing fields.

Publishing reference books and series is another important activity, although the initial editorial development and production costs for a major reference project can be substantial, and fundraising on a heroic scale may be required. But the contribution to knowledge of such large-scale projects can be simply incalculable, as it is for Yale University Press's magisterial seventy-five-volume *Culture and Civilization of China.* Moreover, some reference books have become so well established and widely used that their title is virtually synonymous with the name of the university and its press: The *Chicago Manual of Style, The Columbia Encyclopedia, The Oxford English Dictionary.*

Finally, there is publishing for general audiences, or trade publishing, as it is known from the idea of publishing "for the book trade," or people who buy their books in general bookstores. Regional publishing can be thought of as a kind of trade publishing for local markets, but trade publishing usually implies publishing general-interest books for a national audience. At the lower end of the sales spectrum trade books can sell on the order of 3,000 to 5,000 copies; at the upper end, for a relatively small number of well-known and popular authors, sales can go into the millions.

University presses have had their successes in general trade publishing; Norman Maclean's *A River Runs Through It* (1976) is a classic example from the University of Chicago Press, and Tom Clancy's first novel, *The Hunt for Red October,* (1984) was published by the Naval Institute Press. But historically, university presses have approached trade publishing with caution. The potential sales can be high, but so are the financial risks. In comparison to scholarly publishing, trade publishing requires higher advances to authors and higher advertising and promotion costs; markets are volatile and unpredictable, and returns of unsold stock from bookstores can turn apparent success into fiscal disaster.[15] These and many other factors create an unpredictable business environment in which, generally speaking, only a handful of the largest university presses have been able to compete regularly and successfully.

However, a 1979 Supreme Court ruling about the way manufacturers would be allowed to value inventory for tax purposes created a windfall for university presses.[16]

The Thor decision, as it is known, caused many commercial publishers to put their slow-moving backlist titles out of print, including many of high editorial quality. The availability of these titles created a wave of new publishing opportunities because, as nonprofit enterprises, university presses are not taxed on the value of their inventories, and they saw this as creating an easy, low-cost entry into trade publishing. By keeping in print many of these titles that would otherwise have disappeared, university presses have provided an invaluable cultural service. Yet while general trade publishing by university presses has certainly increased, it has not proved to be the road to financial salvation, nor, given the high-risk nature of most general trade publishing, is it likely that it will.

In sum, university presses have responded to cutbacks in university funding for scholarly publishing by seeking new sources of nonpublishing income and by seeking to publish for more lucrative markets. These changes in publishing and business strategy, though, also need to be seen against the backdrop of changing technology and the extraordinarily swift development of modern electronic communications.

In the early 1970s, computers began to enter publishing, first of all as a back office tool for keeping track of inventories, recording sales and royalties, generating invoices, and keeping accounts receivable records on a single, integrated system. From there, they spread to automated accounting systems; before long they were being used to set up presswide databases that were capable of tracking editorial and production schedules and of maintaining a substantial body of editorial, marketing, and production data about individual titles.

With the rapid development of PCs starting in the early 1980s, the so-called PC-based "desktop publishing" systems also began to evolve. In actuality they were—and remain—essentially desktop typesetting and composition systems. In the beginning their output mimicked that of a typewriter (even the most common font was Courier, designed to imitate the widely used typeface available on the IBM Selectric "golfball"). On current systems, though, it is possible to render text in virtually any font and size, enter images and size them to scale, layout pages, and transmit the resulting electronic files either for display on a computer monitor, for printing out on a home or office printer, or to generate page images that can be used with a variety of printing equipment to make tens, hundreds, or thousands of copies.

However, it is not computers alone but the extraordinary growth and deployment of the Internet in the last ten years that is finally, after centuries of relative stability, transforming publishing. Before the Internet, whatever new possibilities existed for electronic manipulation and formatting of text and images, the final product still had to be embodied in a physical object in order to be distributed to an audience. Traditionally, that object has been a bound book or journal; more recently it might be a diskette, or a digital tape, or a CD-ROM. But the Internet permits the distribution of electronic files—of digital objects, if you will—as a stream of impulses.

This essay is an attempt at history, not clairvoyance, so I won't speculate here about what the university press—or the library, or the university—of the future will look like. I am confident that publishers will still have important roles to play in the creation and dissemination of knowledge, because the most important skills publishers have—helping to weed out good information from bad, putting it in a form most useful to readers, and getting it in the hands of the people who are likely to be interested in it—are always going to be useful. But the publishing universe has definitely tipped on its axis. Within the last fifteen years, the act of writing has shifted from creating a visible, tangible record of thoughts and ideas, like a handwritten or typewritten manuscript, to creating an invisible and intangible electronic file. As long as that file is used to produce a familiar printed record, like a book, this shift may seem like a distinction without a difference, but it is actually quite profound. We are just beginning to explore what it may mean.

The most obvious break with the past is that applying ink to paper is no longer a requirement for written communication. It remains an option—and for a number of reasons, still an important one—but in the future that just began, printed objects themselves are no longer the necessary heart of written communication. The electronic file is, and that change is a done deal. There's no going back.

The good news about this change is that an electronic file, unlike ink fixed on paper, is protean, able to take a variety of shapes and forms. It can be used to generate a printed text through a variety of methods: distributed printing, print on demand, short-run digital printing, or traditional offset. It can even accomplish its purpose without being printed out at all, like most e-mail messages. It can be translated into different file formats and displayed on a computer monitor with varying degrees of visual quality and resolution: plain text, word processing, pdf. It can be deconstructed on one computer, transmitted across the Internet, and reconstructed on another. It can be linked to video and audio files for multimedia display. It can contain dynamic links to other files. It can be incorporated into searchable databases.

The bad news is that, unlike ink fixed on paper, an electronic file is ephemeral. It cannot be read directly, but can only be accessed through a computer, which is a machine utterly dependent on a stable supply of electricity to operate. It must be a computer, moreover, compatible with the computer used to create the file in the first place, running a program that is compatible with the program used to create the file. Storage media for electronic files are notoriously short-lived, so that long-term preservation and access requires the migration of files to new generations of media as they become available—a process that introduces new questions of hardware and software compatibility and of file integrity. Finally, an electronic file can be altered without leaving any evidence that it has been changed.

The inherently ephemeral nature of electronic files means that everything we thought we knew and believed we could rely on about linguistic artifacts now applies only to those that have been fixed in print. A whole new class of such artifacts, digital texts, has come into being, and while we are exploring the new possibilities they offer for scholarly publishing and discovering how to make best use of them, we also have a great deal to rethink and relearn: our ideas about textual authority, accessibility, stability, and preservation; even our ideas about what it means to read and how to use information. We need a new scholarly infrastructure, with tools that will allow us to cite electronic texts, to refer from one to another, and even to identify, number, and catalog them.

At this writing, ninety-two university presses in the United States and Canada belong to AAUP.[17] Among them they publish on the order of 11,000 books a year, and more than 700 learned journals. University presses are also working on the cutting edge of electronic publishing, often working in collaboration with each other, with their university libraries, and with scholarly societies. Johns Hopkins University Press's Project Muse, an electronic journals publishing program that began as a project to publish all 46 of the press's journals electronically, now includes 160 journals from 25 presses. Columbia International Affairs Online (CIAO), a collaboration between Columbia University Press and the Columbia University Library, is a database of literature in international relations that now includes 100,000 pages of content from 150 contributing institutions. MIT Press has started Cognet, a searchable electronic database in cognitive science that links e-books, conference materials including proceedings and calls for papers, and fourteen journals. The University of Illinois Press, the National Academy Press, the American Historical Society, and the Organization of American Historians have established The History Cooperative; their first project is to put the full text of the *American*

Historical Review and the *Journal of American History* on-line. The presses at seven universities (Columbia, Harvard, Johns Hopkins, New York, Oxford, Rutgers, and Michigan), are working with the American Historical Association and the American Council of Learned Societies and five of its constituent societies on a project to publish 85 new electronic books and convert 500 important backlist titles, and reviews of them, into digital form. There are many other projects as well, both large and small, and new ones start weekly.

The history of university presses in the twentieth century largely has been one of growth: growth in both the number of university presses and the number of books and journals they publish. It has also, especially in the last quarter century, been growth against the odds, growth against a pattern of declining support for universities generally. Through this process, university presses have become tough and resourceful, adaptable to changing market conditions, yet as firmly committed as ever to their main job of disseminating the fruits of scholarly research and to helping the university's lamp of knowledge shine ever more brightly. The twenty-first century brings a whole new host of challenges, but it also brings new opportunities for the presentation of scholarship and for its publication, opportunities that for most of the last century were undreamed of outside the realm of science fiction. And the twenty-first century brings with it the opportunity for new relationships and new forms of collaboration between university presses, university libraries, and universities themselves. University presses will, as they have in the past, rise to meet them.

Notes

1. For the early history of university presses I am deeply indebted to Gene R. Hawes, *To Advance Knowledge: A Handbook on American University Press Publishing,* American University Press Services, 1967.

2. As, some twenty years later, no less a publisher than Charles Scribner, son of the founder of the famous New York publishing house and himself one of the founders of Princeton University Press, observed, "What is accomplished if the work of a lifetime grows mouldy in the drawer of a desk?" Quoted in Hawes, p. 35.

3. Here and elsewhere when speaking of the number of university presses, I am drawing on membership data about AAUP. Some small presses continue to publish under the name of their universities although they are not members of AAUP. Their publishing schedules tend to be erratic and, so far as I know, no census of them exists.

4. There is a small handful of U. S. commercial publishers who use the phrase "university press" in their name. When I speak of university presses here, I mean university presses who are members of AAUP, whose Guidelines on Admission to Membership define a university press as "the scholarly publishing arm of a university or college."

5. Hawes, p. 31.

6. According to *The Association of American University Presses Directory,* 1999–2000.

7. Several AAUP member presses have been closed only to reopen and resume operations a few years later, such as Vanderbilt University Press and Northwestern University Press, but at this point, the only one that has closed and not reopened has been Rice University Press.

8. Universities argued that in calculating the amount to be applied for in seeking a federal research grant, the direct costs of carrying out any given research project—new laboratory equipment, research staff, and so forth—are insufficient and ought to be augmented by an allowance toward the cost to the university of maintaining an institution capable supporting top-quality research. These overhead charges are calculated as a percentage of the grant (they can range from 40 percent to 80 percent), and are negotiated between the university and the granting agency. The principle is certainly sound, but the question of what constitutes allowable overheads, and therefore what the percentage ought to be, has been a matter of some political controversy.

9. The Association of Research Libraries has been tracking this shift for some years; for the most recent figures, visit their website, http://www.arl.org; see especially http://www.arl.org/stats/arlstat/1999t2.html.

10. The causes of the run-up of serials prices in science, technology, and medicine are complex. Most scientific and technical journals are published by commercial publishers, and their desire to maximize profits from an essentially captive market may well be one, but growing "shelf weight" as the sheer volume of scientific research has expanded is certainly another, as is the increasing fragmentation of disciplines into subdisciplines resulting in ever-shrinking markets from which to recover the costs of publication.

11. Paulette V. Walker, "Publishers Fear Impact of Arts and Humanities Cuts," *The Chronicle of Higher Education,* 5 January 1996.

12. In a September 2000 informal survey conducted by the directors of AAUP, they found that among members surveyed, 58 percent of the respondents (thirty of fifty-two) reported that they either already had endowments or were actively raising funds to build them. Building an endowment was distinguished from seeking individual title subsidies, which virtually all presses do when a potential source of such funds can be identified.

13. In 1999, this percentage jumped to 5.8 percent. a welcome event and a significant one if it marks the beginning of a new trend.

14. Small presses are much more heavily dependent on such operating subsidies than are large ones—a small press may require a subsidy equal to 50 percent or more of its operating budget; a large press less than 2 percent—so "average parent institution support" is not a concept that has much meaning when applied to individual presses. But for university presses in general, the average is useful for looking at trends in overall funding patterns. From 1988 to 1998, the average parent institution support among reporting presses declined from 10.4 percent of net sales to 6.3 percent, for a loss of 4.1 percent; during the same period, outside gifts and grants increased, as a percentage of net sales, by only 1.6 percent, for a net loss in nonpublishing income of 2.5 percent.

15. The practice of allowing bookstores to return unsold stock for credit began during the Great Depression, as publishers sought ways to gain store shelf space for their books; it is a practice that publishers frequently deplore, but as long as there is competition for shelf space, it is likely to continue.

16. *Thor Power Tool Co. v. Commissioner, 439 U.S. 522 (1979).* The IRS challenged the manufacturer's practice of writing down the value of certain items held in inventory in order to reduce taxes while still continuing to sell the items at full price; the IRS challenge was

upheld by the Supreme Court. The issue in the case is a complex one involving technical questions of both tax law and accounting practice, but the practical effect of the ruling on commercial publishers was to create a tax liability for holding a stock of slow-moving titles in inventory.

17. AAUP has 121 members and includes scholarly societies, research institutions, museums, and international members. Only scholarly publishers affiliated with degree-granting institutions in the United States are counted here as university presses.

·7·

The Creative Role of the Professional or STM Publisher

John Francis Dill

The donor heart arrives, bathed in a saline solution that keeps it at only four degrees Celsius. You must work quickly now to remove the damaged heart. You cross-clamp the aorta, the heart's main artery. You sever the remaining arteries to the heart, working quickly while taking care that your incisions are clean and smooth. Careless work here can endanger the success of the transplant. "I've only got one shot at this," you tell yourself, "so it's got to be perfect." But it's been too long since you've done this, and you realize that you are not working as fast as you should.

You now hold the donor heart in your hands, momentarily marveling at this miniature miracle. Barely bigger than a walnut, it seems far too fragile to be as powerful as the heart in your own chest, and you remind yourself that you must be precise and gentle while sewing sutures that will be strong enough to hold for a lifetime.

As you secure the left atrium of the donor's heart into the girl's chest, you feel the delicate tug of each stitch. You try not to think about the time, but already an internal alarm is sounding. The donor heart is beginning to thaw, and you've only completed the first step in the transplant. You've got to be faster.

"End simulation," you say, pulling off the headpiece. You blink momentarily to adjust your eyes to the light and find yourself staring not at the sterile walls of an operating room, but instead at the banks of monitors and computers of a virtual reality simulation chamber.

Dressed in casual clothes, instead of green surgical scrubs, you exhale deeply. You'll go home, get some rest, and come back tomorrow and try it again. Your two-year-old patient is still on the waiting list, and the real transplant, which you have been practicing for the past ninety minutes, is still several weeks away. You will have several chances to practice it again, to get it right when the minutes really count.

As you think about the practice that you have gone through, you are grateful to the medical publisher who created the simulation software that captures the genius of great surgeons who have preceded you in facing this kind of operating challenge. The transfer of knowledge that has taken place from their intellect and experience has moved through your brain into your fingertips to better prepare you for the real-life situation that you will be confronting in several weeks.

What Is Professional Publishing?

It is easy to imagine that one of the roles of the medical publisher of the future will be to create products not unlike that described above. Such products are even now in the exploration phase. It is just as easy to imagine similar products in architecture, civil engineering and chemistry, and many other subject areas. After all, it is a natural extension of the publishing process offered for centuries by professional publishers to their authors; authors who have discoveries to share, better professional procedures to describe, or new technologies to explain.

The essence of professional publishing, or STM (scientific, technical, and medical) as it has come to be known, is that it identifies, verifies, shapes, packages, and distributes the procedures and research developments in the world's professions. The accumulation and refinement of this knowledge, through the ages, has facilitated the processes and construction of the infrastructure of civilization itself.

It is impossible to look at modern civilization's towering structures, contemplate a bridge over a breathtaking chasm, ponder the complex logic of precedents of law, or perhaps most significantly, consider the transplantation of the human heart; without realizing that the compilation and refinement of human knowledge that makes these heroic feats possible had to be published to be understood and applied.

Historians might debate the origins of professional publishing. It could easily have been when ancient man invented the wheel and then sought to make public to "publish"—that extraordinary feat of mechanical engineering by enlisting friends to draw it in the sand, on the walls of caves, and on animal hides that would be passed hand to hand.

Most often the professional information published in today's world is written by the professionals themselves looking to advance their science and obtain professional recognition. The packaging of the information can vary. It can be in a book, journal article, CD-ROM, database, newsletter, or piece of software. It might be a report on new developments or critical information needed for proper daily execution of one of the professions. In engineering this might be tables of strength of materials; in medicine it might be drug dosage guides; in law it may be the most current precedents with commentary; in business it might be a description of management techniques or an explanation of a new method for economic forecasting.

Whatever the subject of professional publishing, the work is painstakingly detailed, time-consuming, demanding of the highest standards of accuracy and, therefore, expensive. In its most fundamental definition, professional publishing serves the professions such as engineering, all areas of health science, law, business, architecture, science, and the countless number of related technicians and paraprofessionals who facilitate the work of these professions around the world. Yet in its finest moments, professional publishing can be understood either as communicating, with brilliant clarity, the information that gives healing hands the power to save one precious child for loving parents or that translates complex microcircuitry into rocketry that puts the first human footprint on the moon.

Above all, professional publishers exist to serve their authors by providing the complex array of services that focus, polish, and display the technical competence of those authors around the world. In providing this service for humanity, professional publishers can take justifiable pride.

What Professional Publishers Do

Many assume that publishing is just printing and, therefore, are often surprised that most publishing houses do not have printing presses. To be sure, when you read a book it is easy to assume that the author who wrote it simply gave it to the publisher in completed form for printing. So much of what all publishers do is transparent that many individuals assume that publishers are mere conveyors of information and add little to the process.

This perception will doubtless continue, as the speed and seeming ease of communication through databases, CD-ROM, and online interaction become more prevalent. Whether the mode of publication is print or electronic, most of the basic functions of professional publishing remain the same, as the following explanations will make clear.

The Importance of Imprint

The name or symbol of a publishing house is its imprint. Over time, that imprint becomes a statement of quality borne of the many reviews and edits a work must undergo to meet the quality standards of that publishing house. The imprint, therefore, testifies to the suitability of publication of the work.

The administration of an imprint also provides a number of other functions such as:

- Building a list for an imprint. Sometimes a commissioning editor, through experience, may discern a gap in the literature or a need for an update on a particular subject. Following through to find the appropriate author or contributors to bring this information to market can sometimes be the most creative role of the professional publisher. Many works are rejected by publishing houses. Some, when finally published, can turn out to be bestsellers. It is often the administration of the list deemed appropriate for the particular house that guides acceptance of a particular work. In the end, building a coherent list is one of the most powerful things that a professional publishing house does for all of its authors and customers. This is explained more fully below under product advocacy.
- Providing formats or models that authors can follow for books, journals, or electronic modes. Such standardization provides quality control and enhances distribution in both print and electronic forms.
- Filtering material to ensure its quality and accuracy by both internal and external sources.
- Providing quality screens to ensure against low quality, incorrect, or libelous publication.
- Refining content through review and editing.
- Certifying publishable materials that have successfully passed through the above process. Professional publishers will put the works they are creating for their authors through several different rounds of checking and double-checking with professionals who challenge the technical aspect of the theory or practice. In addition, editing serves to recheck and correct the accuracy and presentation of the information. Since the nature of the material being published is technical, accuracy is of singular importance. Misinformation can endanger lives by possibly undercutting the structural integrity of a suspension bridge or causing a malfunction in electronic controls for an airplane or a space shuttle.

The point needs to be emphasized that incoming manuscripts frequently bear little resemblance to the high-quality work eventually published. Professional publishing requires a painstaking process to ensure accuracy and quality. Therefore, it is an expensive process. This explains why the price of individual professional products can be quite high.

Nevertheless, because of the essential nature of the information being provided, quality information from reputable authors typically will find a receptive market. Indeed, significant discoveries or excellent representations of basic information can become professional "best-sellers" through many editions, adding up to hundreds and hundreds of thousands of copies. Then, too, a particular journal may become known as the most respected source of the latest information in a particular subject area.

Enhancing an Author's Presentation

The opening illustration of virtual reality transplantation surgery demonstrates what any professional publisher might do to enhance the author's transfer of knowledge. The same kind of hands-on, virtual reality training devices can be created in almost any other professional discipline published by an STM publisher.

Regardless of format, the transfer of knowledge from the author's mind to the reader's mind is the critical process that publishers are expert at facilitating. A variety of techniques involving artwork preparation, layout, formatting, the use of illustrative materials, typesetting, and packaging of the final product are all part of preparing the work for market.

In electronic modes publishers are actively engaged in experimentation to find the very best techniques to accomplish the same objectives. Much is being developed in this regard that will surely enable future generations to enjoy the transfer of knowledge much more quickly and accurately, compared with the more laborious methods of absorbing print and static illustration from paper as we do today. That does not mean to imply that paper products will not continue to be used even in an electronic world. Like radio in a world of television, printed and bound products of all kinds will no doubt continue to have an important supplementary role.

The Business of Publishing

Professional publishers, as all publishers, manage the myriad details associated with bringing a work to fruition. A substantial number of transactions, royalties, fees to various agencies and permissions must be sought and recorded so that a work can be legally published with full authority. All of this detail requires meticulous care and record keeping.

Product Advocacy

Although it is difficult to be too precise, it is a fair guess that approximately 20,000 or more new STM titles are published each year worldwide in many different formats, including an increasing number in electronic formats. Some might add as many as 18,000 journals to this figure. That represents an amazing amount of information to be absorbed by the world's professional communities.

Overcommunication in modern civilization makes it incredibly difficult to get a message through to professionals who might be interested in a particular new work. What makes one new work more special than another? What makes it different from the countless works already published on the same subject? Just to get a professional to consider the answer to those critical questions is a special creative skill for publishers.

In order to conduct the marketing or targeted communication, that this process requires, professional publishers typically:

- Use well-organized mailing lists, which pinpoint proven and potential buyers by area of interest using direct mail methods. Sometimes these efforts are undertaken in cooperation with bookstores. Solicitation for journal subscribers works much the same way, sometimes in conjunction with relevant professional societies.
- Communicate with potential buyers using descriptive materials such as pamphlets and catalogs to define the product and its uniqueness.
- Use creative skills to develop materials that portray the product in its most distinctive form.
- Use current-awareness services to ensure that the new product listing, in whatever form, is carried by appropriate databases on electronic networks or is listed in print catalogs and advisory services that may be alerting potential customers.
- Support secondary publishing venues such as abstracting and indexing, which supplement or amplify the material being provided.
- Maintain customer-service departments that assist customers in whatever way possible in understanding the products available to serve their needs. These departments also help resolve any potential problems that may occur in trying to complete the transfer of the actual materials involved.

When the mode of publication is through journals, several factors are involved that are of critical importance for the dissemination of knowledge.

- Journals provide faster publication because they are typically issued monthly, bimonthly, or quarterly. Many are now offering services to their subscribers online electronically.
- Journal subscriber lists represent discrete communities of interest. These lists have high value as ready markets for new information of interest. Consequently, experimentation with electronic delivery of journals is

proceeding rapidly through online products, CD-ROM, and other media as it develops.

- Journal articles receive the same type of "expert" or peer reviews as do most other types of professional publishing. However, the "peer review" process in journals is used by the scientific community as an important test of initial credibility of new information. This dynamic may be more fully exploited in the electronic age when instant direct communication and dialogue is possible.

Raising a product to the right level of visibility to be sure its unique utility is clear to potential customers is a very proactive process of advocacy by professional publishers. Unless this process is executed properly, potential customers will never see many products that have every reason to succeed. They will come and go unnoticed.

Distribution of Completed Works

If the completed work is not available for delivery to the customer, the product is not published. The complexity of distribution in professional publishing involves far more than most individuals outside of the business could possibly imagine. This is particularly true when you consider that most works published have distinct differences and, therefore, take on a life of their own, requiring special attention to get them to the correct market segment. Adding electronic modes to the process now requires new skills.

Professional publishing serves discrete markets, meaning its works are very specifically targeted to the professional category that will use them, for instance, civil engineering. Finding the right combination of methods to reach people around the world who have interest in these specific professional categories is quite a task.

- Bookstores that carry only professional titles in good quantity make up a very small group. However, everywhere in the world, the use of professional bookstores for distribution is common. Programs for promoting to these outlets, including appropriate discount schedules and support activities, must be maintained.
- Public, school, and university libraries regularly subscribe to professional publications.
- Special libraries dedicated to professional collections are often found associated with the business or professional society that they are designed to serve. These libraries also maintain extensive journal collections relevant to the business or society.

- Wholesalers, distributors, and library jobbers have become expert in knowing the technical collections of their STM publishers. These specialized channels into the market provide an invaluable service to stores and libraries of all classifications. Their sales forces and catalogs compile the technical products from all STM publishers, allowing the customer to have one informed source from which to obtain their products.
- Convention and exhibit attendance is used as another method of professional marketing. Hundreds of national and international shows are held by professional societies throughout the world in association with knowledge updating and training seminars for their members.
- Publishers' sales forces are also employed to represent published or forthcoming works to public, academic, and special libraries, bookstores, wholesalers, library jobbers, hospitals, offices, conventions, and other places of business for the professional.
- Databases of influential experts, instructors, and other potential customers are used to market published and forthcoming works. Many of these databases and networks represent communities of professionals with similar interests.
- Some professional publishers use specialized book clubs and other vehicles to reach discrete markets, for example, the Mechanical Engineers' Book Club.
- Warehousing, shipping, billing, customer service, credit, and collection services all must be provided, maintained, and operated at reasonable cost if the author's work is to be successfully supplied to the markets for which it is intended.

Professional publishers are serving worldwide professions and, therefore, are international by nature. The global market is critical to the professional publisher and needs to be addressed directly. Licenses for translations are usually negotiated at a host of international book fairs around the world from London, Budapest, Prague, Warsaw, Bucharest, and Beijing to the annual fair in Frankfurt, Germany, to name only a few. These fairs are huge bazaars of publishers from around the world exchanging their wares.

At other times during the year, however, such transactions take place through prior arrangement with publishing houses around the world. Meanwhile distribution agreements, licensing arrangements, joint ventures, subsidiaries in international locations—all are devices used to facilitate the flow of professional information worldwide. In recent years an extraordinary number of acquisitions and mergers of companies around the world have enabled some large multinational corporations to establish international networks of subsidiaries.

The infrastructure for making books, journals, and other forms of professionally published information available to the right market segments around the world has been built up over time and represents a vast network of outlets for print and, increasingly, for electronic modes as well. Agents, networks, established procedures, discounts and policies are all important to the process. All of these factors are involved in bringing works to market and they require investment, experience and understanding in order to make a specific professional publication successful.

The Contribution of Specialization

Professional publishers become recognized by their customers in their various fields through their success in attracting the best authors, providing a critical mass of titles on a list, and becoming the best source of information in their areas of specialization. This leads to efficiencies in marketing and sales as well as reinforcement of the value of a specific imprint. There are, however, many other activities that need to take place to establish this publishing focus and the reputation that arises from it.

- Planning a portfolio of publications in response to market trends and needs determined through market research and other means. This is creative work for publishers, who are often responding to market trends and anticipated future needs by pushing forward products that examine new ideas or subjects. These activities help to shape the course of knowledge in a specific area.
- Establishing publications, such as journals, that help define interest groups and subject areas of research.
- Encouraging other activities that facilitate communication among authors and scientists. These activities are relevant to an intellectual climate and keep standards and respect for the scholarly process high, for example, research grants, symposia, networks, seminars, and awards for excellence.

Vigilance for Rights and Protections

Publishing is supported by a complex code of copyright law internationally that is designed to respect the right of authors to be properly rewarded for their intellectual creativity. As agents for their authors, professional publishers have taken this responsibility seriously and have worked individually and through publishers' associations around the world to defend copyright, enforce intellectual property rights, fight piracy, and prosecute plagiarism or any unauthorized use of published materials.

This vigilance involves activities such as:

- Protecting copyright on behalf of author and publisher. STM publishers have historically been in the forefront of taking action against piracy and copyright infringement.
- Initiating and negotiating license for use or materials for foreign translations or use in databases, CD-ROMS, software, and the like.
- Working with reproduction rights organizations (RROS) around the world to facilitate efficient and mutually satisfactory compensation for authorized use of materials. These major organizations are legally established to collect payments for use of copyrighted materials.
- Administering proper payment of revenue share or royalty to authors.
- Working within the industry to create means of setting quality standards to guide industry practices.
- Working with government agencies around the world to effectively craft new or revised copyright legislation for new electronic modes of communication.

The Future Is Already Here

This is an exciting time for professional publishing because the promise of the electronic age is that the transfer of knowledge will be accomplished more quickly and efficiently than is possible using the printed word and illustration. The Internet is transforming global communication exponentially. Professional publishers worldwide are now regularly digitizing text and illustration for the creation of databases that will be published on world electronic networks.

Digitizing also allows the publisher to quickly "repurpose" works into formats that individual customers require according to their needs.

Much of what professional publishers do is transparent to the end user, who often takes for granted the quality, accuracy, packaging, and availability of the information he or she is using. Therefore, there are those who assume that the marvels of the electronic age will eliminate the need for professional publishers. This is not so.

If one considers that more than 80 percent of our technological inventions have occurred since 1900 and that computers and the World Wide Web are indeed making it easier to create more and faster communication, is it not also conceivable that this tidal wave of information needs to be selected, sorted, assessed, evaluated, checked, packaged, promoted and protected in the same way as the printed word? Is it not also true that authors themselves will require these services as never before?

Professional publishers have endured and taken pride in their profession through the ages. They have taken that pride from their skill in communicating the genius of their authors to those who can use it best.

May professional publishers forever keep their humility in service to their authors and customers, and they shall never want for a future role in the transfer of knowledge.

*   *   *

John Francis Dill, Chairman Emeritus, was Chairman, President, and CEO of the Mosby Company, an international medical publishing corporation and subsidiary of the Times Mirror Corporation. He also served as Chairman of The International Association of Scientific, Technical and Medical Publishers, 1994–1996.

"The Creative Role of the Professional or STM Publisher" was originally published in booklet form in 1994 on behalf of the International Publisher's Association (IPA) and the International Association of Scientific, Technical and Medical Publishers (STM). STM is affiliated with IPA and serves the specialized needs of more than 300 scientific, technical and medical publishers worldwide. The booklet was published as part of a series of booklets describing the roles of all kinds of publishers. It received worldwide distribution and has been translated into German, French, and Spanish.

◆8◆

Diversity and the Growth of
Serious/Scholarly/Scientific Journals

Albert Henderson

Diversity is more than a common denominator of periodicals and other serial publications. It is the essence of the spirit that constantly creates and changes them. It is also a reflection of the systematic variety of nature. New journals, magazines, newsletters, reviews, and the like, are born with increasing regularity, each displaying innovations, refinements, and variations. Each attempts to serve a new audience well, an old audience better, or a community of interests more effectively. Vigorous creation must be nature's way of counteracting the chances of survival being poor. Derek de Solla Price (1963, pp. 6–8) observed that of the one million scientific journals that have come into being since 1665, the majority has died. The National Library of Medicine estimated that the number of biomedical journals rose from 22 in 1775 to about 19,000 in 1973 (Corning and Cummings 1976). Thus, in the first century, they increased by a factor of ten. in the second century growth nears a factor of 100. Publishers are getting better at sustaining life. Six biomedical periodicals were born during the five years ending December 1974 for every one that died.

The phenomenon extends beyond science journals. Frank Luther Mott estimated that some 7,500 magazines appeared in the United States in the twenty years ending 1905; half that number failed or merged during the same period (Mott 1957, Vol. IV, p. 11) Three thousand three-hundred periodicals were published in the United States in 1885. By 1905, the number had increased to 6,000. More recently, Samir Husni (1999) counted a record number of 1,065 consumer magazines launched in 1998, compared to 553 in 1991.

133

Statistics

It is often difficult to understand the scope of our topic. Statistics having to do with periodicals all employ restrictive definitions that exclude more titles than they represent. It appears that no one wishes to bother to count all serial titles and then to classify them by contents, language, audience, frequency of publication, and the like. A task group on the economics of primary publication of the National Academy of Sciences (1970), for example, argued for the exclusion of all publications that are not first communications of new findings and all that have a local but not a really "public" audience. It thus distilled a study sample of 300 to 400 "widely used U.S. primary journals" in the natural and physical sciences. Others estimated 2,800 titles for natural and physical sciences worldwide (Machlup and Leson 1978, Vol. 3, p. 13). Is the sample scientifically representative? Probably not. Whether such reductions are due to elitism, naiveté, indifference, the intent to persuade, indolence, or thrift, they may backfire. Fritz Machlup (1979) faulted the 1970 task group for reaching shaky conclusions. Another prestigious institution, the National Science Board, has also been criticized for its small statistical sample of journal articles that it offers as an "indicator" of science and engineering outputs. It shows output growth levels far short of financial inputs. The input/output contrast invites inferences of poor productivity and wasted money that reflect poorly on the management of government-funded academic research.

Is the Medium the Message?

Diversity, combined with apathy, and other factors, makes the reliability of statistical and reference sources about periodicals somewhat elusive, to put it kindly. Sources of statistics as a byproduct have their own problems. For example, many directories such as *Ulrich's* depend on the cooperation of the publishers. They are partially out of date when they appear. Many bibliographic databases, such as MEDLINE and Science Citation Index, deliberately sample the literature rather than aim for comprehensiveness. Others, such as MLA International Bibliography (1922), depend on volunteers who may delay the insertion of records for many years (Uchitelle 1998). The annual periodical price indexes found in *Library Journal* and *American Libraries* ignore page inflation, a factor that affects certain categories but not others, while making less relevant comparisons to the Consumer Price Index. Some indices ignore foreign publications. Some ignore the Third World and former Soviet zones. There is also the growing "gray literature" problem: tracking elusive low-profile publications. Known best for his statement that "the medium is the message," Marshall H. McLuhan is also often credited for telling the *Washington Post,* "Xerox makes everybody a publisher." The ubiquitous self-operated copier of the 1990s rivals the short-run printing press in quality, cost, and speed. Not only photocopy productions, but popular magazines may be disregarded and discarded by many libraries due to limits of budget, narrow mission interpretation, and theories of value. Arguably, some other categories often ignored include:

1. conference proceedings that are valued as unique sources in areas of applied technology and management;
2. business newsletters and trade journals that may include interviews, profiles, statistics, analyses, and other information found nowhere else;
3. photocopy or computer productions that are distributed by hand, by mail, or by email. 'Zines, for instance, cover many popular subjects and are published largely by hobbyists: they are collected more privately than by libraries. They are reviewed appreciatively by R. Seth Freeman's *Factsheet 5,* which can be found on news stands;
4. comic books, according to the box score feature of *Magazine & Bookseller* (1982), sell millions of copies and are ranked high in terms of profits for retailers. They are imitated by movie and television directors and have a profound impact on popular culture;
5. supermarket tabloids also rank high in sales but lower in influence and opportunities for licensing. There is something about them that bespeaks our society, if not our culture.

More Reliable Statistics?

Perhaps for many readers, library collection data, particularly "current serials," may be a more useful reference to indicate some consensus on the universe of publications that are worth preserving. *ARL Statistics 1998-99* indicates that maximum number of serials purchased by a member library to be 55,924; ten years earlier, the figure was 41,878, indicating a 34 percent growth in spite of the "serials crisis" at many of the Association of Research Libraries (ARL) institutions. The figure of 34,827 serials not purchased (excluding the Library of Congress's 133,093 figure) contrasted with 33,093 ten years earlier indicates a slight decrease. Similarly, totals of 105,837 and 103,075 current serials demonstrate little change. In terms of subject-interest universes, certain collections may be representative (see Table 1).

We find 15 to 17 percent drops in current serials at the Canadian Institute for Scientific and Technical Information (CISTI) and National Library of Medicine (NLM) while the National Agricultural Library (NAL) remains stable. The trend in the number of titles contrasts with increases in research spend-

Table 1
Current Serials in National Topical Collections

	1989–1990	1998–1999	Percent Change
CISTI (purchased)	23,877	28,804	–4.927
NAL (total current)	21,919	22,000	n/a
NLM (total current)	23,078	27,157	–4.079

ing. On closer inspection, it is clear that the reductions occur in the purchased column. These statistics probably reflect trends in financial support more than they signify changes in publishing activity. NAL purchases only 23 percent of its current serials, while NLM purchases 81 percent. (CISTI reported only purchased serials for 1998/99.)

Motives to Publish

The Fable of American Chemical Society and the 1970s

Critics of publishing often argue that new periodicals appear simply to earn profits for publishers. Any serious inquiry should find not only that this inference is inaccurate, but that even if it were, there is nothing wrong with a profit in our free-market economy. Publishers could not succeed based on the profit motive alone, nor could they succeed on the sole basis of compelling non-profit charter. Excepting the producers of free advertising media, publishers must attract authors and readers who recognize good value. As the numbers of readers and their interests multiply, publishers must respond. The growth of new periodicals cannot be stopped by fiat. The ACS once announced a moratorium on new journals (Ballhausen et al. 1973). This strategy probably aimed to force authors to crowd their papers into existing journals with loyal library followings rather than have ACS risk starting a new publication. At the time, academic science and university libraries were suffering a reversal of fortune that was connected more with national politics than with publishers' prices (Henderson 1999). The moratorium naturally failed. On a visit to ACS headquarters in 1981, I learned that it was to start its first new journal in more than a decade in the narrow, but "hot" niche of organometallics. A commercial publisher had already taken over the field, capturing many desirable papers and new subscriptions with a new journal. A sector of the chemistry community was highly dissatisfied with the moratorium and with existing outlets. The society was compelled by its members to scrap its policy and launch a new journal. It then discovered what the rest of the industry knew.

Libraries still had no money for new subscriptions. The ratio of member to library subscriptions was far different than anything experienced before 1970. In the meantime, the Internal Revenue Service (IRS) challenged whether the differential pricing of the ACS, whereby members paid much less than libraries, violated nonprofit standards. At the time, many librarians complained bitterly of their need for such discounts. The IRS alleged that member discounting was "inurement," putting the ACS's nonprofit status into jeopardy for two years, as noted in the society's newsmagazine *Chemical & Engineering News* in the October 4, 1980, issue. In the end, the IRS gave the ACS a clean bill of health. The moral of the story is that when science activity grows, publishing must keep up.

Rites of Passage

Particularly in research, where learned associations are major publishers, the creation of a new journal often resembles adolescent passages characterized by maturation, dissatisfaction, and parental friction with some bitterness perhaps on both sides. When in the 1970s the Indian Academy of Sciences decided to establish *Pramana* (1973), a new physics journal, its members must have debated the needs of a million Indian scientists more than simple financial goals (Arunachalam 1993). Similar debates must have occurred when the United States was a developing country about 100 years earlier. How would scientists handle time-consuming management and routine business matters? What about financial risks and limited resources? Were existing journals not adequate? Apparently, existing journals are often not satisfactory to scientists working on the fringes, whether these fringes are geographic or topical. Publishing is a communal enterprise with social benefits that begin years before actual production begins and continue long after distribution ends. Editorial activity connects an invisible college bonded by topical interest and loyalties to language, locality, and community. To scientists and scholars, publishing means participation in editorial work and production as well as connecting authors with readers. Nearly all publishing is connected to some other activity, whether it be religious, commercial, cultural, medical, technical, or scientific. Publishing may serve a point of view as well as providing information. Good publishing often means entertaining many points of view to draw constructive criticism, to reconcile conflicts, and to establish consensus. Biases that treat some "outsiders" unfairly can hardly be avoided once the editorial team is established. This does not mean that adjustments cannot be made to the mainstream. A change in editors, for instance, made possible the publication of a languishing paper that eventually won the 1997 Nobel Prize in economics (Passell 1977). Researchers in developing countries today—

undoubtedly just as those in the United States 150 years ago—complained that mainstream editors deny them opportunities to participate as referees, as authors, and as editors. United States and European index and abstracting services are equally unlikely to cover publications considered to be outside the mainstream, adding insult to injury (Gibbs 1995). There are also economic concerns for scientists in developing countries because currency exchange values are generally unfavorable. Mainstream publications are relatively expensive, with prices and currency restrictions creating insurmountable thresholds for circulation and readers. International dissemination may be important to an author but not in the best interests of the community. Recognition must begin at home, even if it means starting your own journal.

Science as an Example

Not surprisingly, the dissatisfaction that leads to the creation of new science journals may cut both ways. Every new venture represents a failure of someone to satisfy the needs of authors and readers. Associations, in particular, have a difficult time dealing with such failures. It means arriving at a decision that involves commercial risk and permits dissidents to infiltrate their treasured hierarchies of editors and upset conventional beliefs. They have no problem complaining, however, when someone else succeeds on what they consider their turf. Whether or not a new journal is successful at first, its ancestors may choke on their envy of first-rate authors, highly cited papers, and considerable subscription revenue. Too late, they may wish the new generation to return, like the prodigal son. There may be a happy reconciliation. They may resolve their issues and embrace an acquisition of a journal that they believed to be theirs all along. There are examples of journals, having proven their viability, being acquired by associations. Financial responsibility for the first science journal, *Philosophical Transactions* (1665) was assumed in 1752 by the Royal Society (London) long after the death of its founder, Henry Oldenburg. *Physical Review* (1893) was founded by a group headed by Edward L. Nichols at Cornell University as an American venture of the British publisher, Macmillan. It was eventually acquired by the American Physical Society, which was not fully organized until 1899. The *American Chemical Journal* (1879–1913) started the same year as and was later absorbed by the *Journal of the American Chemical Society* (1879). *Science* (1883), now published by the American Association for the Advancement of Science (AAAS), was created by Moses King in Cambridge, Massachusetts.

The development of professional commercial publishers, who flourished in nineteenth-century Europe, makes such recoveries less likely. Mainstream editors often condemn new ventures with some bitterness, particularly when they are successful. When a new journal thrives, it is often because it provides special features customized to provide a high level of service. Well-focused coverage makes a publication interesting cover to cover and bonds the community it addresses. It assures authors that readers will notice their work without delay and the need for extra indexes. Bibliographies, letters, news, editorials, conference papers, abstracts, summaries, reports of panel discussions, advertisements, and other materials are highly useful to (although rarely cited by) readers and authors within a well-defined niche. Contrary to the presumption of many critics of research publishing, refereed primary reports of research are not the only unit of publication. In contrast to the niche journal, a behemoth such as *Physical Review* carries no bibliographies or review articles in spite of its title, its broad coverage, its strong citation impact, and its relatively low price per article. Its huge annual production of articles makes it mandatory for most readers to consult indexes and review articles—not included in the price—in order to locate material of interest.

Technology as an Example: IEEE

The metaphor of "twigging"—with every branch producing new branches—expresses the inevitability of dissatisfaction with existing journals, institutions, and associations. The "twigging" record is considerable and occasionally ironic. Learned pursuits tend to produce a certain elitism—perhaps even snobbery. New ideas that are perceived as radical may be shut out by the mainstream at first and later adopted as conventional. For example, Gugielmo Marconi's 1895 transmission of radio waves confounded many electrical engineers and scientists. I don't doubt that some sneered at followers of Nikola Tesla and Marconi, perhaps calling them hobbyists and worse. The American Institute of Electrical Engineers (AIEE), which started publishing its *Transactions* in 1884, would have little to do with radio. The result was the Wireless Institute, founded in the first decade of the twentieth century. The Wireless Institute was superseded in 1912 by the Institute of Radio Engineers (IRE), which flourished. In 1963, the IRE merged with a more mature AIEE to form the Institute of Electrical and Electronics engineers (IEEE). Meanwhile, the first computers gave rise to a new discipline: computing languages. True to historical pattern, neither the IRE nor the AIEE could relate to programmers and the other computer people who were developing the now-ubiquitous technology of logic. The Association for Computing Machinery (ACM) emerged in 1947, eventually forming special interest groups (SIGs) to serve the diversity of topical interests related to computers. Its *Communications of the Association for Computing Machinery* (1959), *Journal* (1956), *Computing Reviews* (1962), *Guide to Computing Literature*

(1979), and *Computing Reviews* (1962) serve broad membership interests, while a variety of *Transactions* and SIG newsletters organize technical communications of limited scope. Many other associations also formed subgroups to address the variety of new and divergent special interests harbored by a large membership. Today, the IEEE's Computer Society (perhaps its largest subgroup) and ACM compete for attention and also cosponsor meetings and other projects.

Ethnic Diversity

Dissatisfaction moved African Americans to establish their own press, a movement well documented by the new union list, *African-American Newspapers and Periodicals. A National Bibliography*, compiled by Danky and Hady (1998) and dramatized by Stanley Nelson's *Black Press* (1998). As the first-place newspaper, *Freedom's Journal* (1827) asserted, "Too long have others spoken for us." This alternative coverage included news, people, and issues that were invisible to mainstream editors, giving African Americans a voice, valuable information, and a sense of community. *Freedom's Journal* folded within two years, but not without first having an impact. It paved the way for more than twenty other African American papers published before the Civil War. After the war, southern blacks were no longer prevented from learning to read. This encouraged the development of more than 500 African Americans newspapers before 1900. *The Chicago Defender* (1905) and its publisher, Robert S. Abbott, started by producing 300 copies. By 1920 each of his more than 100,000 copies was read, on average, some five times. Distributed beyond the borders of Chicago, it included train schedules and discussions of opportunities that encouraged a great migration northward. *The Pittsburgh Courier* (1910) also addressed economic opportunities invisible to the mainstream while crusading against stereotypes, southern Jim Crow, and northern racism. During the Great Depression, its publisher, Robert L. Vann, convinced many blacks to "turn Lincoln's picture to the wall" and desert the Republican Party, which took them for granted. This tipped the balance in favor of Roosevelt, who recognized this debt to Vann. The mainstream press met the challenge of the civil rights movement more than 100 years after *Freedom's Journal* by expanding its own coverage. In so doing, it lured some of the best journalists, as well as many readers, away from successful African American media.

Literary Diversity

Cultural interests demonstrate the same growing pains as science and technology, although the "twigging" in this area is subtler. New creative work by young writers may be considered unreliable by mainstream editors, just as new lines of research are in science. Little magazines such as *The Fugitive* (1922–1925), Margaret Anderson's *Little Review* (1914–1929), George Hartley's *Listen* (1954–1962), *The Double Dealer* (1921–1926), and innumerable others have addressed the problem by providing critical venues and opportunities to establish talent. In contrast to science, in which the cumulative building blocks of discovery are the subject of the writing, creative writing is its own end. Thus, each little magazine tends to fail as the cohort of writers it has nourished moves to mainstream publishers with distribution resources, the ability to pay, and to recoup their investment.

Management Diversity

There is a diversity to dissatisfaction, of course. It can be addressed and thereby controlled. *Life* (1936–1972) was spun off by Henry Luce's *Time* (1923), taking advantage of newly developing photojournalism and production technologies. *Physical Review* (1893) spun off its *Letters* (1958) first and then subdivided into four topically differentiated sections enigmatically titled, "A," "B," "C," and "D" (1970) as rising annual pages and prices began to overwhelm both members and nonmember customers. Because of continued growth, most sections today are too big and broad to browse. Robert Maxwell kept his finger on the pulse of the information explosion. In the mid 1970s, he announced a series of Pergamon Press journals entitled "Computers and . . ." even before editors could be recruited, to serving the proliferating technology applied to various fields of science in which Pergamon was active. The real growth in computer publishing has been at the consumer level, where periodicals that offer education about innovation and outreach books for "idiots" transcend the opacity of manufacturer documentation. Who would have thought that Allan M. Meckler's eight-page newsletter, *Research & Education Networking* (1990), would have metamorphosed into *Internet World* by 1993 and have become the basis of a glittering exposition?

Reprints

At the other end of the spectrum we find an industry of re-publication, perhaps best exemplified by *Reader's Digest* (1922), which flourished during the Great Depression years and has led the market ever since, with forty-eight editions in nineteen languages reaching a worldwide total somewhere near 30 million copies and many pass-along readers. It was not a particularly innovative format. It was preceded by *Review of Reviews* (1890–1936) and Funk & Wagnall's *Literary Digest* (1890–1937), the latter boasting circulation of

1,200,000 by 1920. The success of *Reader's Digest* was probably in its competitive selection and presentation. It produced tightly edited versions of articles focusing primarily on contemporary society found in well-circulated publications (Reed 1977). Quality became paramount with several simultaneous editors each producing a few issues a year. Even the jokes and short anecdotes were screened against decades of prior entries to eliminate potential repetition. It developed a formula requiring the mention of sex, for instance, in every issue. DeWitt Wallace and his wife, Lila, minimized costs and kept management simple and prices affordable. They depended entirely on subscription revenue at first. They simplified production by not using illustrations or ads. They carried very little fiction. Their product resembled none of its sources. By 1941, with the help of newsstand sales and the demise of its predecessors during the Depression, *Reader's Digest* could claim a circulation of four million. Applying many of the same principles that made their magazine a success, the Wallaces launched *Reader's Digest Condensed Books* (1950) by direct mail as a subscription service. By this time, the art of direct marketing had taken on many aspects of science. Adopting principles of experimental design from the science laboratory, marketers constantly tested offers, using controls and keeping meticulous records, to establish the most effective presentation and to develop refinements. The success of *Condensed Books* may be termed "primarily a business story, rather than a publishing story," according to Evert Volkersz (1995). Reader's Digest Corporation went public in 1990. It reinvented itself as a direct marketer and added books and compact discs produced and packaged to attract its well-known audience. I think the moral may be that the reprinting is not redundant if it pleases new readers. It amplifies.

Diversity of Gender

Social and political diversity sparks new magazines that may aim to generate movements connected with politics, fashion, culture, ethnicity, and other topics. Many women's magazines, such as *McCall's* (1921), aim to serve traditional interests such as home economics. Others seek new horizons. An important part of Margaret Sander's mission was realized as editor and publisher of *Woman Rebel* (March–September/October 1914) and then *Birth Control Review* (1917–1940). The first one challenged Anthony Comstock kamikaze-style. Comstock had the authority to censor birth control and other information from 1872 until his death in 1915. As a postal inspector, he deemed *Woman Rebel* unmailable and subject to confiscation. The last straw was an article in the July 1914 issue that justified assassination as a tool of reform. Called to court, Sanger fled the country. During the trial of Sanger's husband as accomplice, Comstock caught cold and died, along with him the prosecution. Sanger's were not the first periodicals of what we might call the women's or feminist movement. *The Advocate and Family Guardian* (1835–1941) which notes that it was preceded by *McDowell's Journal* (Edited by John McDowell 1833–1834) was founded by the New York Female Reform Society during the "Second Great Awakening"—a time of moral regeneration. By exposing immorality, the magazine aimed to end prostitution, which it blamed on men, and to educate children against becoming victims or predators. Among the collateral issues it addressed was housing. The publishers actually operated a shelter and playgrounds. In their historical bibliography, *Women's Periodicals in the United States: Social and Political Issues*, Endres and Leuck (1996) cite many notable publications. Women's political interests range from conservative to radical. Historic issues of abolition and suffrage are superseded by such modern causes as gay rights and employment discrimination. Some are more fraternal or professional than political. Many are one-woman projects, while others are the product of a team or a movement. Some existed briefly; others endured. Some had large circulations, while others produced and distributed fewer than 1,000 copies. A few more titles should be listed here, without suggesting that one is more important than another or that the list is complete:

- Amelia Bloomer's *Lily* (1849–1856)
- Jane G. Swisshelm's *Pittsburgh Saturday Visitor* (1874–1854)
- Lydia Sayer Hasbrouck's *Sibyl: A Review of the Tastes, Errors and Fashions of Society* (1856–1864)
- Susan B. Anthony's *Revolution* (1868–1972)
- Alice B. Blackwell's *Woman's Journal* (1870–1917)
- Abigail Scott Duniway's *New Northwest* (1871–1887)
- Ida B. Wells' *Free Speech and Headlight* (1888–1892)
- Rosa Sonneschein's *American Jewess* (1895–1899)
- *National Citizen and Ballot Box* (1876–1881)
- *Business Woman's Journal* (1889–1892)
- *Anti-Suffragist* (1908–1912)
- Charlotte Perkins Gilman's *Forerunner* (1909–1916)
- Woman Suffrage Party of New York City's *Woman Voter* (1910–1917)
- *Women Lawyers' Journal* (1911)
- Dorothy Day's *Catholic Worker* (1933)
- *Equal Rights* (1923–1954)
- *Ladder* (1956–1972)
- *off our backs* (1970)
- *New Women's Times* (1975–1984)

- *Sinister Wisdom* (1976–1994)
- *Harvard Women's Law Journal* (1978)

Advertising Diversity

All is not editorial material. The development of advertising meant that the purpose of content was to attract and deliver an audience of potential customers to producers and distributors of goods and services. By today, mass media such as radio and television have demonstrated this beyond any doubt. For some advertisers, the largest audience is best, meaning the lowest common denominator in terms of editorial allure. For others, the demographics of gender, age, ethnicity, education, income, geography, religion, and the like are tied to sales potential. Ernest Dichter used psychoanalytic theory to tie marketing to personality, lifestyle, and fundamental human motivations (Packard 1957). In advertising, Daniel Starch embraced behaviorism as a means to assess which print ads pulled best. As a reading audience, women are considered by advertisers to be shoppers first. Concerns about food, fashion, and relationships come well before political thought. Men can be drawn by coverage of sports and adventure. Musicians are interested in music, and so on. Magazines that meet readers' needs of entertainment, cultural appreciation, business information, and education also serve advertisers' promotional purposes. The new management of *Youth's Companion* accepted advertising in 1857. *Scribner's Monthly* (1870) carried advertising from its beginning. *Harper's Monthly* (1850) followed suit in 1881. Cyrus Curtis of *Ladies Home Journal* (1883) had sufficient economic advantage to reject ads for products such as patent medicines and cosmetics that he thought cast a shadow on the magazine's respectability. By 1910, with the *Journal* and *Saturday Evening Post* (1839), he felt confident enough to publish his acceptance standards for advertising in a book.

Nineteenth-Century Developments Set the Stage

Technology

In the late nineteenth century, the second industrial revolution produced a fertile environment for magazines as mass media. The entire graphics industry changed, as did many other aspects of industry and consumer life. Richard Hoe, an American, developed a high-speed rotary press in 1847. Later presses used continuous rolls of paper and bindery features that vastly increased production speed, turning out 24,000 copies hourly. By 1897 the biggest British magazines, *Tit-bits* and *Answers* were printed on Hoe presses. The development of wood-pulp paper (that later would cost libraries millions of dollars) began in Germany in the 1840s and 1850s. The American Wood Paper Company, which started operations in 1866, had its own approach, using caustic soda, which further lowered costs and increased supplies. Newsprint was born in 1868, used first by the German-language New York newspaper, *Staats-Zeitung*. Dense black inks that facilitated high-speed printing were developed from coal-tar oils, advances that were related to the creation of the German dye industry.

Speeding words was accomplished by new machines. The first practical typewriter was manufactured by Remington in 1874. The first mechanical typesetter, the Linotype machine, was invented by Ottmar Mergenthaler in 1884, the Monotype machine was first used in 1897. These machines automated the typesetting process, eliminating handwriting and hand-set type (except for advertising and headlines). Electric illumination, invented in 1879 and quickly commercialized, fostered writing, reading, and publishing late into the night. Transportation technology amplified the gains in production. Railway, postal, and telegraph connections across the continent made possible not only delivery of the printed page, but of raw materials and finished goods that were produced for and advertised to a national audience. In the 1880s, refrigeration and its application to wagons and storage meant that beef, beer, and other perishables could be marketed coast to coast by national companies such as Pillsbury, Gold Medal, Heinz, Campbell, and Quaker Oats.

Other technological developments improved illustrations used in ads, editorial material, and covers. The halftone requires a smoother surface than simple text. Several types of paper addressed this need by the end of the nineteenth century. Super-calendared paper produced from ground wood pulp and the invention of the halftone made the illustrated magazine possible. A portrait of Prince Arthur appeared in the *Canadian Illustrated News* (1869) on October 30, 1869 (Reed 1997). In England, *Review of Reviews*, Macmillan's *English Illustrated Magazine* (1884–1913), and *Strand Magazine* (1891–1916) set examples that were widely imitated. The leggotype technique, named after William A. Leggo, is often credited with the first halftone reproduction in the March 4, 1880, issue of *New York Daily Graphic* (1873). French publications developed reticulated gelatin emulsions to reproduce artworks in *Le Monde Illustré* (1857–1948). A British weekly, *Life*, contracted with the French company to produce a portrait of Mrs. Lillie Langtry on September 6, 1879, and then other women prominent in society, on a regular basis. On September 5, 1885, a British magazine, *The Graphic*, published the first photographic picture story titled "An Amateur Photographer at the Zoo" (Reed 1977). *Frank Leslie's Popular Monthly* (1876–1904) initially offered its readers a specially printed print that was bound just inside the front cover. Eventually it introduced halftone color, using two-and three-color printing, as a regular feature in late 1896. The satirical *Puck* (1877–1918), which had editions in both English and German, employed lithographed tints to decorate its pages of caricatures in 1877. Reed (1977) notes, "It can be no coincidence that a new title, that of art director, made its appearance during the 1890s, the decade in which photo-mechanical reproduction took over."

Social and Economic Factors

Social and economic changes also had a profound effect on other aspects of periodical publishing. The U.S. population actually tripled between 1850 and 1900. It surpassed the population of England before the Civil War. It not only grew, it clustered. The number of cities inhabited by more than 25,000 souls increased to 160 by 1900. Combined with the adventure of westward expansion, immigration, and economic optimism, these circumstances generated periodicals of every kind, ranging from the most esoteric to what we might call mass media. The *Postal Act of 1863* and 1879 amendments encouraged magazines. Although North Americans continued to look to Europe for culture and science, they developed their own identity and achieved an economic critical mass that was more than sufficient to sustain their own periodicals. Why would the United States continue to depend so heavily on imported publications when domestic markets were robust, viable, and more interesting?

Modern Popular Magazines

The stage was set in the nineteenth century, one might say, for the modern twentieth-century magazine. *Harper's Monthly* (1850), *Atlantic Monthly* (1857), and many others already had well-established audiences. They provided a stable business model and training ground for the industry. Technology already established contributed refinements. *Life* (1936–1972), for instance, used custom paper produced by the Mead Corporation. Emphasizing the power of photojournalism, it was an instant success. As a child of Henry Luce's *Time* (1923), its original coverage fell quite far from the tree—a digest of news largely rewritten from newspaper articles. *Time* is still going strong, meeting weekly competition from *Newsweek* (1933) and *U.S. News and World Report* (1948). The Crowell organization, which published *Collier's* (1888–1956), owned technology connected with color gravure. In the year's preceding World War II, it used this technique to produce signatures bound into *Collier's*, creating a front/middle/and back zoned effect. *Collier's,* which originally published cheap versions of popular books and novels, increased its interest in baseball and current events with as obvious an anti-Nazi perspective as that of Luce.

Science in the New World

The growth of the science community produced an impressive round of multiple births of scientific journals in North America by the start of the twentieth century. *Journal of Analytical and Applied Chemistry* (1887) was edited by Edward Hart of Lafayette College in Easton, Pennsylvania. *Physical Review* (1893) and *Journal of Physical Chemistry* (1896) appeared at Cornell University. A group at the Massachusetts Institute of Technology prepared a quarterly journal of abstracts titled *Review of American Chemical Research* (1895). Some other science and technology starts of the period include, among others,

- *American Anthropologist* (1888)
- *Astrophysical Journal* (1895)
- *American Geologist* (1888)
- *Journal of Geology* (1893)
- *Transactions of the American Entomological Society* (1867)
- *Transactions of the American Fisheries Society* (1872)
- *Transactions of the American Foundrymen's Association* (1896)
- *American Journal of Mathematics* (1878)
- *American Journal of Physiology* (1898)
- *American Journal of Psychology* (1887)
- *American Journal of Sociology* (1895)
- *American Mathematical Monthly* (1894)
- *Journal of Morphology* (1887)

Notably, the word "American" often reinforces the New World identity. All, I believe, continue to publish.

Development of Secondary and Tertiary Science Publications

The record of science and technology tracks an exponential doubling of journal articles and scientists since the mid-seventeenth century. The ratio of journal articles to the number of authors appears to be constant (Lotka 1926). Soon, too many articles for anyone to follow created consternation over resources wasted by researchers who had missed some news of others' findings. The expansion of research activity created a need for indexes and bibliographies that would help researchers locate useful relevant material (Price, 1963). The first such "secondary" periodicals (to distinguish them from the "primary" publication of original research) was seen in the early nineteenth century. In the United States, *Index Medicus* (1879), *Engineering Index* (1884), and *Chemical Abstracts* (1907) come to mind as pioneers. Equally important innovations in scientific publication were the review journal and the continuation reference work, called by some "tertiary" to distinguish it from "primary" and "secondary" forms. The greatest challenge to science was the gap in knowledge between contemporaries. Indexing was not sufficient to close that gap because the reader was still required to screen out irrelevant and useless sources. Review journals and reference works that evaluate and summarize the state of science were developed by publishers that include Academic Press *(Advances in ...)*, Pergamon Press *(Progress in ...)*, and others. Notably, this approach bore a striking resemblance to German journals with titles such as *Ergebnisse der ...* and *Fortschritte der ...* . The German Reference *Beilsteins Handbuch der Organischen Chemie* (1881) originally described some 15,000 compounds within 2,200 pages. After 100 years of editions and supplements, it occupies shelves all around many chemistry reading rooms. (The Beilstein Institute converted to electronic format in the 1980s and now summarizes organic chemistry through *Beilstein Informationsysteme.*) *Reviews of Modern Physics* first appeared in 1930, published by the American Physical Society. A Stanford University professor, James Murray Luck, founded Annual Reviews Inc. during the Great Depression. Beginning with *Annual Review of Biochemistry* (1932), Luck noted that *Chemical Abstracts* at the time published 6,500 abstracts of papers on that subject; the number in 1979 exceeded 148,000 (Kaufman 1995). The value of reviews was captured by a now-famous article by Conyers Herring (1968) and 1963 recommendations of the President's Science Advisory Committee.

Effect of World War II

Before World War II, Europe was at the center of the world of science, engineering, medicine, and the liberal arts. Most technology and high culture was imported to North America. German publishers such as Springer-Verlag, Akademische Verlagsgesellshaft, and Fischer Verlag were at the center of scientific publishing. German was the language of science, mandatory for an undergraduate degree in science or medicine. French and classical Greek and Latin were required for the arts. Study in Europe was essential for any learned pursuit. Elsevier Science Publishers, with roots in publishing going back to the sixteenth century, and North-Holland Publishing Company, which merged in 1969, were both founded in the 1930s.

Beginning in that decade, political troubles and the persecution of Jews made publication difficult in Germany. German publishers were affected by new regulations. They lost many editors, authors, and staff. In addition, they were soon viewed as unattractive outlets for foreign authors (Sarkowski 1996). The effect was to increase learned publication outside Germany, particularly in the United States, the United Kingdom, and in the Netherlands. For example, spurred by concerns that *Zentralblatt für Mathematik* (1931) might soon fail, a U.S. group created a very similarly organized replacement called *Mathematical Reviews* in 1940 (Bartle 1995). Publication of *Zentrablatt* was indeed suspended during the war years 1941–1944, as were many German periodicals, but it resumed afterward. Many publications were embargoed from export by the German government. Edwards Brothers, of Ann Arbor, Michigan, was authorized to reprint and sell the wartime volumes of German scientific journals. After the war, German publishers continued to endure distressful circumstances. They were taken over by Occupation forces and could publish journals only under special licenses. As of October 1947, many important journals, such as *Langenbecks Archiv für Chirurgie, Archiv für Ohren-, Nasen- und Kehlkopfheilkunde, Zeitschrift für Anatomie und Entwicklungsgeschichte, Zeitschrift für vergelichende Physiologie,* and *Zeitschrift für angewandte Physik,* still lacked American licenses. The requirement of a license ended in September 1949, except in Berlin where it continued until 1952.

Post–World War II

Post–World War II developments had a tremendous impact on periodical publishing, particularly in science and medicine. Research centers shifted from Germany to the United States. The partnership of the U.S. government with larger universities—spurred by Cold War competition with Soviet science—had created a new era. Particularly in basic science, and in contrast to applied subjects where local markets preferred the vernacular, English became the *lingua franca* of higher learning. Dutch publishers such as Elsevier were already publishing in English. Springer-Verlag's *Pflugers Archiv—European Journal of Physiology,* for example, turned to the English language in 1968 after publishing more than 300 volumes in German (Gotze 1977). The exodus from Europe included individuals with special skills, who changed science publishing in the United States: Kurt Jacoby, his brother-in-law Walter J. Johnson, Eric S. Proskauer, and Maurits Dekker. Jacoby and Johnson, whose family had owned Akademische Verlagsgesellschaft and the Leipzig antiquarian Gustav Fock, who fled the Nazis in the 1930s, founded Academic Press in 1942. Johnson also founded Walter J. Johnson, Inc., an antiquarian bookseller that included a subscription agency. It participated in many co-publishing ventures with German publishers such as Springer-Verlag. In the 1960s,

Johnson developed Johnson Reprint Corporation to supply universities with learned journals and books, many published before the establishment of western and midwestern institutions. Johnson Reprint was challenged competitively by other Europeans, particularly the famous antiquarian H. P. Kraus, whose Kraus Reprint Corporation was managed by Fred Altman. Eric Proskauer, who had been an editor at Akademische Verlagsgesellschaft and executive at Nordeman Publishing Company from 1937 to 1940, founded Interscience Publishers in 1940 together with Dekker, who had co-founded Nordemanns Wetenschappelijke Boekhandel in 1925. Working from an apartment in Manhattan, Dekker's son launched Marcel Dekker Inc. in 1963. Soon after the war, the polylingual autodidact from Slovakia, Robert Maxwell, managed to extract Pergamon Press as a prize from his role in a joint venture between Butterworth Scientific Publications Ltd. and Springer-Verlag. That included the Springer-Verlag journal *Spectrochimica Acta* (1939), as well as *Progress in Biophysics and Biophysical Chemistry* (1950); *Progress in Nuclear Physics* (1950); *Journal of Atmospheric and Solar-Terrestrial Physics* (1950); and *Geochimica et Cosmochimica Acta* (1950). An important part of Maxwell's strategy was to make every journal international in nature with American and European co-editors. Many other European publishers followed a similar path. Pergamon Press, headquartered in Oxford, England, opened its U.S. offices in 1952; Elsevier in 1962; Springer-Verlag in 1964. Indeed, international co-authorship is common, and most science journals now consider themselves international in terms of authors and readers no matter where they are edited and printed.

The Cold War

The Cold War produced the House Un-American Activities Committee and McCarthyism. They generated a national obsession on the menace of "reds" and "pinkos." As with Hollywood writers, anyone in the publishing industry asserting First Amendment rights was likely to suffer job loss and blacklisting. At the height of Cold War paranoia, the separation of Soviet science from the West created an opportunity for Earl M. Coleman to create the first cover-to-cover translation journal: *Journal of General Chemistry USSR* (1949) Soviet scientists wrote in Russian and published in Soviet journals. Coleman boldly signed royalty arrangements with the USSR in order to successfully battle Robert Maxwell over rights that were not officially recognized by courts outside the Soviet bloc (Coleman 1994, 1995). By the time Coleman retired in 1977, his Plenum Press was translating more than 100 Soviet journals. Robert Maxwell also negotiated with the Soviets for rights to scientific and medical works during the 1950s, often making payments in barter.

The Soviet Sputnik, the first satellite to orbit, punctuated the Cold War in late 1957. Its unexpected success left Western science, education, and politicians embarrassed and envious of the Soviet achievement. The science bureaucracy confessed at once that science information in the free world had stagnated. A series of reports to the president and Congress blamed the superiority of Soviet science information and education for their success in space (Bishop and Fellows 1989). The role of information was abruptly recognized and tied to the productivity of research. Frank Sisco, director of the Engineering Foundation in New York, was fond of postulating, "If a research job in the USA costs less than $100,000, it is cheaper to do it than to find out if it has been done before and is reported in the literature" (Gaudenzi 1958). President Dwight D. Eisenhower's approach to scientific and technical information helped many secondary publishers to computerize (Kaser 1955). Information services were certainly the first to realize the potential of electronic publishing, far ahead of publishers of primary reports, entertainment, and general nonfiction. Their market was institutional and well defined, with the means to pay and bespoken needs. Science policy also encouraged development of Eugene Garfield's brainchildren, *Current Contents* (1958), which developed as a loose-leaf service for companies like Miles Laboratories, Lederle Laboratories, Warner Lambert, and others, and *Science Citation Index* (1961). Some of the more noticeable effects of Sputnik on publishing came from legislation that emphasized education and libraries. The *National Defense Education Act of 1958* addressed such concerns. Its Title VII was amended in 1964 to finance the purchase of library materials (Krettek and Hubbard 1964). Democratic and Republican platform statements expressed support for libraries in 1960 for the first time in history, according to the *Bowker Annual* in 1961. The *Library Services and Construction Act,* passed in 1964, underwrote development of new buildings (Krettek and Cooke 1965). Title II-A (college library materials) of the *Higher Education Act of 1965* provided important support to collection development, more than $24 million in 1967, 1968, and 1969—a significant figure at a time when collection development spending of all higher education libraries totaled around $200 million (Stevens 1971). Spending on research and development also increased sharply as a result of Cold War competition, generating more journal articles than ever. Federal sponsorship of academic research rose from 63 percent in 1960 to 73 percent in 1965 (National Science Board 1996).

Periodicals after World War II

In the late 1940s and 1950s, several other noteworthy developments emerged. Most important, thanks to the postwar economy, popular magazine circulations broke the four million mark, and publishers enjoyed record revenue from advertising and subscriptions. *Life* posted 5,242,614 in 1950; *Ladies Home Journal* with 4,429,000 and *Saturday Evening Post* with 4,009,587 were both published by Curtis. *Reader's Digest*, which carried no advertising, was privately held, and had no reason to disclose its circulation, reached an estimated eight million copies (Reed 1997). Advertising receipts nearly doubled, reaching $648 million by 1949. Comic books such as *Superman* (1939), which were not recognized by the U.S. Department of Commerce in 1939, surpassed all other categories in aggregate sales in 1947. *Mad* (1952) pushed the satirical level of comic-book publishing beyond the cartoon personality and superhero. The advent of television, competing for advertising dollars, created a market for *TV Guide* (1953), perhaps the most successful new magazine of the twentieth century. Television also probably helped spell the end of many popular magazines like *American Magazine* (1906–1956), *Life* (1936–1972), *Colliers* (1888–1956), *Look* (1937–1971), and *Saturday Evening Post* (1839–1969). Multimillions of advertising revenues notwithstanding, costs were escalating at an astonishing pace. To a periodical such as *Saturday Evening Post*, delivering 6.2 million copies of each issue to subscribers and sending millions of solicitations by mail, huge increases in postal rates can be deadly. Magazines that lose money die (Reed 1977; Peterson 1964).

Post–World War II Technology

In the technology area, photo-offset lithography and photo-typesetting began to take hold. Regional editions such as a West coast edition of *Time*, first produced in 1944, were made possible by flying films—more easily transportable than metal plates. The flexibility of photo-typesetting made it stylish for use in advertising at first. With lower costs and the possibility of using labor with little training, it replaced unionized linotype operators and metal type in many job shops and in-house operations. The Mylar carbon ribbon made "cold" type feasible for production by electric typewriters and paved the way for the proliferation of "desktop publishing." Computerized pre-press processing made great strides toward the end of the century. The combination of the Xerox 914 photocopier's success in the 1960s and the embrace of "fair use" by the *Copyright Act of 1976* rationalized draconian cuts in library spending and set off the interlibrary-loan skyrocket. To deal with dissatisfactions with interlibrary borrowing, a commercial document-delivery industry was born—charging for copies, paying royalties, and using contractors to source articles in large collections. Today, some of the major document-delivery sources for U.S. researchers are located in Europe and Canada. To the consternation of many of the technology advocacies, the authors and the copyright industry have asserted their rights over copied articles. Texaco, Kinko's, and the *New York Times* discovered that royalties and fees must be paid. In 1993 the British Library agreed to pay royalties on its copying. The Copyright Clearance Center, which was organized by science publishers in the 1970s, has handled an ever-increasing business.

The Baby Boom

The population explosion after World War II sent a wave of consumers through all markets. The growth of family-oriented suburbs increased the importance of subscription sales. The maturing of baby boomers created sufficient markets for new products and services across the board, ranging from business and professional categories to home and leisure activities. Higher education enrollments regularly set new records, as did the awarding of PhDs. The new vitality of the social sciences, which explained social and economic changes and provided solutions to problems, contributed to the development of many niche publications, as well as more general titles. Publishers such as Erlbaum, Transaction, and Sage responded with academically oriented specialty publications. Social science is different from physical science in many respects. Social science publications risk intruding on taboo topics such as politics, sex, and religion (Horowitz 1972). Many socially oriented periodicals focused on these, as well as less controversial specialties. The sociologist and publisher Irving Louis Horowitz also pointed out that, "along with the benefits from such niche publishing come the penalties. The basic problem is that the new specialized publishing environment encourages fragmentation and atomization" (1991). Information services such as *Sociological Index* (1953), and *Journal of Economic Literature/Economic Literature Index* (1969) arose to make the needed connections. The growth of sociology is dramatized by the contrast of 14,555 abstracts in the first decade followed by 56,782 abstracts in the second decade of *Sociological Abstracts*. In addition, much as *Scientific American* (1845) had done in the nineteenth century, *Psychology Today* (1967) and *Society* (1962) aimed to bridge the gap between research and the general public.

The Post–World War II Impact of Technology
on Science and Education

The impact of technology on periodical publishing during the second half of the twentieth century was as profound, but not as positive, as it was 100 years earlier. A rival to the printer, the photocopier, proliferated starting in the 1960s. Unfortunately for publishers, the possibility of excellent photocopies and, later, the fantasy of the Internet that individuals would find all the information they needed using their own computers, threatened subscriptions. The "enemies of the library," including librarians as well as bureaucrats well insulated from the actual use of libraries and unconcerned with difficult-to-measure productivity, decided that libraries had too much money to spend (Crawford and Gorman 1995). The growth of library finances suddenly decelerated. The "enemies" carried forward their assault on the latest Standards for College Libraries prepared by the Association of College and Research Libraries (C&RL News 2000). The present revision is hardly a "standard" since it offers only vague notions of adequacy, supplemented by questions without answers. It is now possible for a mediocre facility to claim a satisfactory status. The previous version (C&RL News 1995) provided finite measures by which to judge collections (for example, minimum 85,000 volumes), staffing, facilities, and other factors Among the lost formulas, the revision approved in January 2000 excised the following passage:

> [8.1] The library's annual authorized expenditures shall be at least six percent of the total institutional expenditure for educational and general purposes.

Removing this criterion goes against long-standing recommendations. In addition to fostering subscription cancellations, it encourages the inadequate pay of librarians, as well as the impoverishment of other acquisitions, facilities, training, and services.

Moon Landing and Perestroika

The U.S. landing on the Moon in 1969 sits like a bookend on the other end of the post-Sputnik expansion of instruction, libraries, and publishing. The 1970s saw the devastation of both research and development and libraries. Funding from the Higher Education Act Title II-A (library materials) funding dropped sharply in 1970 and dwindled to nothing by 1983. Support for research, which was substantially tied to defense budgets, was undercut by Vietnam politics. The "Mansfield Amendment" to the military procurement authorization for 1970 eliminated great numbers of academic research jobs (Nichols 1971). It did not stop authors from writing. Submissions of journals articles, however, drawn from all over the world, continued to rise. The National Science and Technology Organization and Priority Act of 1976 began as an effort to find work for scientists. (The unemployment problem resolved itself as policy makers realized the social value of research.) The act eventually focused on dissemination. It required the government "to promote prompt, effective, reliable, and systematic transfer of science and technology information," a mission that it has failed to carry out, according to all subsequent analyses (McClure and Hernon 1989). In spite of this apparent mandate, the National Science Foundation shut down its Division of Science Information by the end of the decade. Cuts in academic libraries' share of university expenditures meant declines in library spending per student, staffing per student, proportions of the library budget expended for materials, and the numbers of books added to collections. Libraries competed with the activities they were supposed to support, and lost (Fry and White 1975; Talbot 1984). The National Enquiry on Scholarly Communication (1979) complained that inadequate library collections were the most severe problem faced by scholars. Meanwhile, support for the expansion of research and development resumed and continued uninterrupted after 1975 (National Science Board 1989).

Serials Crisis

The energy crisis, the Cold War and Star Wars, and eventually an appreciation of the value of technology, medical research, and environmental studies restored the growth of research and development. Nonfederal sponsors increased their participation in academic research from 32 percent in 1980 to 40 percent in 1995. They caused some concern by attempting to control the publication of results that they wished to treat as "trade secrets" or that they felt were bad for business. U.S. research and development spending (in constant dollars) approximated the growth of world science, doubling between 1980 and 1995. Spending on libraries, which had not grown between 1970 and 1980, began to increase, but not enough to keep up with the growth of research funding Title II-A (college library materials) was eventually deleted by the *Higher Education Amendments of 1993*, after a decade of not being funded. In vain the American Library Association called attention to the devaluation of the U.S. dollar and its impact on the purchasing ability of libraries collecting foreign research (American Library Association 1987).

The financial gap between libraries and research and development was taking its toll on publishers as subscriptions to learned books and journals dropped sharply (Henderson 1995). Circulation and price are inextricably linked. As cancellations rolled in, prices shot upward, boosted by increasing submissions. Researchers also suffered. Evidence of collection failure appears in skyrocketing photocopy activity reported widely. The doubling of the mean ratio of interlibrary borrowing to collection size (i.e., access to ownership) between 1974 and 1998 of eighty ARL members should be a cause for concern (Henderson 2000). Raw interlibrary borrowing statistics are even more dramatic. OCLC recorded a fivefold increase in interlibrary loan requests generated by academic and research libraries during the ten years ending in 1988–1989 (OCLO 1989). The Association of Research Libraries reported interlibrary borrowing increased 104 percent between the academic years 1985–1986 and1994–1995 (Association of Research Libraries 1996). In 1989, the Association of College and Research Libraries eliminated assertions that weak collections hampered research in its revised Standards for University Library Collections (ACRL 1989). What is the effect? Inferred insularity may be corroborated by extraordinarily high incidence of citations to U.S. authors by U.S. researchers, a characteristic unique to U.S. authors (National Science Board 1996). I would add that I am always surprised at the ignorance and insularity of some critics of science publishing, as if U.S. universities were the only consideration. They may monopolize U.S. government research contracts, but that is where it ends. According to the National Science Board (1993, p. 421; 1996, p. 207), academic researchers accounted for about 15 percent of world output. Authors in the United States decreased their share of world journal articles from 38.2 percent in 1973 to 33.6 percent by 1993.

Peer Review

The integrity of the scientific record is the burden of science editors aided by peer review. Legal misconduct in science is limited to the relatively small number of projects funded by government contract. The government standard was recently narrowed to "fabrication, falsification, or plagiarism, in proposing, performing or reviewing research, or in reporting research results," as documented in the *Federal Register* of October 14, 1999. This eliminated "other practices that seriously deviate from those commonly accepted within the scientific community" (42 C.F.R., 50.101). Dependent largely on whistle-blowers, the Office of Research Integrity (ORI) of the U.S. Public Health Service recently circulated a booklet to science editors pointing out their responsibility "to ensure that significant suspicions are reported" (2000). Editors have played a valuable role by informing ORI, which was established in 1992, of allegations and by cooperating with the review process. This leaves open questions of misconduct not associated with government contracts.

Formal peer review is most associated with scientific journals, going back to the seventeenth century when the Royal Society of Edinburgh described an anonymous refereeing process. It is not meant to unearth and investigate misconduct. The historian David A. Kronick (1990) pointed out, "peer review (whether it occurs before or after publication) is an essential and integral part of the process of consensus building and is inherent and necessary to the growth of scientific knowledge."

Although the use of formal review has spread to technical and medical management, little was actually known of the process, even by those who practiced it, until studies focused on scientific communications in the 1960s and 1970s. The American Medical Association and the *British Medical Journal* started a series of international congresses on peer review in biomedicine in 1989. The fourth was held in 2001 in Barcelona. One of the major targets of such studies appears to be the mythology of peer review, including allegations of bias, misconduct, and what it means to the various parties involved. Peer review is blamed for rejections of worthy papers that may appear in other "core" journals of equal reputation, contributing to an overall delay in publication (Garvey et al. 1979). Peer review may be lauded as certifying quality when the material actually falls short of the mark. A random sample of papers, for instance, found citations riddled with errors committed by the authors and ignored during editorial review (Evans et al. 1991).

The popularity of the free electronic circulation of unreviewed physics and mathematics papers brought peer review under a new attack (Bederson 1994). The argument in favor is that the gate-keeping function of journal editors is an anachronism that unnecessarily slows dissemination. The counterargument says, in effect, that we are already drowning in information; now you want to spice the flood with raw sewage to hasten our demise. Many feel that the attack lacks the wisdom of experience. Some of us suggest it is based on the "enemies of the library" motive of removing library funding by eliminating collections and the need for librarians. The crucial parts of peer review—reading, checking sources, evaluating, and writing a report—cannot be automated. Supporters of peer review point to its substantial contributions, including revisions based on referees' comments, as well as the value of time saved by researchers who wish for some assurance of quality. Nonetheless, the manager of a physics preprint server, which is funded by the U.S. Department of Energy, soon bragged that the service had "supplanted traditional journals as conveyors of both topical and archival research information" (Ginsparg 1966). Harold Varmus, during his last months as director of the National Institutes of Health, proposed a service for biomedical communications patterned on the physics service run by the Department of Energy. In contrast to the approach of the energy department, NIH submitted its E-Biomed proposal to open review. It was generally rejected by the science community at large. It survives today in a different form under a different name, to the consternation of its advocates.

Perhaps peer review has also come under attack because, like tenure, it is connected to journals and associations that cannot be controlled by the university and science bureaucracies. Clearly, the economic attack by universities on journals and libraries weakens the information resources of referees and assaults the financial resources of publishers.

References

American Library Association. Resources and Technical Services Division. 1987. Impact of Dollar Devaluation. Resolution dated June 29. Reprinted in *Report of the ARL Serials Prices Project*.

ARL Statistics 1989-90. 1991. Washington, D.C.: Association of Research Libraries.

ARL Statistics 1998-99. 2000. Washington , D.C.: Association of Research Libraries.

Arunachalam, Subbiah. 1993. Serials and developing countries: use of serials literature. In *The International Serials Industry* edited by Hazel Woodward and Stella Pilling. Altershot Hamps. Gower Publishing.

Association of College and Research Libraries . 1979. Standards for university libraries: evaluation of performance. *College and Research Library News,* April 1979: 158–167

Association of College and Research Libraries. 1989. Standards for university libraries: evaluation of performance. *College and Research Library News* 50 (September): 679–691

Association of College and Research Libraries. 1995. Standards for college libraries. *College and Research Library News* 56 (April): 245–257.

Association of College and Research Libraries. 2000. Standards for college libraries. *College and Research Library News* 61 (March): 175–182.

Ballhausen, C. J. et al.1973. Too many chemical journals. *Chemical and Engineering News,* 10 December

Bartle, Robert G. 1995. A brief history of the mathematical literature. *Publishing Research Quarterly* 11 2: 3–13.

Bederson, B. *Report to Council on E-Print Archive Workshop, Los Alamos, Oct. 14–15, 1994.* http://publish.aps.org/eprint

Bishop, Ann and Maureen O'Neill Fellows. 1989. Descriptive analysis of major federal scientific and technical information policy studies. In *U.S. Scientific and Technical Information (STI) Policies: Views and Perspectives.* Edited by Charles R. McClure and Peter Hernon. Norwood: Ablex. 3–55.

Coleman, Earl Maxwell, 1994–95. The mass production of translation—for a limited market. *Publishing Research Quarterly.* 10,4: 22–29.

Corning, Mary E., and Martin M. Cummings. 1976. Biomedical communications. *Advances in American Medicine.* Edited by John Z. Vol. 2. Bowers and Elizabeth F. Purcell. New York: Josiah Macy, Jr., Foundation.

Crawford, Walt, and Michael Gorman, 1995. *Future Libraries: Madness, Dreams, and Reality.* Chicago: American Library Association.

Danky, James P., and M. E. Hady, eds.. 1998 African-American Newspapers and Periodicals. A National Bibliography. Cambridge, Mass.: Harvard University Press.

Endres, Kathleen L., and Therese L. Leuck. 1996. *Women's Periodicals in the United States: Social and Political Issues.* Westport, Conn.: Greenwood.

Evans, J. R., H. I. Nadjari, and S. A. Burchell. 1990. Quotational and reference accuracy in surgical journals. A continuing peer review problem. *JAMA* 263:1353–1354. Reprinted in *Peer Review in Scientific Publishing. Papers from the First International Congress on Peer Review in Biomedical Publication Sponsored by the American Medical Association.* 1991. Chicago: Council of Biology Editors.

Fry, Bernard M., and Herbert S. White. 1975. *Economics and Interaction of the Publisher–Library Relationship in the Production and Use of Scholarly and Research Journals*. Washington, D.C.: National Science Foundation.

Garvey, William D., N. Lin, and C.E. Nelson. 1979. Communication in the physical and social science. In Garvey, William D. *Communication: The Essence of Science*. Oxford: Pergamon Press.

Gaudenzi, Nerio. 1958. The efficiency of metallurgical abstracts. *Proceedings of the International Conference on Scientific Information*. Washington, D.C., 1958. National Academy of Sciences–National Research Council, 1959. 393–405.

Gibbs, W. Wayt. 1995. Lost science in the third world. *Scientific American*. 273,2 (August): 92–99.

Ginsparg, Paul. 1996. Winners and losers in the global research village. http://xxx.lanl.gov/blurb/pg96unesco.html

Gotze, Heinz. 1997. The English language in scientific publishing. *Publishing Research Quarterly*. 13,1: 52–72. Excerpted from *Springer-Verlag. History of a Scientific Publishing House*. Vol. 2 1945–1992. Berlin-Heidelberg-New York: Springer-Verlag. 1996.

Henderson, Albert. 1995. Research journals: a question of economic value. *Logos* 6,1:43–46.

Henderson, Albert, ed. 1998. *Electronic Databases and Publishing*. New Brunswick, N.J.: Transaction.

Henderson, Albert. 1999. Information science and information policy. The use of constant dollars and other indicators to manage research investments. *Journal of the American Society for Information Science* 50,4:366–379.

Henderson, Albert. 2000. The library collection failure quotient. *Journal of Academic Librarianship* 26,3:159–170.

Herring, Conyers. 1968. Distill or drown: the need for reviews. *Physics Today* 21,9: 27–33.

Horowitz, Irving Louis. 1972. On entering the tenth year of *Transaction*: the relationship of social science and critical journalism. *Society* Nov/Dec. 10, 1:49–74.

Horowitz, Irving Louis. 1991. *Communicating Ideas: The Politics of Scholarly Publishing*. 2nd ed. New Brunswick, N.J.: Transaction.

Husni, Samir. 1999. *Samir Husni's Guide to New Consumer Magazines 1999*. New York: Oxbridge.

Kaser, Richard T. 1995. Secondary information services. Mirrors of scholarly communication. *Publishing Research Quarterly* 11,3:10–24.

Kaufman, William. 1995. Annual Reviews Inc: A saga of success. *Publishing Research Quarterly* 11,2:80–89.

Krettek, Germaine, and Eileen D. Cooke. 1965. Legislation of library interest. *Bowker Annual 1965* 164–160.

Krettek, Germaine, and Hubbard. 1964. Legislation of library interest. *Bowker Annual 1964*.

Kronick, David A. 1990. Peer review in eighteenth-century scientific journalism. *JAMA* 263:1321–1323. Reprinted in *Peer Review in Scientific Publishing. Papers from the First International Congress on Peer Review in Biomedical Publication* 1991. Chicago: Council of Biology Editors.

Lotka, Alfred J. 1926. The frequency distribution of scientific productivity. *Journal of the Washington Academy of Sciences* 16,12:317–323.

Lottman, Herbert R. 1976. Elsevier: Increasingly international. *Publishers Weekly* February 16:

Machlup, Fritz. 1979. Uses, value and benefits of knowledge. *Knowledge: Creation, Diffusion, Utilization* 2,1(Sept) Reprinted 1993, 14,4:448–466.

Machlup, Fritz, and Kenneth Leeson. 1978. 3 vols. *Information through the Printed Word. The Dissemination of Scholarly, Scientific, and Intellectual Knowledge.* New York: Praeger.

McClure, Charles R., and Peter Hernon. 1989. *U.S. Scientific and Technical Information (STI) Policies: Views and Perspectives.* Norwood NJ: Ablex.

McLuhan, Marshall H. 1964. *Understanding Media: The Extensions of Man.* New York: Penguin Books.

Mott, Frank Luther. 1930–1968. *A History of American Magazines.* New York: Appleton and Cambridge MA: Harvard University Press. 5 vols.

National Academy of Sciences. Committee on Scientific and Technical Communications [SATCOM]. 1970. *Report of the Task Group on the Economics of Primary Publication.* Washington DC: National Academy of Science.

National Enquiry into Scholarly Communication. 1979. *Scholarly Communication. The Report.* Baltimore: The Johns Hopkins University Press.

National Science Board. 1989. *Science & Engineering Indicators 1989.* Washington DC: National Science Foundation.

National Science Board. 1993. *Science & Engineering Indicators 1993.* Washington DC: National Science Foundation (NSB 93-1) 11th edition Appendix.

National Science Board. 1996. *Science & Engineering Indicators 1996.* Washington DC: National Science Foundation.

Nelson, Stanley. 1998. *The Black Press: Soldiers without Swords.* Produced and directed by Stanley Nelson. Half Nelson Productions. California Newsreel. 1998. VCR tape total running time: 85:54 + CD-ROM.

Nichols, Rodney W. 1971. Mission-oriented R&D. *Science.* 172:29–37.

OCLC Online Computer Library Center, Inc. July/August 1989. Resource sharing and the 10th anniversary of the OCLC interlibrary loan subsystem. *OCLC Newsletter.* 180: 12–16.

Packard, Vance. 1957. *Hidden Persuaders.* New York: David McKay.

Passell, Peter. 1997. Two get Nobel for a formula at the heart of options trading. *The New York Times.* (Oct. 15): D1,D4.

Peterson, Theodore B. 1964. *Magazines in the 20th Century.* Urbana: University of Illinois Press.

President's Science Advisory Committee [PSAC]. 1963. *Science, Government, and Information. The Responsibilities of the Technical Community and the Government in the Transfer of Information.* Washington DC: Government Print Office.

Price, Derek de Solla. 1963. *Little Science Big Science.* New York: Columbia University Press.

Reed, David. 1997. *The Popular Magazine in Britain and the United States 1880–1960.* Toronto: University of Toronto Press.

Sarkowski, Heinz. 1996. *Springer-Verlag. History of a Scientific Publishing House.* Vol. 1 1842–1945. Berlin-Heidelberg-New York: Springer-Verlag.

Stevens, Frank A. 1971. Summary of Title II-A grants for academic library resources under the Higher Education Act of 1965. *Bowker Annual,* 1971. 138–140.

Talbot, Richard. 1984. Lean years and fat years: lessons to be learned. College and research libraries. *Bowker Annual 1984.* 74–82.

Uchitelle, Danielle. 1998. Currency of coverage in the MLA International Bibliography. *Publishing Research Quarterly.* 14,1:46–51.

U.S. Public Health Service. Office of Research Integrity. 2000. *Managing Allegations of Scientific Misconduct: A Guidance Document for Editors.*

Voklersz, Evert. 1995. McBook: The Reader's Digest condensed books franchise. *Publishing Research Quarterly.* 11,2: 52–61.

White House Office of Science and Technology Policy. Oct. 14, 1999. *Federal Register.*

◆9◆

From Bibliothèque to Omnithèque

Allen B. Veaner

Introduction: Triumph of the Device

From the beginning of printing until well into the twentieth century—almost half a millennium—library systems changed comparatively slowly. Even instruments as revolutionary as the Dewey Decimal System, the typewriter, and the telephone were absorbed at a tolerable rate that did not drastically disrupt the basic functioning of the institution or make it unrecognizable to staff and users. But over the past half-century, our profession has experienced a series of major technology-driven media revolutions that, together, created what is arguably a new and quite different institution. Most recently, computers and digital data have played the most prominent role in this transformation. But over the past century there have been other players and other systems.

This article first describes earlier nonprint systems, media, and methods that have contributed significantly to library change within the twentieth century. It also examines the impact of these nonprint devices that supplement the book and the journal and that modern libraries are expected to service. In conclusion, it peers into the future.

The major twentieth-century technology and media shifts in libraries reflect the maturation of techniques, most of which were a long time aborning:

- Microforms, invented in 1839, languished for nearly a century, reaching their potential only after the 1950s.
- Although Thomas Edison devised the first practical cylinder phonograph in 1877, mass production of sound recordings became possible only with Émile Berliner's invention of the flat disk in 1888. Starting at the mid-twentieth century, flat disk technology itself experienced a bliz-

163

zard of change—the long-established 78 r.p.m. shellac records were superseded by vinyl long-playing disks, 45 r.p.m. records, wire, and tape media, compact discs (CDs), and lately, flash memory systems that have no moving parts.

- Motion pictures graduated from nearly a century of slow evolution of the optical and mechanical systems pioneered by Edison and the Lumière brothers to fully digital commercial systems, culminating in today's DVD disks and players and the reality of distributing and showing new films via digital transmission.
- Television, having matured in the post-World War II era, by the end of the century had itself become a pervasive social force worldwide and the source of innumerable video recordings.
- Computers and telecommunications, having started on parallel but related paths, began in the 1990s to converge with ever-accelerating speed, so that by the beginning of the twenty-first century, they had become virtually indistinguishable.

For countless eons, human beings communicated "naturally" by voice, employing innumerable languages supplemented by gestures, symbols, and artistic creations. Then, a few thousand years ago, came the earliest revolutionary change: written language, the first communication "device" that enabled humans to communicate independently of a living physical presence. More than half a millennium ago, printing technology resulted in an even more powerful device, one that could infinitely amplify the power of its predecessor by universalizing written languages and by providing a mass distribution system. After printing, communication beyond the interpersonal was no longer the private realm of a privileged elite. All literate people could decode messages from whatever era and widely distribute their own messages. Beginning with the telegraph in 1844, instantaneous electronic communication brought about yet another sea change. Modern technology is now introducing to the library a previously unimaginable proliferation of communication devices, many characterized by incompatibilities of hardware and software or, at least, accompanied by some difficulty or expense in achieving compatibility.

What is the chief characteristic of these modern devices? All convert previously "natural" oral communication into processes that require additional devices. In the technological and post-technological eras, direct communication between senders and receivers becomes nearly impossible. Every contemporary system requires a cast of supporting devices—even the telephone and the handheld computer—whose shelf life is disturbingly brief. Such devices convert an oral culture into one dependent on complex systems, many of whose components rely on expensive, maintenance-intensive apparatus for effective use: slides, microforms, and motion pictures require cameras, projectors, bulbs, and screens; sound recordings need players, amplifiers, and loudspeakers; computers require keyboards, display units, uninterruptible power supplies, and software not always easy to learn; cell phones depend on elaborate support systems on the ground and in space. The combined complex of communication apparatus results in systems that are increasingly fragile and potentially subject to disastrous failures. A distressing and difficult aspect of such supplementary communication media and systems is that each produces units that are indistinguishable from one another. This fact has introduced a completely new challenge to technical processing and collection management. Whereas traditional books and journals differ mainly in size, thickness, color, design, or, in some cases, other comparatively subtle factors, physical units produced by each new technology all look alike: spools of microfilms, packets of microfiches, bundles of opaque microforms, filmstrips, camera negatives and prints, glass lantern slides and 35 mm film slides, boxes of floppy disks, reels and cassettes of tape, collections of sound recordings. Librarians and the public have long experience with distinctive books, but users and managers alike are now confronted with a world of look-alike objects, where a mismarked or misplaced unit essentially means a unit lost. The tedium of accurately applying classification marks, sequence numbers, and property labels to large numbers of comparatively small (and sometimes fragile) objects of uniform size and shape adds to the manager's woes. What an irony: unstandardized books and manuscripts appear to be much easier, simpler objects to manage than "standard" nonbook media!

Yet there are more problems: all of a sudden—it seems sudden, though the transition occurred over six to seven decades—the world of librarianship changed from one dealing with media that were visible and that directly communicated to the literate user, to one that dealt with materials whose contents by themselves are neither visible nor audible. In fact, without a device, the new media are totally unusable. By interposing itself between the sender and receiver of a communication, the device had indeed achieved a supreme triumph: it required *yet more devices,* an intensity of education and depth of training far beyond the seeming simplicity of learning how to read and write, as well as heavy new demands on the budget and serious challenges to library organization and management.

As these changes evolved, there were transitional difficulties. Yet within fifty years librarianship came very far from the 1930s when anything that wasn't a bound volume received about as much welcome as a staph infection. Take, for example, this citation from 1933:

Both [radio and motion pictures] are "throwbacks to something quite primitive." Radio "is a distinct reversion, so far as it is an entertainment medium" and "is one of the things the makers and dispensers of books have to contend against." So are movies, which, at present, tend "to deaden all esthetic taste.... The intellectual achievement of modern drama is not possible in the movies.... This mechanical substitute for drama, and for printed literature in many homes, is omnipresent and influential. Our only hope is to inspire a critical attitude toward it. Nothing else will raise it to the civilized level of our other arts."[1]

Fortunately, more positive voices soon began to concede that with creative marketing, new media actually stimulated reading. Imaginative librarians began to use motion pictures, sound recordings, and other new media to attract more and more users into their service community and to reach out to the unserved. The Library of Congress's National Library Service for the Blind and Physically Handicapped brought books on disk and tape to millions of readers for whom library service had been inaccessible.[2] Throughout this half-century (1930–1980) even the controlled vocabulary for describing nonbook materials changed fairly rapidly. *Phonograph recordings* and *Phonograph records* became simply *recordings*. *Photographic reproduction and projection* branched into *microforms, photocopying*, and other more specific terms; *slide films*, a 1942 term, eventually became better known as *filmstrips*.[3] The emergence of the VCR and camcorder, with their easy playback and recording capabilities and low cost, spawned a wide-ranging nomenclature: *video education, video cameras, video conferencing, videotapes*, and more. Each new device stimulated new vocabulary, challenging subject catalogers and indexers.

As the devices evolved and publications in new formats proliferated, the profession created the same types of tools for them that were long available for print media: acquisition and review guides, technical-processing handbooks, new and revised rules and standards for cataloging, manuals for managing the new media. New professional associations were formed and journals established. For example, in the area of sound recordings, the Association for Recorded Sound Collections (ARSC) was founded in 1966, and the International Association of Sound and Audiovisual Archives in 1969. In further response to the new technology, traditional graduate library schools modified their programs, some introducing degrees reflecting specialization in managing audiovisual materials.

1 W.P. Eaton, "Mechanical Substitutes for Literature and the Theatre," *Massachusetts Library Club Bulletin* 23(October 1933):37-39, quoted from the entry in *Library Literature*, 1933–1935 cumulation.

2 Eventually, the commercial sector entered the field, supplying audiocassettes to the sighted as well, to commuters and others who wished to make dual use of their time.

3 It is interesting to observe that in the *Library Literature* cumulation for 1940–1942, there is no occurrence of the terms *filmstrips, nonbook*, or *slides*, nor any reference to the Society for Visual Education, an early proponent of audiovisual technology.

Key Events

Certain key events of the twentieth century may here be enumerated to set the context of the changes that, by the start of the twenty-first century, had profoundly altered the educational foundations for the profession and radically changed some of its recruiting requirements.

1906: Goldschmidt and Otlet design the microfiche.[4]

1920: Society for Visual Education (SVE) begins to publish a journal, *Visual Education.*

1925: First Leica camera manufactured; scholars begin using it to make their own microfilms.

1930s: Introduction of filmstrips and 16 mm sound movies into public school classrooms.[5]

1936: Recordak, the microfilm unit of Kodak, publishes an experimental edition of the *New York Times* for 1914–1918; Keyes Metcalf proposes establishment of a national register of microform masters.

1938: Harvard University establishes The Foreign Newspaper Microfilm Project (an enterprise subsequently taken over by the Association of Research Libraries); start of the the *Journal of Documentary Reproduction* (Chicago: ALA); University Microfilms founded.

1943: Founding of National Microfilm Association (succeeded by Association for Information and Image Management).

1956: Xerox introduces Copyflo®, a machine capable of producing inexpensive hard-copy prints from roll microfilm.

1959: The first *Directory of Institutional Photoduplication Services in the United States* (Chicago: ALA) is published (recent issues are entitled *Directory of Library Reprographic Services*).

1963: First International Congress on Reprography held in Cologne, Germany.

1964: Publication of *Specifications for Library of Congress Microfilming* (Washington: Library of Congress).

---

4 Robert Goldschmidt and Paul Otlet, *Sur Une Forme Nouvelle du Livre—Le Livre Microphotographique* (Brussels: Institut International de Bibliographie, 1906).

5 Western Electric, the manufacturing arm of the former Bell System, formed a subsidiary, ERPI (Electrical Research Products, Inc.) that, in collaboration with Encyclopedia Britannica, became a major supplier of instructional films for public schools. In the area of filmstrips, the Society for Visual Education (SVE) promoted that medium through the design and sale of specially designed projectors.

1965: Library of Congress begins to publish the *National Register of Microform Masters.*

1966: Publication of *Microfilm Norms* (Chicago: ALA); Association for Recorded Sound Collections (ARSC) founded.

1967: Second International Congress on Reprography held in Cologne, Germany.

1971: Publication of *The Evaluation of Microforms: A Handbook for Librarians* (Chicago: ALA).

1972: Establishment of *Microform Review* (subsequently retitled *Microform and Imaging Review*); ALA publishes Pearce S. Grove and Evelyn G. Clement's *Bibliographic Control of Nonprint Media.*

1973: Northeast Document Conservation Center established.

1975: *Books-on-Tape*™ begins publication.

1978: *Guide to Microforms in Print* first published.

1983: Founding of NISO (National Information Standards Organization), successor to Committee Z-39 of American National Standards Institute.

1986: Commission on Preservation and Access established.

1989: National Endowment for the Humanities (NEH) launches Brittle Books preservation program in which microfilm technology plays a central role in saving the content of some three million volumes; founding of Corbis digital imagery service, which eventually includes the Bettmann Archive and similar archives of photographs.

1992: *RLG Preservation Microfilming Handbook,* edited by Nancy E. Elkington, published.

1993: Yale University Library begins Open Book, a pilot project under the NEH's Brittle Book program, to digitize microforms.

1997: *National Register of Microform Masters* becomes available online.

Dissemination, Publication and Media Management Problems

Virtually all nonbook devices are inherently capable of cheap, easy, and rapid reproduction and distribution: hard metal matrices stamp out phonograph records; high-speed printers generate thousands of copies of motion picture films for simultaneous showing in theaters nationwide; similarly, CD replicators spew out software, video, and data disks by the millions. In almost every case, highly automated packaging equipment prepares the output for shipping. But responsibility for management of the product at the point of use—a very labor-intensive job—is left to librarians and their staffs, who are expected to maintain all the look-alike objects in good order, ready for immediate access by users.

Yet in one major system—that of micropublishing—there is comparatively little automation; manual effort remains at the core. Why? Because micropublishing, almost by definition, involves either single copies to order or orders produced to fill subscriptions; no micropublisher stockpiles an inventory of microforms in the hope of selling enough copies to cover initial costs.

Nonbook devices had another management impact: users' unfamiliarity with the devices' technological features virtually required facility centralization, hence the formation of microtext reading rooms, audiovisual laboratories and screening rooms, computer centers, and the like, along with their specially trained staffs. In the area of electronic devices, this impact has been greatly mitigated by the development of individually owned and controlled mass-produced electronic devices, such as personal computers, VCRs, and DVD players. But in the area of microtext, there has been little research and no practical development aimed at permitting an individual user to personally own the medium or easily operate the companion device, for example, the microform reader. The prospect of mass-producing microform equipment or widely distributing scholarly and research materials on microform is practically nil—large projects cost tens, even hundreds, of thousands of dollars—and thus the market is nonexistent. So we come full circle: no market, no corresponding research and development.

That nonbook materials required bibliographic treatment and service methods different from their print counterparts became evident very quickly. As early as 1937, it was clear to one writer that the filing and cataloging rules for books were "far from being the most practicable" for sound recordings.[6] Since that time, hundreds of titles have been published that counsel librarians on the processing of nonbook materials. Also, recent editions of the *Anglo-American Cataloging Rules* include expanded coverage for nonbook publications. Much of the early work on nonbook materials was written for school libraries, for schools were among the first to seize upon new instructional media, while nowadays, new media rapidly permeate all sectors of education.

A sometimes overlooked or unappreciated aspect of managing both microforms and sound archives—especially for disk recordings that predate the CD—is the substantial floor-loading demands of such collections. Sound recordings on disk and microforms weigh far more per cubic foot than do books. Both may require expensive, heavy-duty shelving and floors strong enough to take the load.

---

6 P.L. Miller, "Cataloging and Filing of Phonographic Records," *Library Journal* 62 (July 1937):544-46.

Permanence and Preservation

Concern about the durability of print library materials increased considerably in the 1960s and later, when the former Council on Library Resources began to research and publicize the deterioration of acid-based paper. But with the new "invisible" media, there was no easy, effective way to determine, using an appropriate optical or electronic device, whether any microform, motion picture film, still picture negative, or magnetic medium would suddenly decline to reveal its contents.

As early as 1955, in a study originating at the Library of Congress, conventional silver halide microfilms emerged as a prominent problem area. In that year, in a widely publicized article, the Library of Congress revealed that a significant number of microfilms purchased from commercial and other sources had badly deteriorated and that the condition of others offered little promise of long life.[7] In the commercial sector, new problems emerged in the 1970s, when the *New York Times* bought a microfilm company and began to sell film copies of its own newspaper that were produced on a controversial new film whose durability was alleged questionable. That the country's acknowledged newspaper of record might not endure caused deep concern within all sectors of the library community. A current article maintains that in certain instances there has not only been no improvement but the situation has actually gotten worse.[8]

For well over half a century the motion picture industry used nitrate film in cameras and for distribution copies. Unfortunately, nitrate film was not only dangerously flammable, but it also degenerated spontaneously within a relatively short time. Innumerable films were lost forever. Although nitrate film long ago ceased to be manufactured in North America and Western Europe, it continued to be used to produce microforms in the former Soviet Union even as late as the 1960s.[9]

Preservation Problems Caused by Technological Obsolescence

The great advantage of printed materials is that only three preconditions need be satisfied for their effective use: (a) good or correctable eyesight, (b) literacy, and (c) sufficient light for reading. All three are achievable at relatively modest expense, compared to the costs imposed by the huge number, variety, age,

---

7 Verner W. Clapp, Donald C. Holmes, and Francis Henshaw, "Are Your Microfilms Deteriorating Acceptably?" *Library Journal* 80 (March 15, 1955): 589–95, 612, 613.

8 Nicholson Baker, "Deadline," *The New Yorker*, July 24, 2000, 42–61.

9 For the safety of its personnel, buildings, and collections, no library can afford to accept any material on questionable photographic film without careful prior examination.

and condition of the hardware and software that device-centered systems demand.

In the Cold War era there was much concern over whether data stored on magnetic media might be catastrophically destroyed by radiation from nuclear weapons. At that time microforms were actively touted as the medium immune from radiation damage. Since the end of the Cold War, attention to preservation matters has moved to the natural degradation of charged particles in magnetic media. Important data may be lost if not transferred to new media. There are at least three causes for such loss: (a) physical deterioration (or total loss) of the medium itself; (b) unrepairability of antique playback hardware; and (c) inability to interpret or update antique software. Degradation can be overcome, in part, by periodically reading and rewriting tapes or by transferring the data to ever more modern media. Nevertheless, as Crawford has pointed out, production technology, especially encryption, has imposed substantial limitations on any end user's attempt to preserve certain types of digital media through copying.[10]

As the CD-ROM was perfected, and vast amounts of data started to be published in that format, the U.S. National Archives, other government agencies, and the library community at large raised questions about the new medium's long-term durability. To date there is no conclusive evidence that commercially produced CD-ROMs will outlast the output of Gutenberg's era, now in its sixth century, or last beyond the hundreds of years estimated for properly processed and properly stored microforms. The durability of CD-ROMs individually produced on CD "burners" is another unknown. (Before the advent of commercial equipment for microphotography, many a scholar made his or her own microfilm using a 35 mm camera. Some of these films ultimately found their way into library collections where they raise the usual questions of whether such privately produced research materials can endure. The same question may be asked about individually produced CD-ROMs.)

Failures and Follies: Vendors, Libraries, System Design Limitations

Vendors, libraries, and system designers are reluctant to discuss their failures. Two mercifully brief experiments with ultrahigh reduction microfiches[11]—one

---

10 Walt Crawford, "Bits Is Bits: Pitfalls in Digital Reformatting," *American Libraries* 30:5 (May 1999), 47–49

11 These ultrafiches, produced by "microfilming microfilm," demanded unusually tight control over production of the first (low reduction) microfilm and even more demanding adherence to high-tech procedures to manufacture the final product, whose image size was often 100 or more times smaller than the original printed page.

promoted by Encyclopedia Britannica and the other by NCR—were surely
among the most egregious fiascos. Both powerfully illustrate the futility of
designing systems without first learning how the ultimate users behave and
without providing adequate hardware.[12] Whatever the reduction from the
original document size, reader/printers ameliorate the situation but, in general, their ease of use, performance, and reliability are substantially below that
of ordinary modern photocopiers. In sum, regardless of how large or small
their images, microform systems cater poorly to casual readers and serve not
well at all most researchers' primary needs: comparing different texts, taking
notes, annotating a hard copy of a specific passage, or incorporating a passage
into a new work. For these latter operations, there is no substitute for hard
copy.

The Future: Speculations, Guesses, and Questions

Although it is risky to speculate in an era of rapid technological development, some trends and questions are evident. As a first observation, we may
at once dispose of what I have called the "fallacy of displacement," the
notion that new media actually do—or ought to—displace old ones.[13] It is
quite unlikely that new systems and new devices will bring an end to books
and magazines. Continuity rather than discontinuity will likely characterize
the future world of recorded materials, with each type finding its own special
and most suitable niche.

We may expect much greater attention to be paid to the preservation of
data and media. This is attested to by the Council on Library and Information
Resources' absorption of the former Commission on Preservation and
Access, by the establishment of the Image Permanence Institute at the Roch-
ester Institute of Technology, and by the implementation of NEH's Brittle
Books program. In addition, ARL, OCLC, and the Research Libraries Group
are strongly focused on the subject. But what should be done with the essential user devices for older, nondigitized media? Will the nation need to establish a museum—possibly with regional branches—dedicated to preserving,
rerecording, and interpreting data stored on obsolete media? As a matter of
fact, for sound recordings, such facilities already exist: archives of recorded
sound routinely maintain many generations of playback equipment so that
researchers may hear wax cylinders, thick Edison records, 78 r.p.m. shellac

---

12 For a devastating critique of the ultramicrofiche projects, see Mark Yerburgh, "Where Have All the
Ultras Gone? The Rise and Demise of the Ultrafiche Library Collection, 1968–1973," *Microform
Review* 13 (Fall 1984):254–261.

13 Allen B. Veaner, "Guarding Against the Fallacy of Displacement," *Microform Review* 15(3):69 (1986).

records, studio transcription disks, long-playing records, and piano rolls.[14] Similarly, motion-picture archives maintain an assortment of projectors to cope with a wide variety of film sizes and formats.

The paperless society, long predicted, has not yet arrived, and the plethora of printers, copiers, and fax machines available at any office supply house suggests that the decline or disappearance of paper is not around the corner. Currently, there is still little joy or comfort in reading on media other than paper. Microforms are certainly the least popular medium for continuous reading and are far inferior to reading from a CRT screen.

Perhaps wireless, handheld computers will soon enable users to obtain bibliographic data from any location, surely a boon to the researcher, whether deep in the stacks or elsewhere. But such systems will be of comparatively little assistance if the holdings themselves have not been digitized or micropublished to a standard suitable for scanning.

Is the whole concept of "book" and "nonbook" about to be redefined? The publishing industry is already on the point of producing any part of a trade book, either in hard or electronic copy, for sale via the Internet.[15] To make their wares cheaper to produce and more salable to a broader readership, scholarly publishers are also mulling over the idea of issuing hard-cover books without bibliographies or footnotes, these latter to be relegated to databases accessible via the Internet. Perhaps book indexes will be the next tool to be pushed out of the book and onto the Internet; such a move will surely hinder research, not help it. Conceptually, these notions resemble an idea proposed by Watson Davis in the 1930s: that a scholarly book's supportive apparatus be issued on microform and maintained in a central repository.[16]

Could the labor-intensive aspect of managing look-alike media be met by the development of large-scale automated storage and retrieval equipment? If history is a guide, the likelihood of such a development is uncertain: between 1955 and about 1975, millions of dollars were spent in attempts to build such devices for a wide variety of standard-size microforms—reels, fiches, and cartridges. The hardware, constructed mostly for the military, proved to be

14 Some current research points to the possibility of applying lasers to reading sound recordings of whatever type. However, if the market is but a few sound archives, it is unlikely that a *universal* device would be developed to read any type of recording. Thus, the need for the "museum" remains.

15 On-demand printing of portions of travel guides is already a reality. There are also indications that publishers may soon have the capability to control each and every instance of access to their materials, a development that could totally change the economics of scholarly communication and higher education.

16 The proposed central repository, although never implemented, formed one impetus to the founding of the American Documentation Institute (ADI), now the American Society for Information Science and Technology (ASIST).

astronomically expensive and, in almost every case, thoroughly unreliable; all the products were abandoned. However, the situation may be quite different with the modern CD-ROM, a medium that seems far more tractable for automated handling than are microforms.

May we expect higher quality microfilm in the future? There have been encouraging developments. Within the past dozen years, the Association for Information and Image Management (AIIM) has published numerous newly revised microfilming standards covering newspapers, public records, raw film stock, inspection of finished film, and the characteristics of original documents.[17] Many of these standards did not exist when microfilm laboratories were established in North American research libraries six to seven decades ago, and lab practices were sometimes far from topnotch. Conditions are quite different today. The Northeast Document Conservation Center plays a leading role in producing high-quality microforms that follow national standards; Yale's experimental Open Book project was founded upon production of microfilm that already met national standards; the Research Libraries Group plays a central role in promoting high standards for producing microforms. Presumably the dozen or so research libraries and networks microfilming brittle books under NEH grants all follow these modern high standards. These advances suggest that early in the twenty-first century, we may surely expect the quality and durability of microfilm to rise, at least in comparison with what was produced from the 1930s to the 1980s.

Could regional centers service large collections of microforms regardless of format? As with sound archives, regional centers might have to maintain their own museums of microform readers. Such centers could hold vast collections of infrequently used research materials and might use scanners to transmit copies of less used materials to distant libraries. Agencies of this kind already exist, for example, the Center for Research Libraries. But without inexpensive, reliable, high-quality automatic microform handling equipment—just the devices that industry has thus far been unable to produce—such a service is unlikely to be developed.[18] The future lies with the microfilm master negative (or better, a high-quality working copy) as an intermediate source document for digitization. The resulting digital media may indeed be stored, managed, and retrieved (if suitably cataloged and indexed) by relatively inexpensive automated equipment, such as software-driven high capacity CD jukeboxes.

17 The pertinent documents are equivalent to ANSI standards and some have been adopted as Federal Information Processing Standards.

18 Kodak has recently introduced a scanner to transfer to a PC images from 16 mm film mounted in their proprietary cartridges. Whether such a device will ever be adapted to accommodate 35 mm microfilm on reels or microfiches remains to be seen.

Could the JSTOR Project, which provides full-text versions of some journals, be broadened indefinitely to cover the complete span of research library holdings? This also seems an unlikely prospect, for the physical condition and variability of much of the world's retrospective collections inhibit any easy mechanization of data recording, whether by scanning or by microphotography. Years ago, at a meeting of the National Microfilm Association, a speaker presented the foolish suggestion that all the nation's preservation and collection development problems might be solved simply by microfilming the entire contents of the Library of Congress! At that time there were not enough microfilm cameras in the United States—to say nothing of production personnel—to implement such an idea within a reasonable time frame and at an affordable cost. The proposal instantly reached the oblivion it deserved.[19] For the same reasons, the idea of digitizing everything in sight is not practicable.

Despite decades of pleading and complaint within the profession, the problem of adequate bibliographical control for microforms specifically, both current and retrospective, has not been solved. Enormous collections of microforms still exist with few finding aids to help users navigate through them. Furthermore, at this stage, it seems improbable that decades of neglect in providing tools for intellectual access can be undone. Early micropublishers were in business to make money, not to make their products easy and convenient to use. Hence, users of retrospective microforms will, by and large, still be forced to continue wasting their precious time. Perhaps the most cogent comment on this vexatious matter was made by Conway in 1996, who said, "without improvements in intellectual access to microfilm collections that support subject-oriented retrieval, digital conversion of these collections may prove to be quite feasible technically and quite untenable intellectually. The consequence of failure to build a truly useful and useable digital collection is irrelevance."[20]

Naturally, Conway's observation applies equally to many large microfilm collections: for want of appropriate access tools a significant number may have become irrelevant.

---

19 The same idea came up in Britain. In 1986 Lord Dainton estimated that to microfilm ten million books would take 110 cameras working nonstop for a century and cost half a billion pounds. See *Conservation in Crisis* (London: The British Library, 1987), 8.

20 Paul Conway, *Conversion of Microfilm to Digital Imagery; A Demonstration Project* (New Haven: Yale University Library, 1996), 8.

Summary

Emergence of the CD as a device for recording sound, video images, and text is not likely to cause sound and video archives to close up shop or put an end to vital programs of preservation microfilming. Publishers will reissue on CD only those audio and video products deemed profitable, that is, recordings with mass-market appeal. Thus, sound and video archives with their rare works and museums of playback equipment will remain, as will libraries of printed books of interest to researchers. However, intensive current research on achieving data permanence, if successful, may alter this picture.

As a serious publication and preservation methodology, microform technology emerged in the 1930s as a highly promising approach. Its full development was hampered by several factors: many commercial publishers were unwilling to provide adequate bibliographic tools or internal finding aids to facilitate its practical use; most academic institutions declined to invest the huge sums essential to creating, maintaining, and staffing professional-level laboratories; there were no means of enforcing technical standards among producers; manufacturers failed to develop truly satisfactory reading and printout equipment; the scholarly public continued to assume that microfilming was a simple, almost automatic process and remained generally uninformed about—even indifferent to—the highly challenging difficulties of microform technology. In the end, decades of promotion did little to rebut what has been fairly obvious to users for a long time: microform systems, in their present embodiment, are "a misery" and the "bane of the scholar's existence."[21]

Vannevar Bush's 1945 dream of a microtext-based Memex, the researcher's universal storage and access tool, has been overtaken by events. Such a device is clearly in the future—perhaps even within reach very soon—but its active components will surely not be based on microforms. The most valuable future role for microforms is for them to serve as vital intermediates in digital and electronic distribution systems. It is in this way that microforms can contribute most effectively to the goal of creating a serviceable national digital library. To accomplish this goal, existing and future master negatives—assuming they are products of proper camera work, processed to archival standards, stored under secure archival conditions, and equipped from the outset with proper access tools—must be integrated into well-designed systems that take

---

21 Observations by two scholars, forty-one years apart, confirm how most academics feel about microforms. D.W. Ewer's paper, "A Biologist's Reflections on Libraries and Library Service," in *South African Libraries* 29 (October 1961):53–56, 74, calls working with microforms "a misery." A letter from Arthur Schlesinger Jr, published in *The New Yorker*, August 14, 2000, 5, states baldly that "Microfilm is the bane of the scholar's existence."

into account ergonomic and other human factors that have heretofore been ignored. Revolutionary new systems and devices will certainly facilitate improved access, ready consultation. and convenient printout. None of this is achievable with conventional microform systems.

As long as human beings create, they will work in a variety of media. No one medium can satisfy the range of human artistry, intellect, inventiveness, and resourcefulness. It is the function of the library as an institution to provide a permanent home for all kinds of recorded creative work, regardless of medium. Each new medium, in its time, did indeed seem revolutionary. But revolution is nothing new to librarianship whose business has always been the preservation and communication of ideas, ever since Alexandrian days. For over a century, libraries have coped successfully with new formats: the *microphotothèque*, the *phonothèque*, and the *cinemathèque*. It remains only to continue transforming the traditional library from *bibliothèque* into *omnithèque*.

·10·

Development of Public Libraries

Barbara Carol Dean

The twentieth century has seen the development of the public library from an institution that existed in a minority of communities to one that is present in a majority of towns and cities. During the same period, the library has expanded and refined its services in order to educate and entertain all of its users, regardless of age, needs, or background, by providing materials that represent all sides of an issue and in all available formats. The following is a brief description of the development of public libraries in the United States—their growth, funding, services, and collections.

Origins

At the beginning of the twentieth century, much of the activity surrounding public libraries centered on establishing library service in local communities. Just as they had in the nineteenth century, women's clubs were often the first organizations in communities to establish libraries. Their efforts were augmented by membership in the General Federation of Women's Clubs (GFWC), established in 1890. One of the federation's primary areas of interest was the creation of library service.

The first library in a community was often a traveling library begun by local women's clubs to share books among themselves to support their study of a wide range of topics. Library services were later extended to other women in the area. It was common for a traveling library system to exist before a library commission or state association had been created.

Recognition of the need for a library for all citizens was the next step. The clubs raised money to establish a public library through bake sales and various community functions similar to those used by women's clubs today. Members or townspeople donated books, or books were purchased with money

179

raised. The clubs often continued to support the public library after it was established with gifts of money, books, or furniture. Members often acted as the first librarians. They realized early on, however, the need for training. They either arranged it for themselves locally or hired a librarian with formal professional education.

As clubs worked to establish local public libraries, they also became involved in advocacy for various forms of legislation. These included enabling municipalities to provide tax support to libraries, lobbying for state support of library extension activities, and forming state library commissions. The state federation of women's clubs would support the commission whether or not they had a hand in developing it. For its part, the commission often looked upon the federation as its strongest ally. Women's clubs continued their work, sometimes being the driving force behind the formation of state library associations.

In 1901, women's clubs controlled 4,655 traveling libraries with a total 340,961 volumes in thirty-four states in which the federations belonging to the GFWC. These numbers decreased dramatically by 1904, to 1,016 libraries with 46,208 volumes, because of the number of libraries that had gained state support.[1]

The American Library Association (ALA) was aware of the work of women's clubs. In 1914, G. B. Utley, executive secretary of the ALA, reported that half of all libraries in the United States were established through the influence of American women. In 1933, Sophonisba Breckenridge reported that ALA considered women's clubs responsible for initiating 75 percent of the public libraries in the United States.[2]

Buildings

The history of the public library would not be complete without reference to Andrew Carnegie. From 1901 to 1917, he donated about $50 million to construct 1,412 public libraries in the United States. His generosity gave a major boost to the development of public libraries. "In many states Carnegie buildings form the basis for large portions of existing library services." In Wisconsin, for example, almost half of the public libraries that existed in the late 1980s started with a Carnegie building. In Arizona, 40 percent of the buildings began with Carnegie money. Even in well-established Massachusetts, the figure is 12 percent.[3]

Leading citizens of the community, sometimes women's club members, made a case to Carnegie for receiving a grant. If he decided to donate money, he paid for the building, and the town bought the books, maintained the building, and hired the librarian.

The benefit of Carnegie's generosity did not stop with buildings. His example led to contributions from other wealthy people. Between 1890 and 1906 about $34 million was donated to fund various aspects of public libraries.[4]

Like so many other statistics, those recording the growth in numbers of public libraries vary from source to source. According to one source, by 1926 there were 5,954 public libraries in the United States, which served 57 percent of the population. By 1936 that figure had risen to 6,235 libraries, which served 63 percent of the population.[5] Although, growth in the number of libraries slowed during the middle of the century, by 1990 *The Bowker Annual* reported there were 14,998 public libraries in existence.[6]

As the number of public libraries grew, so did the number of buildings in which one library might be housed. The development of branch libraries began when the Boston Public Library established its first branch in 1876. During the remainder of the nineteenth century and on into the twentieth century, large cities established an increasing number of branches. Four factors spurred their development. There was a need to take the pressure for providing popular material off the main library so that its collection could develop more depth and breadth. Services were needed in sections of the city where inhabitants were not heavy users of the central library. Establishing a branch made it possible to make the library more accessible to residents who could not afford public transportation. Finally, a branch library made it allowed libraries to serve special population groups, such as non-English speakers. Smaller cities began establishing branch libraries as housing patterns became more dispersed and differentiated.

After World War II, the economic boom, development of tract housing, and the availability of inexpensive cars led to a decline in central libraries in urban centers, as people moved out. Consequently, branch libraries became a primary source of service.

New Model

Beginning in the 1930s, branches were sometimes organized into public library systems, which were developed to provide larger service units. A system is very like the branch model in that it has more service outlets under a central administration and is established to serve a larger portion of the population. Unlike the branch model, there is no single central library, and systems sometimes cross political boundaries by providing library service to several counties under one administration.

The model is based on an argument presented by Carleton B. Joeckel. He noted that libraries working together could develop more efficient and broadly based library services than they could if they worked as individual units. Joeckel and Amy Winslow wrote *A National Plan for Public Library Service,* published in 1948. Although the term "library system" is not used in it or in Leigh's *The Public Library in the United States* (1950), the theme of cooperation among libraries and the development of larger library units does. The term itself was adopted by 1956.

Joeckel's ideas gained broader acceptance in the 1950s and 1960s with the publication of the ALA's *Standards for Public Libraries* (1956, with a revised edition published in 1966), and with the passage of the *Library Services Act in* 1956 and the *Library Services and Construction Act* of 1964. The concept continued to broaden in the 1970s and 1980s, with the trend away from library systems limited to one type of library and toward those encompassing more than one type. In the mid 1970s, systems limited to public libraries made up 75 percent of the library cooperatives in the United States. Ten years later, that number had dropped to 62 percent.[7]

Financial Support

Public libraries depend on three sources for financial support: public, private for-profit and private nonprofit. In the twentieth century, most of the support came from public sources, although the ebb and flow of government support was closely linked with that from the private sector, which was encouraged to contribute as government funds diminished.

Before World War II, government funds for public libraries ranged from hugely inadequate in small towns to never lavish elsewhere. But the economic boom after the war and the work of librarians led to increases in government funding. In the first half of the century, librarians were afraid of being contaminated by contact with government, but in 1949, Oliver Garceau commented that this attitude had to change, and change it did. Librarians became more active in lobbying for state and federal aid and continued to increase their political activity. Between 1945 and 1965, operating expenditures for public libraries increased fivefold, far above the inflation rate.[8] In 1956, the Congress passed the *Library Construction Act,* which provided money for outreach programs to rural areas. That marked the beginning of a period in which library legislation "offered unprecedented federal funding for a variety of libraries and programs, and encouraged inter-library loan cooperation."[9] It was followed by the *Library Services and Construction Act of 1964.* The amount of money allocated in the federal budget for public library operations under the act varied each year, but it was as high as $75 million during President Lyndon Johnson's administration. The funds were given to state libraries for distribution within each state. They were used primarily for interlibrary loan cooperation and consortia, library buildings, and services to the disadvantaged.

Federal and local government support for libraries eroded in the 1970s and 1980s because of the financial drain caused by the Vietnam war, double-digit inflation, a tax revolt among property owners, and the development of a conservative antigovernment mood. Although public libraries as a group did better in the 1980s than in the late 1960s and 1970s, no libraries were well supported. They struggled to meet higher costs, and, in certain areas, suffered significant budget cuts. As the recession deepened in the early 1990s, libraries also had to make room in their budgets for new technologies and new services.

As discussed earlier, private donations from women's clubs, Andrew Carnegie, and other wealthy donors gave the public library movement a great deal of help at the start of the century. At the time, Carnegie's grants were controversial. Some people thought his money was tainted because his wealth was accumulated at the expense of his workers, although most towns did not go so far as to reject a grant on ideological grounds.

Growth in private philanthropy increased after 1980. In 1955, 300 Friends of the Library groups existed in the United States. By 1990, there were 2,300.[10] Library administrators also began spending time cultivating members of the official power structure, private donors, foundations, and library advocates. The ALA aided the movement to encourage more private giving by accepting $100,000 in grants from the Kellogg Foundation and the Carnegie Corporation in 1995. The purpose of both grants was to train small to medium-sized public library directors and library board members in fund raising.

The century closed with another successful entrepreneur, Bill Gates, providing millions of dollars to libraries through the Bill and Melinda Gates Foundation, established in 1997. Its purpose was to provide public libraries in low-income communities with the funds to buy computers, software, and Internet access for users, and included technical assistance and staff training over a three-to-four-year period. His gifts were also controversial because his company, Microsoft, was viewed by some as an illegal monopoly.

Services

Many public libraries began as resources for adults, but services to children quickly became equally important. These services grew during the Progressive Era when child-welfare advocates began supervising children's physical and moral well being in such institutions as settlement houses, juvenile courts, public health programs, and public libraries. Many children's collections began as "home libraries," that is, cases of books and magazines placed in homes. The service waned as more branch libraries were built, but home libraries continued to be used in classrooms, institutions, and hospitals. At the end of the nineteenth century, the model developed of juvenile services with specialized collections housed in areas or rooms separate from those for adult materials and services designed to bring children and books together. By 1950, about one-third of the collections in public libraries consisted of juvenile materials.[11] The purpose of such collections changed over the years from that of discouraging moral decline and providing children with "proper" materials for social development to that of encouraging literacy and reading habits and supporting formal education.

Services to young adults developed more slowly and did not have the same continuing level of success as those for younger children. The model in place by 1910 was focused on children who had left school, and combined reading with other activities such as games, outings, and athletics. Mabel Williams is considered the first librarian to systematically work with teenagers. She was named the supervisor of the "Work with Schools" program at the New York Public Library in 1919. Jean Roos set up the first separate room for young adults in the United States at the Cleveland Public Library in 1925. Margaret Alexander Edwards instituted "Y Work" at the Enoch Pratt Free Library in Baltimore in 1933. It was not until the end of the 1930s that young adult collections were established in separate alcoves, rooms, and buildings throughout the United States. In contrast to juvenile collections, only forty separate rooms, sixty-three alcoves and ninety-four special collections existed by 1947.[12] In the mid to late 1960s, many new programs were established to bring more young people into the library. Also in the 1960s, librarians, alone or in cooperation with youth agencies, began creating decentralized libraries in nontraditional settings.

In the late 1970s and the 1980s, young adult services were in jeopardy. Fewer and fewer libraries employed young adult librarians. Almost all the separate collections created in the 1930s and 1940s had been removed or closed, leaving young adults being served by generalist librarians.

Collections were not only created for specific age groups, but also to meet specific needs. The development of specialized municipal reference services was inspired by the growth of legislative reference services begun in Wisconsin in 1901. Charles McCarthy was hired that year as a documents cataloger for a library established to serve the Wisconsin legislature. Later, he began a campaign to provide proactive reference service for members of the legislature. His success led to the creation of comparable services in other states. By 1915, thirty-two states had such services.

Municipal governments also adopted the concept of proactive reference service. The first was established at the Enoch Pratt Library in Baltimore in 1907. Following the first was Milwaukee in 1908, Kansas City in 1910, St.

Louis in 1911, and New York City in 1913. These early services were frequently established as separate branches of the library situated near city hall. By the early 1930s, sixteen municipal libraries offered reference services. Although the Great Depression temporarily ended expansion, such services were revived in the 1960s and 1970s with the revived economy.

At the beginning of the century, the United States was experiencing a great influx of immigrants. Unlike earlier immigrant waves, most of the immigrants were coming from non-English-speaking European countries. Professional librarians saw the public library as a tool for curing society's ills, and they made Americanizing immigrants a major priority. The primary question was how to accomplish the task. Should the library provide materials in the immigrants' native tongues and assume they would soon learn English; or should they purchase only English language materials? Around 1900, public libraries began buying books in foreign languages on the theory that people who forgot their history and never read their country's literature would not make good citizens.

By 1906, the discussion had moved to the topic of what information immigrants needed. One group said libraries should provide information about local laws so that people would not get in trouble. Others pointed out such information was not easily available. Another faction maintained that libraries could not afford to buy all the books needed by native-born Americans. Consequently, it was best to buy books written in English and foreign language dictionaries and ask civic and patriotic societies to donate foreign-language materials concerning American history and civics. The debates were never satisfactorily resolved and returned to the forefront in the 1980s as another large group began immigrating to the United States.

The debate not only involved what materials to provide, but also how to encourage people to use the library. Ways to make the library more accessible included employing foreign-born library assistants whose origins represented the nationalities of the neighborhood in which they worked. Libraries participated in and sometimes sponsored neighborhood celebrations that drew together people of different nationalities. Articles were published in foreign-language newspapers; presentations were made at night schools and national clubs. Library programs on American citizenship were provided; slide shows were presented in native languages to describe library services. Programs targeted toward immigrants were developed on great American leaders. Children's programs were augmented to include storytelling in English of tales from other countries. In some cases, the library offered rooms for English classes. By 1916, Immigration Publication Society Director, John Foster Carr, said his organization knew of 500 libraries with programs for the foreign born.[13]

Many of the same methods were reestablished in the latter part of the century as a wave of immigrants began coming from Asia and Central and South America. Libraries revived the practice of hiring library assistants or volunteers from the nations represented in their neighborhoods. They published articles in local foreign-language newspapers and made contacts with national civic groups in order to recruit staff and to tell people about the library. Libraries were again sponsoring celebrations to introduce people to the library. These were not always the sedate adult programming that people were used to, but festivals of food and entertainment for the whole family.

The debate over whether to provide foreign nationals with material in their native languages or to meet only their immediate needs with such material raged once again. This time, as in the past, libraries began buying materials in the languages spoken by their user communities. The materials included not only popular works, but also materials on obtaining U.S. citizenship and other needed information. New technologies allowed libraries to go beyond supplying foreign-language dictionaries to providing audiocassette or compact disc sets teaching English as a second language. They were also able to provide videos and recorded books for those cultures with a strong oral rather than written tradition.

Another group with special needs was the blind. Gratia Countryman, director of the Minneapolis Public Library from 1904 to 1936, is credited with being the first to include Braille books in a library collection. Services increased in the 1950s when captioned films and books incorporating sign language began appearing in libraries. Some of these developments were written into the *Standards for Media Centers* adopted in the United States in 1967.

One of the first libraries to begin delivering books to individuals who couldn't come to the library was the Webster City (Iowa) Public Library in 1935. The Kansas City (Missouri) Public Library quickly followed with a similar service established in 1936. In 1941 the Cleveland Public Library created a professionally run service that became the model followed by other libraries.

In the latter part of the century, budgets did not increase although services had been diversified. Consequently, many public libraries began targeting their services more specifically. In the 1980s Lowell Martin said that librarians had to identify the users' needs that they would meet, rather than trying to be all things to all people. If they did not, he predicted that libraries would become mediocre in all areas. As a result of his work, the Public Library Association (PLA) developed *Planning & Role Setting for Public Libraries* (1987). Eight roles were identified as being appropriate to public libraries:

1. community activities centers in which libraries would provide meeting space and equipment for community and library programs;

2. community information centers with the library acting as a clearing-house for current information on community organizations, issues, and services;
3. formal education support centers that would function by providing materials to support students in elementary and secondary schools, as well as colleges, community colleges, universities, technical schools, training programs, literacy and adult basic education, and continuing education;
4. independent learning centers for individuals of all ages pursuing sustained independent learning outside formal education;
5. sources of current, high-demand, high-interest materials;
6. preschoolers' doors to learning, which encourage young children to develop an interest in reading and learning;
7. reference libraries; and
8. research centers to assist scholars and researchers in conducting in-depth studies.

Libraries were encouraged to limit themselves to no more than two primary roles and no more than two secondary roles.

Evidence indicates that in the 1990s many public libraries did adopt primary and secondary roles based on those listed above. The *Public Library Data Service Statistical Report '93* showed that more than half of the libraries surveyed reported having selected roles on which they would focus. A survey by Kenneth Shearer revealed that libraries were focusing their attention primarily on popular materials, reference, and preschoolers' doors to learning.[14]

Formats

Public libraries purchased materials in a variety of formats for most of the century. *The Bowker Annual* reported that in 1950, the 6,028 libraries that provided information for the report housed 24,272 films; 52,523 microfilms; 201,582 slides and film strips; 320,660 sound recordings; and 8,062,186 photographs, pictures, and prints.[15] As the technology changed, so did library purchases. For the most part, slides and filmstrips were replaced by VHS videos, with DVDs beginning to make an appearance. Books on audiotape and compact discs augmented print collections, and many libraries began to or considered purchasing electronic books. Online databases were added to augment serial collections.

Library in Society

The public library has always reflected the society in which it exists—its constancy, evolution, strengths, and struggles. One of the ways that this is illustrated is in the discussion of censorship. It began in the late nineteenth century when advocates of progressivism sought social and political reforms, and huge waves of European immigrants posed challenges to intolerance and bias against different cultures and ideas. At that time public libraries were viewed as an institution for social stability. The majority of librarians promoted that image by trying to control access to controversial materials, but a growing number began to think that such practices were too restrictive and that a more inclusive approach to realistic fiction and competing ideas was important in a democracy.

During World War I, the debate over selection was dropped. In fact, if anything, censorship increased as patriotic librarians believed that they must remove any publications that seemed to question American traditions.

The 1920s reignited the debate. Suspicions and fears about communism, immigrants, liquor consumption, and demands of racial and ethnic minorities for political and social reform led many to advocate for a continuance of the traditional approach. On the other side was the rapid change in fashion, sexual mores, and women's rights. The period also saw the growth in mass communication with radio broadcasting, motion picture production, newspapers, magazines, and books making censorship less possible. The public library community, as a group, still held that censorship should be practiced in material selection, based on morals and control. Even if some librarians believed greater access was appropriate, many could not practice it because of community pressure and their own individual biases.

During the 1930s, an unprecedented amount of propaganda was distributed through the mass media in the struggles among communism, fascism, and democracy. Liberals and leftists were calling for economic and social change. A growing number of young librarians in particular wanted to publicize and solve the country's social and economic problems. Many librarians began providing access to mainstream and controversial ideas, particularly foreign and domestic political propaganda. Sympathizers for continuing with traditional policies and those advocating change could both say they were giving the public what it wanted or ought to have and that librarians were practicing their role as "responsible educators"[16]

The ALA responded to increasing censorship by adopting the first national libraries "Bill of Rights" at the annual conference in San Francisco on June 19, 1939. It was patterned after the Des Moines (Iowa) Public Library Bill of Rights written by the director, Forest Spaulding. The national bill states that reading materials should be purchased based on "value and interest" to the community served and not on the basis of "race or nationality or political or religious views of the writers." It established the principle of selecting materials covering various sides of controversial issues and said organizations could use library facilities for "socially useful and cultural activities and the discussion of current public questions." It is not as radical as the Iowa bill and gave local trustees the ability to make broad interpretations. It was also not widely adopted by library boards. Librarians who embraced the view that there should be access to information representing all points of view continued to be limited by funding, the traditions of the community served, personal biases, and the traditions of librarianship.[17]

In response to World War II, librarians developed reading lists to guide patrons through the mass of conflicting information. This was the beginning of readers' advisory services.

Also reflected in public libraries was the struggle for equal rights. When southern cities and towns began building public libraries in large numbers, some excluded black patrons. After a decade or two, black leaders approached many city library boards or city councils and asked for the creation of black branch libraries. White philanthropists helped in getting the branches built, and black and white church and civic groups undertook the work of construction and organizing the collections.

In 1961, the U.S. Commission on Civil Rights sent investigators to twenty-two counties in the South to study library service to blacks. Five counties had no libraries; twelve had one or more libraries for whites only, and five operated separate libraries for blacks and whites. The commission also sent a questionnaire to 256 southern libraries that received federal funds. Only 109 responded. Thirty of those reported segregated facilities with those for blacks being open an average of fifteen hours a week, compared to the whites' thirty-three hours. Black branches held collections of about 4,400 books compared to those in excess of 28,000 in branches serving whites.[18]

One of the factors in securing desegregation of southern libraries was the use of protests by such groups as the National Association for the Advancement of Colored People. Black leaders used two methods for opening southern libraries to black citizens. They secured numerous federal court orders mandating desegregation and handled the publicity in targeted cities so that if city governments closed the libraries or created delays, their reputations as progressive, popular cities would be destroyed. Many white business leaders worked to promote desegregation in order to maintain their community's reputation as a calm, prosperous place in which to invest. By 1964, federal laws requiring desegregation in the South had been enacted.[19]

The ALA moved slowly and cautiously on this issue. It feared that its involvement would hinder the progress being made in some southern communities where libraries were quietly being desegregated. In 1962, The ALA moved to evaluate the freedom of access to American libraries with the "Access Study." The report was published in 1963. It showed good progress was being made in the South, but northern libraries were, in effect, segregated because of residential patterns. A sample of ten northern, urban library systems showed that branches in black neighborhoods had fewer staff members, lower funding, and smaller collections than those in white neighborhoods. The resulting controversy led to a call by some to officially reject the study.

By the end of the century, the struggle for equal rights was no longer dominating newspaper headlines, but equal access was still not a reality for all. Traditions of the community served and individual biases remained roadblocks to continued progress.

Conclusion

At the beginning of the twentieth century, public libraries in the United States were relatively rare. They primarily served adults, although juvenile services were available in some libraries. Urban libraries were grappling with the needs of the many immigrants arriving in the country and beginning to develop services for young adults, the disabled, and municipal governments. Librarians were discussing how best to serve their constituencies. Should only popular materials be purchased for adults, "good literature" for children, and no foreign language publications?

By the end of the century, most of the population had library services available, although some areas were still underserved. Whether the library should provide only popular materials or supplement them with high-quality literature and nonfiction had become a classic argument with most librarians believing the latter. Services targeted to a variety of specific user groups were well established.

The challenge of providing high-quality service was both helped and hindered by technology. How could the library afford the new and ever-changing technology while continuing to provide traditional services? The answer for many librarians was to streamline services and to look to private sources for financial support.

Perhaps the most significant change in public libraries between 1901 and 2000, besides an increase in the amount of service, was the difference in librarians' attitudes. The purpose of the library was no longer to represent the status quo. Instead, its purpose was to provide easy access to information as equitably as possible and materials representing multiple viewpoints.

Bibliography

American Library Annual for 1955–1956, s.v. "Library Statistics."

Billington, James H. "American Public Libraries in the Information Age: Constant Purpose in Changing Times." *Libraries and Culture* 33 (winter 1998): 11–16.

The Bowker Annual: Library and Book Trade Almanac. 1991. 36th ed., 1991, s.v Number of Libraries in the United States and Canada.

Cresswell, Stephen. "The Last Days of Jim Crow in Southern Libraries." *Libraries and Culture* 31 (summer/fall 1996): 557–573.

Dain, Phyllis. "American Public Libraries and the Third Sector: Historical Reflections and Implications." *Libraries and Culture* 31 (winter 1996): 56–84.

Encyclopedia of Library History s.v. "Children's Services, Public" by Christine A. Jenkins. "Public Libraries" by Charles A. Seavey. "Young Adult Services" by Susan Steinfirst.

Lincove, David A. "Propaganda and the American Public Library from the 1930s to the Eve of World War II." *RQ* 33 (summer 1994): 510–523.

Marcum, Deanna B. and Stone, Elizabeth W. "Literacy: the Library Legacy." *American Libraries* 22 (March 1991): 202–205.

Sager, Don. "Before the Memory Fades: Public Libraries in the 20th Century." *Public Libraries* 39 (March/April 2000): 73–77.

Notes

1. Paula D. Watson, "Founding Mothers: The Contribution of Women's Organizations to Public Library Development in the United States." *Library Quarterly* 64 (July 1994): 242.
2. Ibid. Watson notes she could not find the primary source for Breckenridge's percentage.
3. *Encyclopedia of Library History,* Garland Reference Library of Social Science, vol. 503 (New York: Garland, 1994), s.v. "Public Libraries," by Charles A. Seavey. 521.
4. ibid.
5. ibid.
6. *The Bowker Annual,* 34th ed. 378.
7. ibid., 67.
8. *Encyclopedia of Library History,* 523.
9. Phyllis Dain notes in her article, "American Public Libraries and the Third Sector: Historical Reflections and Implications," *Libraries and Culture* 31 (Winter 1996): 68, that it is difficult to find consistent historical and current statistics.
10. ibid., 69.
11. *American Library Annual for 1955–1956* (R. R. Bowker) s.v. "Library Statistics."
12. *Encyclopedia of Library History* s.v. "Young Adult Services," by Susan Steinfirst.
13. Deanna B. Marcum and Elizabeth W. Stone, Literacy: The Library Legacy, *American Libraries* 22 (March 1991): 204.
14. Kenneth Shearer, "Confusing What Is Most Wanted with What Is Most Used: A Crisis in Public Library Priorities Today," *Public Libraries* 32 (July/August 1993).
15. *American Library Annual.*
16. David A. Lincove, "Propaganda and the American Public Library from the 1930s to the Eve of World War II," *RQ* 22 (summer 1994): 511.
17. ibid. 517.

18. Stephen Cresswell, "The Last Days of Jim Crow in Southern Libraries," *Libraries and Culture 31* (summer/fall 1996): 558.

19. ibid. 557.

◆11◆

The Growth of Scholarly and Scientific Libraries

Hendrik Edelman

When G. Marvin Tatum and I wrote on the development of the collections of America's research libraries in 1976,[1] the intent was to capture the major trends and events of the past century. Now, a quarter of a century later, it is an opportune time to try to find out if the added perspective has changed our views and what changes have taken place during the past period. Much good work has been written and published on early American library history in recent years[2] and we don't need to go into much detail here. Research libraries are a product of their setting, the research environment, and the world of scholarly and scientific literature. Most research in the United States in the early to mid-nineteenth century was performed by private scholars or by research teams funded by the government. The latter, of course, often took the form of various major expeditions and explorations.

Publicly accessible research libraries were lacking, however, and the earliest efforts to establish such collections were done in the form of public libraries. The Astor Library (1839) in New York, forerunner of the New York Public Library, was first. Boston Public Library (1852) followed, and in subsequent years many of the public libraries in all major American cities developed substantial research collections. Funding, in most cases, came from private sources in the form of bequests and endowments. The tradition of research support in public libraries would last a long time. But erosion of public support ultimately set later in the twentieth century, with the notable exceptions of Boston and New York. Of course, the Library of Congress, under the

---

1 Hendrik Edelman and G. Marvin Tatum Jr.1976. "The Development of Collections in American University Libraries." *College and Research Libraries* 37(3).

2 Wayne A. Wiegand. 2000. "American Library History Literature, 1847–1997: Theoretical Perspectives?" *Libraries and Culture* 35(1).

direction of Ainsworth Ran Spofford from 1864 to 1897, acquired many valuable collections as well.

In the age of the enormous concentration of wealth in the hands of a few major entrepreneurs it is not surprising that education and research became a favorite philanthropy. Carnegie (1911) and Rockefeller (1913) were among the most influential, particularly the latter in funding medical research both in the United States and in Germany. Many others lent their names to the colleges and universities they sponsored. Yet others built their own research collections and established "public" libraries and museums. John Crerar (1894) in Chicago, Henry Huntington (1919) in California, and J. Pierpont Morgan (1924) in New York are good examples of the ultimate public benefit of the publicly much-maligned robber barons. Only in America!

Inspired by the success of German research methods and support in the latter part of the nineteenth century, early American librarians such as Joseph Green Cogswell (Astor Library), Edward Everett (Boston Public), and George Ticknor (Boston Public) trained there and began to apply their experiences at home. Newly established universities with their dynamic presidents such as Cornell (Andrew D. White), Johns Hopkins (Gilmore) and Chicago (Harper) set the tone initially, paralleled by the land grant colleges such as California, Michigan, Wisconsin, and Illinois. But the major existing colleges, especially Harvard, Yale, Columbia, Princeton, and the University of Pennsylvania, adapted quickly as well.

By the turn of the twentieth century, the modern research library as we now know it became the common standard, although actual practice still varied greatly. Collection development was at the center of the professional activities. Annual budgets allowed for the acquisition of current books and periodicals. Gifts and special allocations were used for retrospective acquisitions for which there was much demand. Librarians, faculty members, and even university presidents participated actively, and the European book trade rose to the occasion. Sets of major periodicals, reference works, and, especially, the private collections of scholars and scientists, complete with their specialized off-print collections, were much in demand. Martinus Nijhoff from the Netherlands opened an office in New York in 1904, and several of the German antiquarian booksellers, such as Fock, Harrassowitz, and Brockhaus established close relations with American libraries. As a result, they added new book and subscription services to their repertoire.

At the same time, efforts were made to standardize cataloging and classification rules, while professional reference service became an established feature. Other significant improved standards in service were open stacks, at least for researchers, liberal opening hours, and borrowing privileges. New, specially designed, central library buildings were constructed. The debate on the advantages and disadvantages of centralized collections would range from campus to campus with differing results and, perhaps not surprisingly, it continues today without clear resolution. Library cooperation was a much-discussed issue, and indeed the establishment of interlibrary loan protocols was a unique accomplishment. The more so, because competition for resources played, and continues to do so, a dominant role in the research library world. Even before World War I, critical academic voices were heard about the enormous duplication of research resources among university libraries. Competition and emulation, however, remained the practice.

If American research efforts were being established firmly at the beginning of the twentieth century, they were boosted into international prominence during and after World War I. The National Research Council (NRC), established in 1916, became the instrument of university-based research. Directing private research support, rather than government resources, the NRC de facto became the sponsor of a small and elite group of research universities, which in turn helped develop national library resources.

But industrial research became a powerful establishment as well. General Electric (1900), DuPont (1902), Bell Labs (1912), and Eastman Kodak (1912) all became major research centers, and their scientific libraries developed rich international resources and capabilities.

With research and higher education booming, with the boycotting of German efforts, and boosted by large amounts of private support, American universities and their libraries began an unprecedented decade of growth and development. The established universities set the pace and the standard. New library buildings abounded; current acquisitions now routinely covered the scholarly and scientific publications from the prominent research centers in Germany, Great Britain, France, Italy, and Spain. The emphasis on retrospective collection development continued. Competition for the now scarcer resources led to higher prices and the beginning of academic complaints about unfair American competition in Europe, where the research economy was quite different. The European book trade responded, but American booksellers, often founded by German immigrants, began to play a role as importers as well.

Buoyed by these ever-growing markets, the German publishers, already a dominant power, upped their production significantly. In the aftermath of the World War I, major consolidations had taken place in German publishing, and with the erosion of the traditional publishing by not-for-profit academies and societies, a model of private sector scientific publishing emerged. With new research specializations opening up, publishers were quick to establish new journals and book series with paid academic editors. With the diffusion of knowledge, the need for review literature, compendia, and handbooks became stronger; especially needed were comprehensive bibliographical tools. All of this required considerable capital, and it is thus not surprising that only a very few publishers, notably Springer in Berlin and the Akademische Verlagsgesellschaft in Leipzig, emerged as the leaders through extensive acquisitions of existing lists and expansions thereof.

The increase in production and the cost thereof began to worry American and European librarians, most of whom were trying to keep up on all fronts. Actually, already in 1927, many science librarians reported that most of their budget went into serial publications.[3] The matter of unbridled increase in production and the subsequent higher price tag became an international library controversy in 1928, which was not resolved until the Nazi regime reached a compromise negotiated by the American librarian Charles Harvey Brown. The compromise included reduced production and a considerable state subsidy for export[4]. By that time, of course, German science was already seriously compromised. American, British, and French scientific publishing, including indexing and abstracting services, remained firmly in the hands of the scientific and scholarly societies, and their development was much more conservative.

The period of splendid library development supported by private funds came to an abrupt end in 1929, but it took the libraries some time to come to terms with their now-limited funds. Without a common blueprint for collection development, each institution understandably began to cut back in areas of least priority to their faculty's interest. It didn't take long before librarians became uneasy over the fact that many of the cutbacks were similar, and an increasing share of the world's scientific and scholarly output was no longer being acquired.

Discussions about cooperation emerged once again. It was recognized that the American Library Association was not necessarily the right forum for the debates among research librarians, and in 1937 the Association of Research Libraries (ARL) was formed. Many plans were hatched, including one by the ubiquitous Douglas MacMurtry, that would divide the country into several collection development regions, but it all remained a discussion, and no action was taken.

Increased interlibrary loan traffic, however, triggered major bibliographical initiatives in the form of national, regional, and local union catalogs. They took the form of card catalogs—for instance, the National Union Catalogue at

3 George A. Works. 1927. "College and University Library Problems: A Study of a Selected Group of Institutions Prepared for the Association of American Universities." Chicago: American Library Association.

4 Hendrik Edelman. 1994. "Precursor to the Serials Crisis: Conflict and Resolution in German Science Publishing in the 1930s." *Journal of Scholarly Publishing* 25(2).

the Library of Congress—as well as publications such as the Union List of Serials (1927) and Union List of Newspapers (1937).

Cost reductions also were a driving force for librarians to abandon the practice of including the bibliographical contents of major periodicals in their card catalogs. Indexing and abstracting thus became the exclusive domain of scientific and scholarly societies and commercial publishers. A third set of cataloging principles, those practiced by archivists, remained separate from the library profession as well. It would take more than half a century before the three cataloging methods were reconciled.

Meanwhile, space as well as information retrieval had become a major consideration, and the application of microfilm technology in the 1930s was seen as a breakthrough on all fronts. The expectation of a future in which all information would be in microform for storage and retrieval fueled the imagination of information scientists and librarians. The now statistically discredited report by Fremont Rider in 1944[5] in which he calculated that research libraries were doubling their holdings every sixteen years was a major factor in the planning process.

The lack of availability of basic German scientific publications manifested itself quickly after the American entry into the war. In a repeat from World War I, copyrights of major journals and reference works were confiscated by the U.S. government under the aegis of the Alien Property Custodian and assigned to interested publishers. Using a new printing technology of photo-offset for short runs, Edwards Brothers in Ann Arbor developed a specialty in this field. A substantial number of prominent German periodicals and reference works were thus brought onto the market at very low prices because no copyright fees were being paid. It was the beginning of a revolutionary scholarly and scientific reprint industry.

If the period from 1935 to 1940 was largely dedicated to planning, it took the outbreak of World War II and the entry of the Americans therein to take the collection development cooperation plans a step further. Faced with the actual cut-off from overseas resources, American research librarians developed a plan of shared acquisitions based on (perceived) collection strength and research interests. Under the leadership of the Library of Congress, the Cooperative Acquisitions Project for War Time Publications was started in 1945. It was a considerable success, and it was followed by the Farmington Plan in 1948. Lack of evaluation mechanisms, drastic changes in institutional research priorities, and a changed fiscal environment made the plan a practical failure, although it took a very long time before that was publicly recognized.[6]

5 Fremont Rider. 1944. *The Scholar and the Future of the Research Library: A Problem and its Solution.* New York: Hadham Press.

6 Hendrik Edelman. 1973. "The Death of the Farmington Plan." *Library Journal* 15.

However, it established firmly the concept of blanket orders as a valid means of comprehensive collection development, and the expertise gained by the various European suppliers to the Farmington Plan had already been put to good use.

Much of the professional library occupation during the war was particularly centered on operational issues due to the lack of manpower. Nobody was quite prepared for the future when it happened, except perhaps the scientific research world. The increased involvement of the federal government in research in the 1930s culminated in a total engagement during the war years. The plans for the postwar efforts were laid out clearly in Vannevar Bush's report for the National Research Council in 1945.[7]

But the academic library world was several steps removed from the development. Their immediate concerns were the need for resources to meet the dramatically increased size of the student body. Library buildings were inadequate; so were the collections and, especially, the staff. Fortunately, the armed forces had trained a large and very bright corps of men and women in various branches of intelligence and communication services. Many of their information organizations and linguistic skills were transferable, and the influx of this new talent was felt almost immediately.

Collections were quite inadequate to meet the new demand. With most of the selection decision-making authority vested in the faculty, it took a while to gear up. Building activity was generated on many campuses. Domestic production was the first priority, and the nation's book wholesalers and subscription agents began to flourish. European contacts were renewed within some cases the pleasant surprise that some dealers had accumulated subscriptions during the war.

But perhaps the most significant planning document was the report by a most prominent trio of academic librarians on the status of the Cornell Libraries in 1947.[8] This document became the national blueprint for research library development. It called for a complete re-cataloging of its holdings into the Library of Congress classification system. This far-reaching decision was later copied without question by numerous, but not all, large and small university libraries. It also addressed the issue of selection authority, recommending increased library responsibility and accountability, budgets, staffing, and buildings. The new model was defined and accepted by the profession, and the emulation process was set in motion around the country.

7 Vannevar Bush. 1945. "Science: The Endless Frontier." Washington, D.C.: U.S. Government Printing Office.

8 Louis R. Wilson, Robert B. Downs, and Maurice F. Tauber. 1948. "Report on the Survey of the Libraries of Cornell University." Cornell University Press: Ithaca, N.Y.

The existing research libraries quickly expanded their collection and service profiles. Among the library solutions for the unexpected influx of undergraduates was the creation of separate undergraduate libraries. This concept was based on the recognition that collection and service needs for undergraduates and graduate and research support were incompatibly different. Such new libraries were built at Harvard, Cornell, Michigan, and Berkeley. While Cornell bought a bookstore to provide its core collections, the others went through a careful title-by-title review process with input from many academics. The core list that ultimately emerged quickly became a buying list for three newly founded campuses of the University of California and other existing and emerging libraries. Thus, Books for College Libraries was created, and it became the academic library selector's bible.

But the national capacity to meet the needs of the incoming flow of students under the G.I. Bill was still completely insufficient. State after state proceeded to improve their higher education programs. This was done in several ways. Often existing schools such as teachers' and agricultural colleges were upgraded to full university status. Southern Illinois and Michigan State are examples of such decisions. In other cases, such as New York and New Jersey, the states actually took over existing colleges in order to create a state university system. But whole new universities were created as well. California, Ontario, New York, Florida, Wisconsin, and many other states built brand-new campuses and libraries in geographical areas considered underserved.

Many professional challenges emerged. The shortage in qualified staff was addressed through the quick expansion of existing library schools and the start of several new ones. The Master's in Library Science degree had now become the standard terminal professional degree, while PhD programs in library and information science were created to supply the necessary teaching and leadership capacity.

But the biggest challenge was in the area of collection development, a term that did not yet exist. The decision-making problem first had to be addressed. In the past, selection decisions had been made by faculty members, library directors, or special curators, most of whom had solid academic credentials. The sheer volume of decisions forced other solutions. Several libraries, such as Cornell, Harvard, Yale, and Stanford had already appointed academically and bibliographically trained librarians to coordinate the selection and acquisition process, and that practice multiplied quickly.

Much actual power resided in the acquisition and serial sections of the libraries because fiscal control was often located there. Shrewd librarians learned how to reward and punish their academic colleagues in the quest of improvement of the collections.

The availability of needed materials became a major issue. The quick expansion of the market, especially for retrospective books and journals, led to severe shortages. We have earlier alluded to the European situation, where already scarce resources were often destroyed during the military campaigns by either side. But the domestic front was not much different. During the 1930s and the war years, publishers printed shorter runs and often did not maintain their backlists. The U.S. Government Printing Office was no exception. The antiquarian book trade, not very well organized in the United States at the time, could not cope either.

Soon, this cottage industry came into full bloom.[9] Existing libraries supplied originals, and cozy relations emerged between some librarians and dealers. But the market responded, and soon dealers were able to supply new college libraries with complete opening day collections. But not only hard copy reprints came on the market. Various types of microforms were used to reproduce books, journals, and governmental publications. Unfortunately, there were no approved national or international standards on format or quality. Their unique brand of microform readers was often supplied free with the sets to entice the librarian customers. Both European and American entrepreneurs, including some big ones like the Encyclopedia Britannica, entered this market with so-called complete collections. Unfortunately, poor quality filming and lack of proper bibliographical control often made many such collections obsolete upon arrival.

The availability of large sums of money, often end-of-the-year funds, made such large-scale purchases attractive to understaffed libraries. During my extensive series of collection reviews in recent years, the archeological sediments of such imprudent purchases of big reprint and microform sets are painfully in evidence. An added professional black mark of this period was the use of library directors as paid (in cash, kind, or discount) consultants to this branch of the publishing industry. Even the appearance of impropriety should have been avoided. The ALA's ethical standards for library acquisitions had not yet been issued!

Ultimately, large corporations who were seeking a belated share in the growing library market bought out the small-time entrepreneurs in the reprint and microfilm industry. Most of them, however, had to absorb their losses when the markets closed down after this boom period around 1970.

New Research Frontiers

The massive government involvement in research during the war continued afterward. New discoveries in physics, chemistry, earth and space sciences, life sciences, mathematics, and engineering funded by various government

9 Carol Nemeyer. 1972. *Scholarly Reprint Publishing in the United States.* New York: Bowker.

agencies led to tremendous expansion of the nation's research efforts. The need for qualified people led to further investments in graduate education. The production of books, articles, and conference proceedings grew proportionally. But the existing publishing structure in the heavily subsidized scientific societies could often not cope with this growth. New fields were opening up all the time; the need for speedy publication increased. Conservative editorial policies and practices and slow publication schedules led to other paths.

The previously described German entrepreneurial model had not quite died during the Nazi regime. Former owners and staff members had moved to Holland, Switzerland, Scandinavia, England, and the United States. Starting initially in small corporations, sometimes with funds invested by enterprising scientists as well as with pre-paid subscription funds, they began to take advantage of the new research world that was rapidly becoming international. Holland emerged as a true incubator, partly because of its sophisticated typesetting capabilities in mathematics and chemistry that has survived the war, partly because of its low printing costs, and partly because of its core or prominent internationally oriented scientists.

But the new businesses began to thrive on both sides of the Atlantic. It was a small world where everyone knew each other, and there was considerable cooperation in distribution that rapidly became worldwide, a phenomenon unfamiliar to most traditional U.S. publishers. New journals, reviews, and book series, as well as indexing and abstracting services, came into the market at a rapid pace. Research libraries in the United States with their valuable dollar budgets were eager to absorb this increased production. The scientific societies were encouraged as well, and many of their publishing programs began to expand to meet the publication needs of the research world.

Fueled by the Cold War and subsequently by the Sputnik phenomenon (1956), government investment in research in the United States and Europe kept expanding. Big science had arrived, and big publishing was an essential consequence. But there were other dramatic changes taking place in research libraries as a result of changing government policy. The National Defense Education Act of 1958 opened the way for extensive government support for so-called area studies. These included Asian, Eastern European, Latin American and African studies. With these programs, which included language teaching as well as an array of social sciences research areas, came a considerable investment in library collections, their acquisitions and cataloging. For most research libraries this was an entirely new venture. New staff with foreign language expertise had to be recruited and trained and new acquisitions channels and methods had to be tested. The Library of Congress quickly took a leadership position because of its previous international contacts and a small core of extremely dedicated and creative librarians.

A clever 1958 amendment of a law passed in 1954 made it possible to use accumulated surplus foreign currency for library acquisitions. Such programs, particularly in India, Indonesia, and Egypt, brought large amounts of vernacular language materials into the country. Many research libraries participated, and it took a number of years for library administrators to recognize that possibly more was being acquired than was needed. Vast arrays of cataloging backlogs developed. The need to coordinate these activities became apparent and, once again, the Library of Congress took the initiative. The National Program for Acquisition and Cataloging (1965) allowed the library to open offices around the world to guide the activities. Local staff was used in the cataloging process. Dealers' expertise, especially in Western Europe, in blanket orders already there because of the Farmington Plan, was vastly expanded, and other libraries soon began to take advantage of the new services.

Latin America had always been a challenge in the areas of collection development and acquisitions. Lack of a strong bookselling tradition, lack of national bibliographical coverage, and continuing currency problems were serious impediments. But increased academic interest at many universities forced librarians into action. Buying trips, both by faculty members and librarians, became a necessity, but it proved to be expensive and lasted but a short time. Under the auspices of the 1956 Seminar of Acquisition of Latin American Library Materials (SALALM), a new plan was developed. The international bookselling firm of Stechert-Hafner proposed to serve as the buying agent for American research libraries. Thus, the Latin American Cooperative Acquisitions Program (LACAP 1960) was born.[10] It lasted until 1972. Never without problems, especially about selection criteria, the program did succeed in bringing a considerable amount of material to U.S. libraries. Many of the collaborators, such as the University of Texas and the University of Florida, developed impressive research collections.

Other cooperative programs were established as well. The Center for Research Libraries, founded in Chicago in 1949 as a common storage facility for the "Big Ten" universities, expanded its range of activities as a national library membership resource to include nationally coordinated acquisitions, initially of foreign dissertations, foreign language newspapers, textbooks, and other types of previously stored specialized material. It also entered the microfilm market with the purchase of particularly large and expensive microform sets.

The need for more cooperation in collection development was frequently expressed at library meetings and in the literature. Several regional efforts were made, often with considerable publicity, but very little came of these

10 M. J. Savary. 1968. *The Latin American Cooperative Acquisitions Program ... An Imaginative Venture.* New York: Hafner.

efforts. The three primary conditions for success in cooperation, common bibliographical access, adequate delivery services and effective evaluation methods, were lacking in most cases. The introduction of the MARC format in 1965 as a national cataloging standard began to address the first of these concerns, and soon a number of regional cooperative cataloging networks came to life. Many had cooperative collection development in their mission statement, but no one quite knew how to proceed.

Other changes were taking place in the research library world as well. The rapid growth of collections and the increased specialized needs of researchers once again brought to the forefront the issue of centralization or de-centralization. On one side, administrators saw in centralization a way to utilize staff and space resources more effectively while claiming to achieve improved access for all. Researchers and aligned librarians, however, recognized the need for specialized disciplinary collections and service patterns, as well as the need for immediate physical access. Different campuses tried different models with varying degrees of success, although in most cases, the physical and life sciences as well as the more prominent professional schools retained their own separate collections.

Specialization also became a necessity in the area of rare books, manuscripts, and archives. Although some of the older institutions had established such departments and even buildings, the practice slowly penetrated the profession. The need was greatest in those institutions where research on primary sources was particularly valued, and as a result, such materials were included in collection development programs. The different bibliographical needs, especially in the manuscript and archival areas caused considerable difficulties to the user communities. Different staffing requirements brought a group of more academically trained individuals into the profession. The nation's preeminent independent research libraries, such as the Huntington, Newberry and Morgan libraries, played a leadership role in setting the highest professional standards and training a group of outstanding librarians and archivists. Moreover, successful fundraising allowed for new programs such as exhibits and fellowships, which led to much more visibility in the scholarly community.

The Role of the Book Trade

The remarkable rise in the rate of growth of new books and periodicals and in purchasing power of academic libraries had a strong effect on book and periodical dealers. Although European dealers had successfully specialized in services to the research library world, domestic agents lagged far behind. Most of the book dealers were wholesalers, also often called jobbers, who catered to the book trade as well as to libraries. But public and school libraries, with their predictable collection development requirements, were the main focus of their inventories. Subscription agents similarly carried only a limited, high-profit number of titles in their service repertory.

But this would change. Automation became the key factor for change in the subscription business. With the early assistance from IBM, the Faxon subscription agency began to develop a more specialized capability in the 1960s. Competitors soon came along as well. As their capacity increased more and more, academic libraries began to use their services. Consolidated billing and automatic renewals became standard.

In the book business it was the enterprising initiative of the Portland, Oregon, bookseller Richard Abel whose company revolutionized the domestic book trade. With a more academically oriented stock, reliable back-ordering and continuation services, Abel began to address the common needs of the academic library community. In addition, Abel began to successfully introduce a series of approval plans based on the model used by the Europeans. The innovative and expanded bibliographical services soon became an essential component of the academic library's service expectation spectrum. and, albeit reluctantly initially, other dealers began to follow. As in the case of the subscription agencies, automation of the bibliographical services made the difference. Both book and periodical dealers ultimately added cataloging and other bibliographic services to the repertoire.

Doomsday

The remarkable decade of growth and innovation came to a rather abrupt end in 1971. The drastic devaluation of the U.S. dollar by President Nixon caused an overnight fiscal and decision-making crisis in the larger academic libraries, which were used to spending over 60 percent of their budget abroad. Political turmoil on university campuses and lagging enrollments caused a decline in public support for higher education. Nearly simultaneously and perhaps related, concerns about the seemingly unbridled growth of library budgets and collections and the subsequent need for ever-more staffing and space became a favorite topic among university presidents. Moreover, the aftermath of the 1960s revolution had raised the expectations of library staff that they would play a more active role in the management of academic libraries, which had heretofor remained heavily concentrated at the top. Automation of library services moved from experimental status to implementation, causing considerable shifts in budgetary priorities.

All of these converging trends led to effects that in many ways would determine the academic library agenda for decades to come.

Although the dollar devaluation was the immediate cause of the fiscal disruption in library budgets, the real origin lay deeper and had started earlier. The production of scholarly and scientific books and periodicals had always been, and continues today, to be driven by supply rather than demand. Ever-increasing national and international research production, combined with a tradition of considerable subsidies at various levels, made it an information system with built-in default lines. Although it is a fallacy to state, as is still often done, that once upon a time, academic libraries were self-sufficient, the profession was unprepared to face the sudden de facto underfunding of a program expected to grow.

Almost immediately after the dollar devaluation, the remedy was sought in reduction of subscription costs. This is not surprising; the consolidated periodical bill, often supplied from abroad, was the most visible and available victim. Ever since, research libraries have lived in the so-called serials crisis. Caught between rising production and academic demand on the one side and shrinking resources on the other, the profession lacked the proper decision-making capacity. Particularly in the sciences, librarians did have fiscal responsibility, but often lacked the authority to make decisions. Understandably, fiscal issues prevailed, and in the cancellation spree that followed, untested criteria such as duplication, language, and price were used in the effort to balance the budget. Some in the profession turned their frustration and even anger toward the publishers, the intermediaries through which reduced subsidies and markets were increasing their prices as well as their production. A spiral of acrimony followed. When some in the American research library world proposed a subsidized National Periodical Center to relieve pressure on individual libraries, publishers, already weary of perceived library infringement of copyright, defeated the proposal in Congress.[11] The Linda Hall Library in Kansas City, Missouri, ultimately assumed the practical role of such a center. Founded in 1945, it acquired early on the extensive collections from the American Academy of Arts and Sciences, including its international exchange programs, and, more recently the holdings of the Engineering Society Library.

In another move to counter the effects of the budget shortfalls, several libraries banded together in efforts to share periodical resources. The most notable of these was the founding of the Research Library Group (RLG) in 1974. But the massive and frustrating effort to commonly reduce subscriptions against the backdrop of an unwilling and powerful academic clientele made it an almost immediate failure. Subsequently, the RLG repositioned itself as a bibliographic utility, keeping shared collection development as a public but undefined object.

11 Mary Biggs. 1984. "The Proposed National Periodicals Center, 1973–1980: Study, Dissension, and Retreat." *Resource Sharing and Information Networks,* Vol. 1 (spring/summer): 1–22.

From Collection Development to Collection Management

Academic library management became a major issue at the same time. Top-heavy management style increasingly came under fire in the changed academic atmosphere. The ARL established a special office that helped the inevitable transformation to a more appropriate participatory process. Academic librarians increasingly began to take charge of collection development as part of this new empowerment. A group of collection development librarians at major universities met at ALA in 1971 and set out an ambitious agenda to define and codify proper collection development procedures. Using a comprehensive definition of the field, collection development became a planning process. This certainly was needed in the field because many management questions emerged in the changed environment. The diminishing role of faculty members in the collection decision process led to the appointments of specialized librarians, often called bibliographers, who began to take charge. Blanket orders, approval plans, and other bibliographic and selection support provided by the book trade did much to streamline procedures. In later years, shrinking resources forced many of these selectors back into mainstream public service functions, leading to a decline in the professional profile. In many academic library organizational charts, collection development has remained a staff, rather than a line, function, in which other professional duties such as bibliographic instruction and reference work are shared. The term collection management gained prominence in classified ads.

One of the emerging issues in the 1970s and beyond was the physical condition of the collections. In various surveys, it was found that the paper in large parts of the collections was deteriorating at an alarming and threatening pace. Poor paper quality, especially from foreign countries, poor environmental controls, and open stacks and indiscriminate use—all combined to create a troublesome situation. The profession rose to the occasion. Education and training programs were established, and preservation became an established organizational entry in many libraries. Effective lobbying led to the acceptance of acid-free paper in the publishing industry. Similar efforts, notably by the Council of Library Resources in Washington, led to considerable funding for various preservation projects. A combination of commercial and cooperative efforts rapidly added to the wide availability of microfilm as an alternative. However, despite many efforts, no real national plan emerged, and large scale preservation efforts largely remained in the realm of the so-called "great library theory." This is counter to the results of long-established bibliographic research that shows the nation's unique holdings to be distributed among hundreds of collections. In recent years, the prospect of reformatting in digital formats has reenergized the preservation efforts, but like the never-quite-accomplished microfilm solution, many questions for the future remain.

Collection management concerns also manifested themselves in a revised view of public access to the collections. Open stacks had been the hallmark of American academic libraries. But chronic space problems and low use of certain classes of materials led to the consideration of off-site compact storage. Although often controversial on individual campuses, the practice is now commonly established in large research libraries. As increasing numbers of older books and periodicals can now only be accessed through computer-based bibliographical means, their low usage thus is ironically further confirmed.

Although library acquisitions budgets fluctuated during the 1980s and 1990s, a relatively calm new equilibrium was reached at most of the universities. Only the biggest and richest libraries maintained a comprehensive collection development profile; most other academic libraries scaled down their expectations. Reductions in periodical subscriptions and series standing orders combined with substantial reductions in foreign language acquisitions were continuing. Some libraries, however, continued to retain as much title power as they could and unwisely eliminated needed duplication. Collection management research overwhelmingly points to the need to protect copy-depth in heavily used areas. The current group of users should not be sacrificed for an uncertain future.

But a new addition to the budget burden emerged when more and more serials appeared on the market in electronic format. In one generation of academic librarianship, many prominent periodicals have appeared on the market in four different formats: the original, the reprint, the microform, and now the electronic version. The content obviously did not change. Making the right format choices became a difficult issue, not helped, of course, by the publishers who were not prepared to sacrifice their academic credibility, expense recovery, and profit margin by offering electronic versions only.

But after a period of considerable uncertainty in the market place, a new acquisitions model emerged. Purchasing consortia were formed that negotiated with the major publishers' comprehensive coverage of journal packages in which existing hard copy subscriptions would be preserved at existing levels while electronic access was guaranteed to a large user audience. In many states, these initiatives were subsidized, thus bringing relief to budgets, while also increasing access to many library patrons who were formerly disenfranchised.

The availability of new electronic resources and their appeal quickly demanded considerable sums of money in library budgets. In a period of some ten years, the percentage of funds allocated to electronic resources rose in many libraries from zero to more than 20 percent. It is probably too early to observe for which kinds of information the electronic format will be the one of choice. For reference sources, which need to be up to date, this has become clear. Much experimentation is currently taking place, and the coming decade will undoubtedly see a changed mix of formats for research materials for academic libraries. The economic consequences also remain uncertain, as the cost of developing economic products remains very high, while the market, even globally, appears small.

Meanwhile, extensive paper collections need to be cared for even if fewer people are using them. If one were to walk the stacks of several major research libraries recently, one would not have been able to escape the notion that in another fifty years, most of these collections will become "special collections" with extensive preservation needs and, undoubtedly, much more limited physical access. It will be a considerable managerial, technological and architectural challenge.

·12·

Appearance and Growth of Computer and Electronic Products in Libraries

Ralph M. Shoffner

"What's it all about, Alfie?"

When Richard Abel approached me about writing this paper, I knew that to complete it, I would need an organizing theme. I knew that I wanted to review the past in order to decide where I think academic libraries should be headed today. So I began with the thought of tracing the evolution of computer and electronic products in libraries from their inception to the present day. As I got further into the data, I realized that the path of development has not been straightforward. Indeed, the path has been more than crooked; it resembles a maze. In some cases, opportunities and logical paths of development have been missed or for some reason, not taken; in others, technical solutions that seem less elegant have won the day. So, after feeling my way through this maze, here is what I've found:

- Academic library patrons are better served today than ever in the past;
- The electronic library is in its infancy; there are great opportunities for improving service;
- The methods of reimbursement of electronic authors and publishers need further work;
- The need for academic library service is so great that it must still be significantly improved.

S.R. Ranganathan's five laws of library science still stand as the most elegant statement of the library's purpose:

Books are for use.

Every reader his book.

Every book its reader.

Save the time of the reader.

The library is a growing organism.

http://instruct.uwo.ca/mit/026-98/026w02.htm

Of course, the language is a bit dated. For example, if we rewrote Ranganathan's fifth law, we might come up with a formulation similar to the statement made by the MIT Media Lab:

> If anything can be certain about the future, it is that the influence of technology, especially digital technology, will continue to grow, and to profoundly change how we express ourselves, how we communicate with each other, and how we perceive, think about, and interact with our world. These "mediating technologies" are only in the first stages of their modern evolution; they are still crude, unwieldy, and unpersonalized, poorly matched to the human needs of their users.

http://www.unesco.org/education/educprog/lwf/links/learn.html[1]

Let us keep Ranganathan's original language and understand that book is a metaphor for any type of material, in any format, that libraries make available to their patrons.

Use of computers by and for libraries can benefit library patrons in three ways: by providing services not previously possible, by making services more convenient, and by reducing the cost of the services so that more service can be provided. But first, since we live in a world in which costs of innovation and of operation are of substantial import, let us follow the money.

Although we can't say what academic libraries would be like if there had been no Cold War and no Sputnik, we do know that they would be radically different than they are today. The growth of academic libraries, of computing, and of library research were all fostered by funding from the federal government responding to the perceived threat of the USSR and the inferred need for better education and, as a corollary, for improved libraries. Much of this funding had an intelligence operations rationale and was provided through the military and the intelligence agencies. In some cases, the projects were funded directly; in others, the funds were transferred to other agencies, for example, the National Science Foundation and the Office of Education, which then awarded the grants and contracts. This was natural because it was the intelligence agencies that first experienced the need for immensely increased information (library) services and who had funding available to support the needed innovation. This funding supported far more than hardware development. For example, this was the source of funding for research and development of optical character recognition (OCR), machine translation of language (MT), and selective dissemination of information (SDI). Such research was supported because there were serious bottlenecks:

- OCR: a lack of people to key information into computers
- MT: a lack of people fluent in other languages, e.g., Russian.
- SDI: a lack of time to search and find all the material of potential use to the analyst

Most of the research funding for these activities was terminated before the end of the 1960s. Were the problems solved? Someone with access to that portion of the record will need to answer that question, but if so, there was no public awareness of the achievements. One might speculate that the solutions obtained were good enough to meet the immediate need, and support was terminated to avoid having the results escape the intelligence community. In any event, significant progress had to await the revolution created by microcomputers. Although all are potentially important to the academic library, only OCR, as used in the Kurzweil Reading Machine, has reached routine use.

By the mid 1960s, computer applications development had spread throughout the library community. In addition to the federal government, state and local governments, foundations, and the libraries themselves began to fund the computer transition. The National Institutes of Health supported both internal and external projects. The Library of Congress, the National Institutes of Health, the National Library of Medicine, and the National Agricultural Library stimulated the development of computer-based products and services. Companies that were providing products and services to libraries were developing the use of computers; many research libraries had development projects underway; and most planning for new academic libraries incorporated the use of computers.

With the coming of the 1970s, the funding of computer applications development began to shift away from the federal government and toward the standard sources of library funding—private foundations, local governments, and the institutions themselves.[2]

As this shift advanced, the developers began to look for ways to recover at least some part of their development costs. Once computer-based goods and services were considered as potential sources of revenue, venture capitalists, for-profit and not-for-profit firms all began to participate in the information revolution. In the intervening decades, development has continued to shift to the commercial model, until today, virtually all innovation in the use of computers for libraries is done with a view to recovering more than the costs of innovation through sales of the results.

The Introduction of Computers to Facilitate and Control
Internal Library Operations

The initial use of computers for libraries was primarily to automate tasks already being performed by other methods. This is common for any new technology and is due both to the attempt to generate some cost savings to offset at least part of the cost of introducing the technology and to limited understanding of potential new uses of the technology. During the 1960s, the primary method of input of new data into a computer was still the punched (Hollerith) card. Magnetic tapes were used both for master files and for backup. Output was to line printers, that is, printers that were set up to print an entire line, not only a single character at a time. This architecture defined the mainframe computer. As a result of its architecture, the mainframe computer was used primarily for batch processing. The processing tasks were performed periodically. For example, to maintain the master file, all of the transactions (adds, changes, deletes) from the time of the last maintenance run to the present run were sorted into the order of the master file. Then, the update program would start at the beginning of the master and transaction files, read each record in sequence from both files, match the records and apply any updates indicated; all records, changed and unchanged, but not the deleted records were written out to a new master file.

In the mid 1960s, the first commercial minicomputers were developed. These computers were the first to provide immediate random database update, based upon interaction through keyboards and video monitors with several operators at the same time. By the end of the 1960s, virtually all of the larger libraries had some sort of automation program under way, most of them dependent upon interactive computing pioneered by minicomputers.

Acquisitions and Serials Control

On first consideration, acquisitions might seem a poor application for batch-oriented computers. However, in the 1960s, the workflow of most acquisitions departments was organized along batch lines. It was normal for orders to be gathered and held before they were prepared and sent to the vendors. Although many libraries employed a weekly acquisitions cycle, the hold period could stretch out to months! Without delving into the reasoning behind such organization, let us simply observe that even a batch computer application could provide operating improvements. As I recall, in the mid 1960s, Baker & Taylor arranged for Computer Usage, Inc. of Los Angeles, to produce an acquisitions system for Baker &Taylor to provide to libraries. The libraries would use the software on an IBM mainframe and then send their book orders to Baker & Taylor in the form of a set of punched cards to be processed on that company's computer. To accomplish this, Computer Usage developed the specifications for the content of these punched cards. To see what that content looked like, you need only print out (at eighty bytes per line) a file of acquisitions order records that are encoded in the current standard BISAC Fixed format. When the BISAC committee was trying to set up standard order records in the early 1980s, Baker &Taylor's record format was grand-fathered in as the BISAC Fixed format. Note that because these records were originally defined for punched cards, carriage return and line feed characters are not used to end each line. As a result, these records can't be used readily with standard text or word processors, because the entire file displays as a single continuous line.

Most vendors immediately set up the capability to accept BISAC Fixed, so that they had parity with Baker &Taylor. And I am not aware of any vendor capable of accepting the more sophisticated BISAC Variable format who lacks the ability to handle BISAC Fixed as well. Even though we immediately incorporated the BISAC Variable format and provided the enhancement without charge to our Nonesuch Acquisitions clients, the BISAC Variable format deserved to be ignored. By the time that BISAC Variable was developed, the MARC-II communications format had been an international standard for two decades and there were probably between 10 and 20 million titles in that format. Yet MARC-II was completely ignored-perhaps someday one of the insiders will tell us how that came about. Of course, as long as they get their books, librarians may not much care about the engine under the acquisitions hood.

In the 1960s, work commenced on serials control, particularly control of claiming, check-in, and binding. For the academic library, claiming has always been tough, particularly due to the widely varying publication patterns, plus the distinct tendency of some serials publishers to ignore the stated publication pattern. The UCLA Biomedical Library, with funding from the National Institutes of Health (NIH), developed a claiming system based upon an extensive formal definition of publication patterns that they also developed. After that, the definition of publication patterns was the basis on which claim decisions were made.[3]

In the 1970s, much of the library system development shifted to minicomputers. This was true of acquisitions as well as the other applications. The first system that CLSI installed was a minicomputer-based acquisitions control system at Cleveland Public Library. Although the installation was said to be successful, CLSI did not try to sell any more acquisitions systems. Instead, they shifted to the development of their circulation control system.

At Ringgold, we licensed the Wang minicomputer based multiuser order control software that Academic Book Center, Inc. had developed for their in-house use. We modified it, added fund accounting and management reporting, and installed the first Nonesuch Acquisitions system at Wayne State University in 1981. In 1985, we ported the system to MS-DOS PCs and then moved it to network operation when Artisoft's Lantastic network became available. Today, Nonesuch operates under Windows NT and Windows 2000. And yes, it still produces order records in the BISAC Fixed format. So picture this: by uploading the Ingram order file to their FTP server, we're using the Internet to send transfer card images.

http://www.ringgold.com/

The first product developed by Innovative Interfaces, Inc was a microcomputer-based backup system to be used when the CLSI circulation control system was out of service. Acquisitions control was the second product. The software was developed for use on a microcomputer and was released in 1983. Innovative Interfaces, Inc. has continuously supported the software since that time and is probably the most successful vendor of acquisitions software.

http://www.iii.com/

Dogs That Didn't Bark

Neither OCLC (now stands for the Online Computer Library Center, Inc.) nor Faxon (now part of RoweCom, Inc.) took advantage of opportunities to create near-monopolistic positions in information handling relating to acquisitions of books and serials. Although they developed acquisitions and serials control services, it seems that they were unable to exploit their unique positions to obtain dominant positions. As an observer, I didn't understand it at the time, and I still don't.

In the early 1980s, OCLC began operation of their centralized acquisitions subsystem. Many libraries found it useful, particularly because preorder search could be carried out against all of the OCLC titles including the library's holdings in a single operation; OCLC then took care of sending the orders on to the vendors selected by the libraries. For some reason, OCLC made the decision to develop a PC-based acquisitions-control system, and once this software was in place, to terminate the operation of the centralized acquisitions service. Perhaps at some time, an insider will reveal how this decision came about, because on the face of it, it appears to be self-destructive. OCLC was in a virtual monopoly position with respect to their ability to offer acquisitions services bundled with their cataloging services. In contrast to distributed catalog support via their MicroEnhancer software, which required continued use and enhancement of OCLC's database, release of the PC-based acquisitions software obviated the need for continued use of OCLC.

This is not meant to denigrate OCLC's local software. Whatever the reasons for discontinuing their central position, in about 1983, OCLC acquired the serials control system developed by Maurice Leatherbury and Bud Eaton (MetaMicro Library Systems, Inc.) and had them migrate it to OCLC's version of the IBM PC, where it became SC350. About a year and a half later this team rewrote SC350 to make it multiuser, using IBM's new PC LAN. After that, OCLC contracted with them to design and develop a microcomputer-based acquisitions system. Like SC350, it was multiuser, ran on IBM PCs, and was christened ACQ350.

Then, having terminated their centralized acquisitions services, OCLC proceeded to sell their local acquisitions software to Ameritech, which subsequently terminated their software support. And in the last chapter of the acquisitions story, after OCLC acquired WLN, the WLN Acquisitions Subsystem was closed to libraries on July 1, 1999. By this time of course, the situation for the libraries was entirely different than it had been in 1983. Many had been through an acquisitions cycle with OCLC, and most of the larger libraries had some sort of acquisitions control as part of their integrated systems.

> http://library.calumet.purdue.edu/acqart.htm
> http://www.oclc.org
> http://www.wln.org/transition/number8.htm

In the late 1970s, Faxon was still the dominant vendor of serials subscription services to academic libraries. They developed Lynx, a centralized serials control system. Although the system was a bit pricey, Lynx had excellent functionality and was well received by libraries with significant serials operations. However, it didn't take advantage of its centralization to alert the other participating libraries when any one of the participants received a new issue of a serial. Of course, given their unique position vis-à-vis the serials publishers, they could have gone a step further and arranged that the publishers would update their titles in the Lynx database when new issues were released. This should have been a win-win-win situation for all three parties: The libraries and the publishers would have benefited by eliminating unnecessary claims, yet signaling nondelivery when the publisher still had time to do something about it and, Faxon would have solidified its central position in serials information exchange. Instead, Faxon released microLynx software to be used in the individual library and as a result, placed itself in direct competition with the offerings of Innovative Interfaces and OCLC.

Cataloging

It is probably impossible to overstate the beneficial effect that the existence of an international standard format for catalog records had on the development of computer-based catalogs and cataloging. With that standard in place, institutions throughout the world have been able to invest significant amounts of money in converting bibliographic records with reasonable assurance that the conversion would never have to be redone. From a financial viewpoint, the technical aspects of the MARC-II record format are beside the point. The fact that it is an international standard means that it can only be replaced by another international standard and that it will be possible for a computer program to translate the existing body of records in the MARC-II format into the new international standard format.

In 1964, Verner W. Clapp, Council on Library Resources, Inc., funded Lawrence F. Buckland (Inforonics, Inc) to ". . . demonstrate that bibliographic information in general and in particular Library of Congress catalog card information can be so recorded in machine form as to make possible the subsequent automatic printing of such information in all required typographic and bibliographic forms."[4] This seminal work was followed by the effort spearheaded by the Library of Congress to develop a standard format for the communication of machine-readable cataloging. Henriette D. Avram was the point person for LC, both heading up LC's internal effort and marshaling the support of the library community. LC's MARC distribution service and the international standard MARC-II formats were the results.[5]

Interestingly, John Knapp, one of the authors of the original standard, suggested that after ten years of experience, the standard should be subjected to a formal review, for the purpose of developing a new standard. At the end of the century, the development of a new standard had not been undertaken, even though many stresses on the record structure were recognized.

http://www.acctbief.org/avenir/evmarc.htm

http://www.loc.gov/marc/

http://lcweb.loc.gov/catdir/lccn/lccn0613.html#5

Work on the automation of cataloging in the 1960s did not wait for a standard format to be developed and accepted. On one side, it was by no means assured that a standard record format could be negotiated because it required political, as well as technical, accomplishment. On the other, there were both immediate needs and the money available to try to meet them.

The lowly catalog card presented one such immediate need. In 1964, Richard Abel & Co. was supplying cataloging with their approval books. They accomplished this by using Friden Flexowriters, which, at the time, was one of the principal methods of producing input for computers. The Flexowriter resembles a typewriter, but it can both read and produce punched paper tape. So, at Abel, the cataloging for each book was typed into the Flexowriter. After review, editing, and testing, the paper tapes were duplicated, by sending the output tape from one Flexowriter to the input of the next. The approval books and the punched tapes were then sent to the libraries. In the libraries, the tapes were loaded into Flexowriters, reviewed, edited, a master tape punched, and catalog cards printed. These final tapes could be saved until the library had a computer available in which to load them.

The Flexowriter production system was highly effective, even though it was of Rube Goldberg caliber. The major cost was input, which was proportional to the number of titles being handled; there was then a relatively small marginal cost associated with each copy handled. The limits were production time and space. Thirty Flexowriters are still slow and take up a lot of real estate. Instead, computer processing and transfer to magnetic tape was required in order to supply hundreds of libraries. By 1967, Abel's bibliographic record processing was operating on an IBM System/360. Then, after the MARC-II format was released, Abel's system was converted so that all subsequent catalog records were maintained and distributed in this format. As soon as the format became available, authority control using the MARC-II format for authority data was incorporated in the software. In addition to its internal use for building and maintaining the databases for Opening Day Collections, this software was provided to three of the University of Texas campuses, so that they could continue to maintain their databases in MARC-II. This software continued to be used by Abel, and then by Blackwell, North America, until it was sold to OCLC in the late 1990s.

During the 1960s, printed book-form catalogs enjoyed a resurgence that had not been experienced since the nineteenth century. This resurgence was due to the increased desire to make use of library collections over a wide geographic area, primarily through interlibrary loan. For example, in response to pressure from the aerospace industry for a research library system to serve industry, the California legislature assigned the libraries of the University of California to act as research libraries for California business and industry as well as for their traditional clientele. To meet this new responsibility, one of the system's responses was to produce printed book catalogs of the existing UCLA and UC-Berkeley collections, using the manual method of laying out the catalog cards in pages and then photographing them to produce a page master. This was done in 1963, and from then on, a catalog card was saved for each new monograph title added to any of the campuses. In 1972, a printed book catalog was produced, representing a five-year supplement of all Roman alphabet titles added to all the university's libraries since the first book catalogs were produced. To accomplish this, the catalog data were retyped using the OCR-A font. These forms were scanned into the computer via optical character recognition. The resulting records were submitted to a format recognition program, which converted them to MARC-II format records. The MARC-II records were then fed through software to detect duplicates and consolidate the holdings for the duplicates. The final step was to sequence the MARC-II records into author-title and subject sections and then format the pages ready for photocomposition. The resulting catalog contained 798,000 different titles in MARC-II format, of which 675,000 were held by one campus only.[6]

Circulation

Circulation was one of the earliest library computer applications. Even before the advent of the digital computer, some libraries had been using punched cards for circulation control, so it was convenient to transfer the application to computer control. The batch orientation of the 1960 mainframes was not a severe drawback, since most lending, other than for reserves, was for periods of a week or more. Also, it had long been the case in the larger libraries that their availability information was rarely completely accurate.

As soon as minicomputers became available in the1960s, they were seen as natural machines for circulation control. In 1965, Scientific Data Systems (SDS) made a proposal to the University of California to use SDS minicomputers, equipped with video terminals and bar-code readers. Although an intriguing proposal, it was not accepted, due to concerns about cost and reliability. This technology waited until the 1970s, when CLSI successfully combined it into a complete package—hardware, software, installation, training, and ongoing support.

During the 1970s, circulation system development was stimulated by more reliable and less expensive minicomputers, as well as transaction recorders to input the patron and item identification numbers. At the beginning of the decade, punched card readers and patron (punched) badge readers were the primary methods of transferring the transaction information. Although bar-code scanners and OCR scanners had been available in the 1960s, their costs were high and their production limited until the 1970s, when they began to be used in quantity in banking and manufacturing. At that time, libraries began using them for circulation control. By the end of the decade, numerous institutions of all sizes and types had developed their own circulation control systems.

Ideas Whose Time Has Come and Gone?

Optical character recognition was developed for the Defense Department in the 1960s as a method of creating text input for computers. It can be produced using relatively inexpensive typewriters equipped with a special type font, OCR-A. Not only is the relative input cost low, but also, the input is readily checked for accuracy because the font is directly human-readable.

These same characteristics would seem to make OCR-A labels more appropriate than bar-code labels for the identification of books in circulation control systems.

In the 1970s, Bucknell University in Pennsylvania made imaginative use of OCR-A labels to create an interesting system, written in FORTRAN for the Xerox Sigma 7. Their design used the item's call number as the item identification number; as a result, they could perform their database conversion on the fly. If a book without an OCR-A label appeared at the circulation desk, the label could be typed, put on the book, and scanned, immediately charging out the book. With this approach, circulation of the collection was not impeded during the conversion process even if that process required several years to complete.

Despite the apparent desirability of OCR-A labels for library use, bar-code labels continued to be used more heavily and are the current transaction standard. Certainly, the makers of optical character recognition equipment were focused on full-page scanning, as opposed to scanning a single line of text on a label. Quite possibly, the market for label scanning equipment was considered to be too small to justify the needed investment for development. The OCR-A equipment of the 1970s had a breadboard appearance. used about 100 watts of energy, and had a high failure rate.

Whatever the reason, OCR-A label scanning has virtually disappeared and bar-code labels are now standard for item identification in libraries and throughout industry. And since most books in most library collections now have bar-code labels, it is difficult to imagine any circumstances that would cause their replacement by OCR-A.

Bar-codes have also had some competition from magnetic cards. In the 1980s, magnetic cards were used for some patron identification, and it was thought that this would increase, particularly for student patrons. For example, in the late 1980s, Baldwin-Wallace College began using Ringgold's Nonesuch Circulation system with magnetic identification cards for the college students and staff, and bar-code labels for the books and for the off-campus patrons. However, in the 1990s, it seems that the direction went more toward dual identification cards, that is, magnetic cards that also have the identification number in a bar-code as well. As a result, it now seems unlikely that magnetic cards will replace bar-codes for circulation control.

Due to the crowds that develop at checkout just before the next class, undergraduate libraries would seem to be strong candidates for self-charging. But intriguing as the concept may be and even though self-charging is widely used to purchase gasoline, there has been little progress toward self-charging of library materials. In the 1970s, Innovated Systems[7] built a most interesting system for the University of Texas at Dallas. The system had self-serving checkout that included deactivation of the security strips in the books. The patron inserted his badge in the reader, then placed his books one at a time on a sloped platform with a lip, so that it would hold one book at time. The barcode was scanned and the database checked. If there were no problems, the database was updated. and the book's magnetic security strip desensitized. Unfortunately, the system began operation in 1975, just as there was a crunch in library funding. Although the system was well conceived (for example, individual components could be replaced easily when better ones came out), Innovated was not able to find libraries interested in pursuing this path. Since that time, at least two firms, Checkpoint and 3M, have installed self-charging terminals, but it appears that these systems have generated limited interest.

Integrated Library Systems

The term "integrated library system" has come to refer to those systems that support acquisitions, circulation control, cataloging, and public access to the catalog. Serials check-in and serials binding control and the control of interlibrary lending are usually covered as well. At present, there are a substantial number of vendors of integrated systems.

In the late 1960s, Northwestern University began the development of the system that became NOTIS (Northwestern Online Total Integrated System). Although using a mainframe computer (IBM System/360), it used the on-line terminal model of computing, not batch processing. Beginning with circulation control, NOTIS was later extended to include acquisitions and cataloging.

During the 1960s and 1970s, there were often cases in which one institution would base its development on software obtained from another, for example, Ohio State University from University of Buffalo, University of Illinois from Ohio State University, Oberlin College from Bucknell University. However, Northwestern University was one of two universities that went beyond this approach and ultimately created commercial software.

In the late 1970s, Northwestern University undertook a special project that resulted in the installation of NOTIS in Venezuela for the National Library of Venezuela. In the early 1980s, the university began licensing NOTIS to several other institutions. The University of Florida was the first, followed by the University of South Alabama and Washington University in St. Louis. Jane Burke, a librarian with extensive marketing experience with CLSI, was hired to head NOTIS marketing. NOTIS became so successful that in the late 1980s, it was transferred to NOTIS Systems, Incorporated, a for-profit corporation wholly owned by Northwestern University, with Jane Burke as president and chief operating officer. In the early 1990s, Ameritech

Corporation bought both NOTIS and Dynix and formed Ameritech Library Services. Then in late 1999, SBC Communications acquired Ameritech and subsequently sold Ameritech Library Services to a private investment group led by 21st Century Group, LLC, and Green Leaf Ridge Company. In 2000 the name of the company was changed to epixtech, inc.

Meanwhile, Jane Burke and several NOTIS veterans left Ameritech in the mid 1990s and set up a new company, Endeavor Information Systems, Inc. Endeavor designed and developed Voyager, an integrated system that operates over the Internet. Endeavor is now competing strongly in the integrated library system market. And finally, Northwestern University has replaced NOTIS with Voyager.

> http://www.library.nwu.edu/lms/notis/notisdev.html
> http://www.library.nwu.edu/lms/notis/history2.html
> http://www.ameritech.org/community/loc/bio.html
> http://www.ilsr.com/fyi9911.htm
> http://www.library.nwu.edu/lms/
> http://www.endinfosys.com/

In the mid 1970s, Virginia Polytechnic Institute and State University began the development of an integrated library system, VTLS, based upon the HP3000 minicomputer and using COBOL and the IMAGE relational database technology. This was a systems concept similar to that being pursued by Dataphase, Inc., which used the Data General minicomputer platform. From the beginning, VTLS was planned for installation in other libraries, although it was being developed in a single university environment. As a result, the VTLS design incorporated configuration controls so that its operation could be modified to fit different library environments. The development was carried out under the direction of Vinod Chachra, director of systems development; the application requirements were supplied by the library, directed by Gordon Bechanan. In the mid 1980s, VTLS was spun out of the University. Chachra formed Virginia Tech Library Systems, Inc., with Virginia Tech holding an equity interest in the firm. At the end of the 1990s, VTLS was privately held with annual sales of approximately $11 million, with 65 percent of its products delivered outside the United States.

> http://www.state.va.us/governor/newsre/vtls0526.htm

Within the available resources—time, space and energy—for this article, it is not possible to identify all of the individuals and institutions that have played a role in the development, much less discuss the role that each played. For example, a version of a system originally developed for internal use at the National Library of Medicine, has been installed in other medical libraries by a commercial organization and recently has been offered for general library use.

GEAC, a Canadian computer manufacturer, developed and sold a complete system, hardware and software, with its first installation at the University of Guelph. It is hoped that those that are covered will convey the main threads of development. Of course, the Internet is an excellent resource for those who may wish to go further. For example the following is a list of library automation suppliers compiled by Thomas Parry Library, as of October 1996.

http://www.aber.ac.uk/~tplwww/e/auto.html

Outsourced Services—In Acquisitions, Cataloging, Systems, Specialist Bookseller

Development of Integrated Purchasing Services

In the 1960s, Richard Abel & Company changed the way academic libraries could acquire their books. The elements of these services had existed before, but Abel extended them and combined them in ways that allowed the libraries to reorganize their operations. There were three parts to these order services, firm orders, standing orders and approvals. A "firm order" is the traditional order for a specific publication and is still the common method of ordering. An order for a specified title is sent to the vendor, the vendor sends the book (and the invoice) to the library, and the order is filled. A standing order is an open order for a sequence of books to be published, books that have some common characteristic, for example, having a series title or being designated as part of a publisher's series. As books are published, the vendor must identify each of the books that share the common characteristic, send the book to the library with an identification of the standing order to which it belongs, and then keep the order active for subsequent publications. Given the nature of publishing, a book can be a member of more than one series. And of course, the same book can be published at the same time by more than one publisher—and, of course, with different prices. Approval orders extend the order concept in two ways. First, they are not quite orders in the same sense as firm or standing orders. When the library receives a book sent against an approval order, it may decide to keep or return it; thus, it approves the book after seeing it and before paying for it. Second, the vendor decides to send a book on approval, based on a description of the collection interests of the library.

Approvals represent outsourcing part of the acquisitions process, the part that involves selecting from all the materials published the subset that in all likelihood should be acquired by a particular library. Certainly, the library has the final say on whether the individual item is acquired. But for the program to be successful for both the library and the vendor, there should be few returns, and most of the items that ought to be included should be selected. For this to occur, the library must be able to describe the nature of the materials that it wishes to add to its collection. Desirable though it may be, this is not required in a traditional firm order environment, where the collection may simply represent the accumulation of the individual books acquired. Once collection interests are described, it is up to the vendor to match those descriptions against the books as they are published, then send them to the appropriate libraries for their approval. Abel did three new things to make approvals successful:

1. Formalized the process of describing collecting interests. Description went beyond the publisher and subject categories to include other aspects of the work—the nature of the treatment, the level of the work, and other elements.
2. Reviewed the book before deciding on the distribution of the copies. The nature of publishing demands that the book be described in the most appealing way possible. Therefore, it was as true for Abel as for the libraries; description was best done with the book in hand.
3. Placed all information on the computer and matched the book description to the library's collecting interests to determine ordering and distribution; this gave the economy of scale over which to distribute the costs of review and description.

It is no surprise that some of the most desirable books meet the specifications to be included in all three of the ordering categories for a given library. Because the library normally wants only one copy of such a book, the library could specify that at most, one copy was to be sent to the library. In this case, Abel would send the copy against the most specific order category (i.e., firm order, then standing order) and suppress it from being sent in the other categories.

The concepts implemented by Abel in the 1960s and 1970s are still the dominant methods of supplying books to libraries. In 1974–1975, Abel metamorphosed into Blackwell, North America (BNA). BNA continued until 1999, when it became Blackwell's Book Services (BBS). BBS then purchased Academic Book Center, Inc., a firm started in 1974, by four former Abel employees. Of course, to survive, vendors must continue to be competitive, so it is no surprise that other academic vendors have offered similar services.

Although there has been a great deal of integration in purchasing services associated with in-print books, out-of-print (OP), and serials backfiles have not yet been integrated. During the 1990s, the Internet had a substantial impact on OP acquisition. For example, by the end of 1999, Powell's Books could accept a file of "wants," provide machine matching against their inventory, and quote on the hits found. Bibliofind, acquired by Amazon in 1999, offered the ability both to computer match against wants and to send the wants on to their nonautomated participants. Doubtless, these services will be revised. For example, they were not organized to recognize either MARC-II records or X-12, but certainly they will do so in the future. There are other such websites, and the economies of the Web operation make it likely that most OP vendors will soon be using the Internet.

http://www.powells.com/
http://www.bibliofind.com/

Recently, there has been rapid change in the community of vendors providing books and serials to libraries. For example, Baker & Taylor acquired Yankee Book Peddler; Rowecom acquired Faxon, and Blackwell Limited and Swets & Zeitlinger completed the merger of Blackwell's Information Services and Swets Subscription Service to create a joint venture, Swets Blackwell. Much of this ferment was caused by changes in business models due to electronic commerce on the Internet and in this regard, everyone was watching Amazon and Barnes & Noble to see what effect they would have upon services to libraries. To date, these two firms have not had much impact on library acquisitions, primarily due to their discount structures and to their order process, which is essentially the firm order.

http://www.blackwell.com/
http://www.lib.pku.edu.cn/98conf/paper/a/RedmanLau.htm
http://www.amazon.com/
http://www.bn.com/

Development of Related Cataloging Outsourcing

American libraries have always strongly supported the concept of centralized cataloging, particularly that of the Library of Congress. Before the computer revolution, the Library of Congress Card Division and the National Union Catalog were the two major sources of catalog information. In most libraries, original cataloging was done only when cataloging could not be found from a reputable source. And when the computer epoch began, it was a key requirement of the Library of Congress that the MARC format be capable of supporting the activities of the Card Division.

A major motivation behind the development of OCLC was the desire to begin the conversion of library collections to MARC-II records from the Library of Congress, while also filling the immediate need for catalog cards. OCLC accomplished this for its participants, and when LC cataloging was not available, its online cooperative cataloging minimized the amount of original cataloging needed. Part of the drive for the development of the Research

Libraries Information Network (RLIN) was the perceived need for a wider range of cataloging than was available through OCLC, joined with a concern for the performance of the OCLC network during its extremely rapid expansion. And in contrast to OCLC, authority control was an integral part of WLN, whose objective was to provide coherent cataloging of consistent quality. It was only after many years of operation that the WLN policy was revised to allow records to be added to the database that had not been put through authority control and full quality-control review.

Auto-Graphics did not have a catalog card phase, but became a library vendor from the publishing side. Their first large library publication was the book form of the University of California Union Catalog in 1972. Since that time, they have published both union and individual catalogs on microform, in CD-ROM, and in magnetic online catalogs.

The first product of The Library Corporation in the early 1970s was microfiche produced from LC MARC-II records and used to print catalog cards. Following that, the firm moved to providing CD-ROMs containing these records, together with software that printed cards or extracted the MARC-II records for other use. And from there, the firm began producing union catalog databases and supplying library automation software.

http://www.tlcdelivers.com/tlc/company/history.htm

Beginning in the 1960s and continuing on into the 1970s, the expansion of college and university campuses meant that whole libraries needed to be created in the space of twelve to thirty-six months. Abel responded to this need by contracting to provide opening day collections, that is, books processed to shelf-ready condition, sorted into shelf order, and with associated cataloging. There is a natural progression from providing opening day collections to ongoing provision of shelf-ready materials, together with MARC-II records processed to reflect these materials. This new form of outsourcing improved effectiveness by making a single order entry function to provide both the book in fully processed form and the associated cataloging. Although the volume of these integrated services continued to build, so that most of the academic vendors were offering shelf-ready books with cataloging by the end of the 1990s, traditional firm orders were still the most common form of purchasing.

Development of Contract Library Operations

In the progression of outsourcing of library services, the next step beyond contracting out technical services is to contract out the entire operation of the library. By the end of the 1970s, some federal libraries were operated under contract by private companies. For example, even though primarily concerned with computer systems development and integration, Informatics, Inc. set up a group to provide contract library operations to its government clients. And there was at least one time in the late 1980s, when NASA had libraries operated by the agency's employees, plus libraries operated by two different contractors. Some corporate libraries have also been operated under contract. For example, in 1999, the library of Dow Corporation was operated by GCI Information Services, Inc., which was purchased in 2000 by Stanley Associates, Inc.

http://www.stanleyassoc.com/Default.htm

Although this may have been the next logical step in outsourcing, no academic or public libraries that I am aware of that have been operated under contract.

Introduction and Growth of Electronic Products in Library Collections

Media for Storing Information

As soon as a new medium for storing information is developed, libraries incorporate that medium into their collections. As a result, during the decades of computer system development, libraries have collected punched cards, magnetic tapes, and most recently, CD-ROMs and high-capacity magnetic disks. For a time in the 1980s, it seemed that CD-ROMs in particular would be important for the storage of bibliographic tools. However, by the 1990s, the rapid development of the Internet had reduced their importance because the bibliographic tools could be held at a few locations that were easily kept current and accessed over the Internet. By the end of the 1990s, the primary importance of CD-ROMs was for archiving information from PCs, not for a library's bibliographic tools.

Introduction and Growth of Services to the Blind and Visually Impaired

Before the advent of the digital computer, books printed in the Braille alphabet were the primary method of delivering library service to the blind. The computer was hardly developed before Bell Labs began doing research into speech recognition and speech synthesis. Their initial focus was on spoken numbers because if they could recognize them with a high degree of reliability, then telephone handsets would not need dials and dialing errors would be eliminated. By the early 1960s, they were able to recognize spoken numbers with a satisfactory degree of reliability, but the power of the computers then available did not allow them to recognize the numbers in real time. That is, with the speed of computers at the time, it took about a day to recognize ten spoken numbers. By the end of the 1980s, PCs had been fitted with microphones and software that would allow the recognition of limited vocabularies. By the end of the 1990s, Corel's WordPerfect program incorporated speech recognition in its standard version. In spite of this progress, I am not aware of any library-specific applications that are yet capable of being driven by speech. However, research and development is continuing.

http://userwww.sfsu.edu/~swilson/emerging/artre488.voice.html

Practical use of speech synthesis by libraries had to wait until the 1970s, when the Kurzweil Reading Machine was developed. This was a print-to-speech reading machine, combining optical character recognition of scanned printed text, with text-to-speech synthesis. Essentially any book in a library's collection could be placed on the flatbed scanner and processed in real time. As a result, these machines represented a major breakthrough in library service to the blind. For the first time, virtually the entire collection became immediately accessible. In 1980, Ray Kurzweil sold Kurzweil Computer Products, Inc. to the Xerox Corporation, which continued the development and marketing of the Kurzweil Reading Machine. To create a new generation of reading technology, Ray Kurzweil started another company, Kurzweil Educational Systems, Inc. in 1996 and then sold it to Lernout & Hauspie (L&H) in 1998. As of this writing, L&H is continuing the development and supply of reading tools for the blind and those with reading difficulties.

http://www.ccs.neu.edu/home/elan/ray.html
http://www.kurzweiltech.com/raycv.htm
http://www.lhsl.com/kurzweil1000/
http://www.lhsl.com/kurzweil3000/

Introduction and Development—Automatic Indexing of Spoken Materials

To date, the indexing of spoken materials, for example, oral history tapes, has been manual. However, speech synthesis could be applied to this process. At the 1999 COMDEX, Dragon Systems, an L&H company, previewed AudioMining technology that uses voice recognition software to build an index of the text from an audio or video stream. Like other indexes, it gives a reference location so that the user can search on keywords and then jump to the relevant points in the original stream. It has normally been the case that products shown at COMDEX are pre-production versions. Therefore, it may be the case that this product was not in general release. As of this writing, this speech recognition capability has not been incorporated into a library application.

http://www.speech.cs.cmu.edu/comp.speech/
http://www.wired.com/news/mp3/0,1285,32628,00.html
http://www.lhsl.com/audiomining/

Introduction and Growth of Electronic Data Services

Shared Cataloging

Throughout the twentieth century, the Library of Congress fostered shared cataloging. Until the late 1960s, the National Union Catalog was the principal method of distributing shared cataloging. Following the successful development of the MARC-II format, LC began its MARC Distribution Service, distributing its new English language cataloging, approximately 100,000 titles per year. LC's commitment to supply these records provided a sound basis on which other organizations could develop computer-based shared cataloging. By the end of the twentieth century, LC's MARC Distribution Service covered almost all English-language imprints; it distributed cataloging from the national libraries of the United Kingdom, Australia, Canada, Japan, and Germany. It also provided some materials in hundreds of other languages and in some languages that do not use the Roman alphabet—Chinese, Hebrew, Japanese, and Korean.

http://lcweb.loc.gov/cds/
http://www.loc.gov/catalog/

Although numerous organizations began shared cataloging efforts, the following were probably the largest at the end of the century: OCLC, RLIN, and Auto-Graphics. OCLC (now Online Computer Library Center, Inc.) was founded in the late 1960s by the presidents of the colleges and universities in the state of Ohio as the Ohio College Library Center to develop a computerized system to share library resources and reduce costs. Frederick G. Kilgour was the first director and oversaw its successful growth from serving solely Ohio libraries to serving libraries worldwide. Much of the credit for the initial success of OCLC should go to the technical director, Phil Long. He successfully designed and implemented a custom operating system, a custom database, a custom cataloging terminal, and a custom communications protocol. At the time, it was the most efficient cataloging system, bar none. By the end of the century, OCLC had become an independent nonprofit organization providing information services to some 30,000 libraries throughout the world. Throughout OCLC's history, shared cataloging has been one of its most important activities. In 2000, the main database, WorldCat, contained over 750 million holdings representing 45 million different titles.

http://www.oclc.org/oclc/menu/history.htm
http://oclc.org/oclc/menu/home1.htm

The Research Libraries Group (RLG) was founded in the mid 1970s by Columbia, Harvard, and Yale Universities and The New York Public Library. James E. Skipper was RLG's first president and John F. Knapp, its first technical director. Its purpose was to improve access to information that supports research and learning. Subsequently, RLG developed the Research Libraries Information Network, RLIN, which first used Stanford University's SPIRES-BALLOTS bibliographic utility, itself based upon SPIRES. SPIRES was originally developed at Stanford for use at the Stanford Linear Accelerator Center (SLAC). If memory serves, SPIRES was developed under funding from the National Science Foundation. SPIRES's initial development predated the MARC-II format; however, it was subsequently modified to support the format when it became the SPIRES-BALLOTS database engine for the Stanford University libraries.

Although continually expanding in membership, RLG's focus has remained on large research libraries and on other libraries with specialized collections. Resource records for RLIN come from the Library of Congress, the National Library of Medicine, the National Libraries of Australia and Canada, the British Library, the U.S. Government Printing Office, the United Nations, and OCLC (preservation masters, CJK records). Individual members also provide original input. By 1998, RLG had an international membership with a union catalog of nearly 88 million items representing over 30 million different titles.

http://ublib.buffalo.edu/libraries/units/cts/olac/newsletters/march98.html
http://lyra.rlg.org/toc.html#toc
http://lyra.rlg.org/dtlpolicy.html
http://domin.dom.edu/students/mcgudenn/final_paper.htm

In addition to these not-for-profit membership organizations, shared cataloging was also supported by for-profit organizations. For example, Auto-Graphics was founded in the 1950s as a printing firm servicing publishers. In the 1960s, it moved into computer-based photocomposition, and then in the late 1960s, it expanded into computer input services for libraries. In the 1970s, it produced catalogs for libraries in printed and microform formats and then in the 1980s, moved to CD-ROM and online database formats. From the 1980s on, it provided regional online shared catalogs, for example, in Maine, Maryland, and Texas. Although most of participants in these regional catalogs were public and school (elementary and secondary) libraries, many academic libraries were also included. Libraries used the Auto-Graphics database for conversion as well as for sharing; for example, the California State Library recognized Auto-Graphics (in addition to OCLC, RLG, and WLN) as a reimbursable supplier of MARC records for libraries converting their collections.

In the late 1990s, Auto-Graphics formed A-G Canada Ltd. and purchased the Library Information Services Division (LIS) of ISM Information Systems Management Manitoba, formerly Utlas International. The University of Toronto designed, developed, and operated the University of Toronto

Library Automation System (UTLAS) in the early 1970s. It had features that made it an excellent system for both individual catalogs and shared cataloguing (or cataloging):

- Support for both USMARC and CANMARC formats (the latter has bilingual tagging and content)
- Hierarchical authority control—allowing libraries to use different authority records for the same shared bibliographic record
- Online real-time updates of its system
- Immediate downloads of identified MARC records

By the end of the century, Auto-Graphics reported that it had a database of over 57 million bibliographic and authority records from 2,500 libraries worldwide and that over 1 million people a day used its software to access library information.

http://www.auto-graphics.com/agcanadapr.html

Document Delivery

Throughout the twentieth century, the most common library use was for the library patron to obtain an item from the library's collection and then either use it in the library or borrow it for use elsewhere. To improve service to the libraries' patrons, interlibrary loan was developed to share materials among libraries. For example, the Library of Congress began lending its materials to other libraries in 1901. As different technologies became available, it was common for libraries to adapt them to improve their sharing activities. Thus, teletype, telephone, facsimile, and finally the computer were all pressed into service in support of sharing.

Although publishers sometimes saw libraries as a threat to their potential revenues, by midcentury, most publishers had revised this opinion and sometimes even viewed them as allies. For some publishers, this changed again after the Xerox Corporation radically reduced the cost of photocopying in the 1950s. At that point, libraries began to photocopy shorter works, particularly journal articles, instead of lending the entire bound volume. In addition to being less costly than lending the volume, it was also more effective because the volume continued to be available for other use. The availability throughout the society of relatively inexpensive, on-demand reproduction sent a shock wave through the publishing industry. After all, on-demand reproduction posed a direct threat to the revenue structure of the industry because a publisher's revenues were commonly based on the number of copies sold.

The publishing industry chose to sue to try to maintain their rights (and revenues) under copyright law in a changed technological environment. After much "Sturm und Drang," the U.S. government passed a new copyright law, the *Copyright Act of 1976*. Although some photocopying continued to be considered fair use, much of the copying on behalf of other libraries was not. To conform with the law, many libraries, particularly those supplying large photocopy volumes to other libraries, set up tracking of their photocopying and made arrangements for reimbursement of copyright holder(s).

http://www4.law.cornell.edu/uscode/17/
http://www.benedict.com/

Following the passage of revised copyright laws in the 1970s, publishers and other interested parties worked on the development of organizations to operate as middlemen in the process of providing text reproduction permission and collecting and redistributing royalty revenues. By the end of the 1980s, these centers were called Reproduction Rights Organisations (sic), and an independent not-for-profit association, the International Federation of Reproduction Rights Organisations (IFRRO), was set up as a formal federation eligible to speak on behalf of its constituents before various international bodies. By the end of the century, IFRRO had twenty-one full members. The U.S. member, Copyright Clearance Center, Inc., managed rights relating to more than 1.75 million works from about 10,000 publishers and distributed to more than 10,000 licensed customers in the United States.

http://www.ifrro.org/
http://www.copyright.com/
http://www.mcgrawhill.ca/copyrightlaw/collect.html

In the 1980s and 1990s, the developing electronic information environment continued to present new problems for protecting authors and publishers in the United States and other nations. In Europe, protection of intellectual property can be traced back to the 1883 Paris Convention for the Protection of Industrial Property and the 1886 Berne Convention for the Protection of Literary and Artistic Works. These international treaties were intended to protect patents, trademarks, industrial designs, writing, music, and art. The United International Bureau for the Protection of Intellectual Property (BIRPI) was set up to administer these treaties at the end of the nineteenth century. In the 1970s, BIRPI was transmuted into the World Intellectual Property Organization (WIPO); subsequently, WIPO became a specialized agency of the United Nations, administering intellectual property matters recognized by the UN member states. By the end of the century, WIPO had 175 member states from eighty-three countries.

http://www.wipo.int/
http://www.wipo.int/about-wipo/en/index.html?wipo_content_frame=/about-wipo/en/gib.htm

During the 1990s, there was continuous pressure on the U.S. government to increase and clarify copyright protection in the electronic environment, as well as to bring the protection into correspondence with European law. For example, copyright holders wanted an extension of the term of protection from life of the author plus fifty years to life plus seventy years, the law in European nations. Authors in the United States would then receive full protection of European law. Another concern was to limit the liability of the Internet service providers for any infringements resulting from materials placed in their systems by their subscribers. At the same time, libraries and academic institutions had other concerns. Libraries wanted to make digital as well as facsimile copies and did not want to have their usage curtailed due to longer periods of protection, while academic institutions wished to facilitate, not impede, distance education via the Internet.

In late 1998, the U.S. Congress passed two new copyright laws, the *Sonny Bono Copyright Term Extension Act* and the *Digital Millennium Copyright Act* (DMCA). The Term Extension Act extended copyright protection by twenty years in order to bring it into conformance with European laws. The DCMA also had the title *WIPO Copyright and Performances and Phonograms Treaties Implementation Act of 1998*. This law:

- Restricted devices or processes to overcome a copyright owners technology to limit access
- Limited the liability of Internet service providers for copyright infringement in which they had no knowledge
- Permitted libraries and archival institutions to preserve materials in digital formats

This law left a number of issues up in the air, especially database protection, fair use, and distance education. Database protection was removed from the final bill with the understanding that it would be addressed by the Congress in 1999. Distance education was to be studied by the Copyright Office and a report made to Congress by April 28, 1999.

http://lcweb.loc.gov/copyright/
http://www.lib.umich.edu/libhome/copyright/dmca.html
http://arl.cni.org/info/frn/copy/dmca.html
http://arl.cni.org/info/frn/copy/primer.html
http://www.law.nyu.edu/engelbergcenter/legislativewatchnational/wipotreaty.html

As this paper was being written, the 106th Congress was considering two measures to provide electronic database protection: the Consumer and Investor Access to Information Act of 1999 (HR 1858) and the Collections of Information Antipiracy Act (HR 354). At that time it was unclear whether either would make it into law.

http://www.nhalliance.org/ip/
http://www.perkinsgroup.net/articles/0003.htm

In the arguments over copyright, authors and publishers sometimes disagreed. For example, authors began to feel that they were not being fully compensated by the publishers for republication in electronic formats. *Tasini v. The New York Times* was a lawsuit brought by members of the National Writers Union against The New York Times Company, Newsday Inc., Time Inc., LexisNexis, and University Microfilms Inc. It charged copyright violation regarding the electronic reuse of work produced and sold on a freelance basis. On appeal in 1999, the case was decided in favor of the writers: a publisher may not put a freelancer's work on-line or otherwise reuse or resell it without explicit written permission. In 1999, the National Writers Union set up a Publication Rights Clearinghouse (PRC) similar to the music industry's ASCAP, to license electronic rights to publishers, and to receive and distribute revenues, both for new articles and for material previously put on-line. In April 2000, the U.S. Court of Appeals denied publishers' request for a rehearing of the case. The case eventually went to the U.S. Supreme Court and was decided in June 2001, with the Court upholding a September 1999 unanimous ruling by the U.S. Court of Appeals, Second Circuit, which found that the *New York Times* and other publishers had committed copyright infringement when they resold freelance newspaper and magazine articles without the authors' permission or paying additional fees, via electronic databases such as LexisNexis.

http://www.nwu.org/tvt/tvthome.htm
http://www.nwu.org//prc/prchome.htm

While all of the arguments were being made about protection of intellectual property, the library community continued to improve document delivery. From the beginning, shared online catalogs were intended to make more effective the sharing of materials located in other libraries. It was envisioned that online catalogs would increase the speed and reduce the cost both of determining where desired material was held and of requesting the material. From the volume of use, it certainly appears that online catalogs had the desired effect. By the end of the 1990s, OCLC was being used to arrange 8 million interlibrary loans annually. The Library of Congress, which operated as a library of last resort (i.e., libraries were supposed to borrow from other libraries wherever possible), handled more than 40,000 requests a year, four-fifths of them transferred electronically from OCLC and RLIN.

http://oclc.org/oclc/ar96/oluc.htm
http://oclc.org/oclc/press/20001023a.htm
http://libws66.lib.niu.edu/libstats/NATIONAL.HTM

Libraries in Canada and the United Kingdom also used their online systems to enhance their sharing programs. By the end of the 1990s, Canadian libraries were borrowing 1 million items annually from other libraries. In the United Kingdom, there were 1.3 million interlibrary loans annually. The British Library Document Supply Centre (BLDSC) developed as one of the leading document providers in the world. Virtually all of the collection of 3 million English-language books was available via interlibrary loan. It should be noted that there was a cost for this service. For example, in April 2000, a registered U.S. customer could obtain a four-week loan (from date of receipt and shipped via airmail) for $21.25.

http://209.217.90.93/top/whatsnew/libraries/010300libs6.htm
http://www.lboro.ac.uk/departments/dils/lisu/about.html
http://www.lboro.ac.uk/departments/dils/lisu/list98/gen.html
http://www.bl.uk/
http://www.oclc.org/oclc/new/n232/mem_80mil_ill.htm
http://library.ukc.ac.uk/library/papers/jwts/d-journal.htm

Indexing

Throughout the twentieth century, there were different levels of access to monographs and to serials. Traditional access to monographs was provided by the catalog record, which described the entire work. In the United States, it was usual to assign a single classification number and as few subject headings as possible to reflect only the major topics of the work. Although this level of access may have been acceptable for monographs, it was inadequate for serial publications, especially journals and periodicals. To fill the need for improved access, indexes to these materials were developed and published. First, the publishers of the journals began to provide indexes to their publications and include them as part of the subscriptions. Then, other organizations began to publish combined indexes that covered a group of journals, in broad subject areas. The best-known general index was *The Reader's Guide to Periodical Literature*; publication began in the late nineteenth century and continued throughout the twentieth century. Early in the twentieth century, the American Chemical Society (ACS) began publishing *Chemical Abstracts*. This publication went beyond assigning index terms to journal articles and provided abstracts for these articles. As computers became practical for text manipulation, it was natural for ACS, as well as the index publishers, to apply them to index production and maintenance. And as with catalogs, the next step after that was setting up online access to the index databases. At the end of the century, ACS had a strong publishing program, providing online access to members and to the general public.

http://www.acs.org/

The beginning of large-scale funding for medical and health sciences research by the U.S. government predated Sputnik. Although there were predecessor organizations dating back to the nineteenth century, in the late 1940s, the size and scope of the National Institutes of Health (NIH) was changed dramatically. The NIH was given a dual responsibility: to carry on its own research and to providing funding to the rest of the medical (later called health sciences) research community. To give some sample numbers for the expansion: from 1947 to 1957, the grants program went from just over $4 million to over $100 million, and from 1947 to 1966, the overall budget of NIH went from $8 million to over $1 billion.

http://www.nih.gov/
http://www.nih.gov/od/museum/exhibits/history/full-text.html

The increased research in the 1950s led both to increased production of research literature and increased demand for retrieval of relevant information. In turn, this created a demand for automatic alternatives to indexing and abstracting, alternatives that could operate directly from the text of the articles, bypassing the manual tasks that required specialized training. To respond to this demand, permuted title indexes were created—by "permuting" the title and using each of the title words as an index entry. Later, this same process was applied to the body of the text. I think it was H.P. Luhn of IBM who coined the names "key word in context" (KWIC) and "key word out of context" (KWOC) indexes to refer to these indexes. Once the idea was formulated in this manner, it became increasingly common to use the actual words of the text for indexing and searching. At the end of the century, most of the Internet search engines were using simple matching of terms in the document (e.g., the Web page) with the terms in the search specification.

The National Library of Medicine (NLM), whose roots trace to the founding of the library of the surgeon general of the Army in 1836, was one of the pressure centers during this expansion of medical research, publication, and dissemination. The interest in improving the health of the nation had been translated into government funding of research at levels that had never been seen other than for national defense. One of the responses was to produce Index Medicus, which provided increased access to medical literature. In the 1960s, NLM was funded at a level that allowed it to pursue a strategy of providing online access to health sciences information. In addition to its government funding, NLM was legally authorized to charge for its information services. As a result, it could, and did, set up differential fee structures that gave it some cost recovery, as well as feedback on the usefulness of its information services to the health community. The NLM developed the MEDical Literature Analysis and Retrieval System (MEDLARS). This system provided both the database content for the production of Index Medicus and the initial system for automated retrieval. A new indexing controlled vocabulary was at the heart of the system: MEdical Subject Headings (MESH). MESH provided terms at different levels of specificity and contained explicit pointers to more detailed and to more general terms. The NLM's indexing strategy was changed to increase the number of index terms applied to a document, so that all applicable terms, at all levels of specificity, were to be applied. At the end of the century, this library continued its preeminence in providing access to medical and health sciences literature. For example, it made its MEDLINE database of 11 million references and abstracts available for free searching via the Internet.

http://www.nlm.nih.gov/

In the late 1950s, Eugene Garfield formed a new company, the Institute for Scientific Communication (ISI) and brought the concept of citation index-ing from the literature of law to the literature of science and technology. Because of the importance of precedent in American law, citation indexes were produced to allow legal researchers to move forward in time, finding cases that commonly cited one or more prior cases. This same concept is useful in science and technology: if a searcher finds an item of interest, then any other item citing that item has a strong chance of being of interest as well. This adaptation, followed by many years of hard work, resulted in the suc-cessful commercial development of the Science Citation Index, as well as other computer-based information products. At the end of the century, ISI was a subsidiary of the Thompson Group and Science Citation Index covered more than 3,800 journals and serials.

http://www.garfield.library.upenn.edu/overvu.html
http://www.isinet.com/
http://www.isinet.com/isi/about/timeline

By the mid 1960s, many computer-based indexes were being developed— many of them with unique structures and search procedures. Anyone requir-ing cross-disciplinary information (e.g., almost anyone engaged in govern-ment-sponsored research) had to either learn multiple search systems or engage an information specialist who kept up to date on these systems. Roger Summit at Lockheed obtained government funding to develop a new system, Dialog, which used the same search procedures to search disparate indexes obtained from their producers. Once operational, Dialog was avail-able online to researchers working under government funding throughout the country. Dialog became the "lingua franca" to replace the "Tower of Babel" of the individual indexes and search systems. As use of Dialog increased, the support shifted from direct government subsidy to cost recovery through fees charged to the users. Later, Dialog was sold by Lockheed; it was operating as an independent corporation at the end of the century; and in 2000, the Information Services Division was sold to Thomson Corporation. Whatever its corporate configuration, Dialog was one of the important suppliers of information access from its inception through the rest of the century.

http://www.pa.utulsa.edu/nfais/miles.d/1996.html
http://www.dialog.com/
http://www.exo.net/ref/uce/revisions/note1.htm

Given the importance of precedent (i.e., the decisions made in prior similar cases) to the U.S. legal system, one might have predicted that the legal community would have provided early support to apply computers to the organization and search of legal information. Even though there was automation of the processes of publishing case law, there was not the level of interest or the breadth of investment that existed in the scientific and technical fields. In retrospect, this seems more reasonable than it did at the time. First, there was no huge increase in government funding driving the legal community as it did the defense and health communities. And second, the legal community has its intellectual roots in the liberal arts, and it values in maintaining consistency with the past. In contrast, the defense and health communities are rooted in science and technology and value innovation, that is, breaking with the past.

In this environment, the work of the Mead Corporation to create practical online search of legal information is impressive indeed. The Mead Corporation was an early user of computers for manufacturing and process control as well as for business information. As a result, Mead had a close working relationship with National Cash Register, a near neighbor, and, at the time, a strong competitor to IBM in some areas of computing. Due to the nature of its business, Mead had a substantial legal department, so the costs and results of its legal activities were of interest at the highest levels of the company. In the late 1960s, Mead undertook the development of LEXIS, an online system providing direct text searching of case law. Although the system became operational in the early 1970s, it was not an immediate commercial success. Part of the problem appeared to be the high initial cost required, for example, specialized terminals were required that were used only for LEXIS. Some of the problem may also have been due to the financial structure of legal services. LEXIS provided the potential of less expensive legal searching, but under the usual billing structure of legal services, the staff costs (including overhead and profit margins) for searching were billed directly to the client. Therefore, LEXIS presented legal firms with the problem of how to reduce their clients' costs and at the same time, retain their own profit margins. In spite of such problems, Mead persisted, and the second version of the product was a technical and commercial success. For a time, Mead virtually cornered the market for online access to legal information. Like Lockheed and Dialog, Mead ultimately sold LEXIS and its other legal products. At the end of the century, LexisNexis was a division of Reed Elsevier, Inc. It reported over 2 billion documents available for searching in over 11 thousand databases, with 700 thousand daily searches by 2 million subscribers.

http://www.law.du.edu/coall/bintliff.htm
http://www.colorado.edu/Law/lawlib/ts/legpub.htm
http://www.lexis-nexis.com/lncc/

By the end of the twentieth century, academic law libraries had already been strongly affected by the availability of on-line legal information. For example, at the website for the University of Denver College of Law, the collection and services of the Westminster Law Library were described as follows: " . . . resources from heavy tomes of knowledge to lightning-fast, on-line data. And if we don't have it right at your fingertips, we can get it through interlibrary loan. No matter what you need, you can count on us to help you find it." On another page, it described the database access available, and listed more than eighteen access points for everything from Encyclopedia Britannica to LexisNexis and Westlaw and stated that access to the databases was available from home or work.

http://www.law.du.edu/lib/index.html

From ARPANET to Internet

The technological heart of the Internet began in 1960, with Paul Baran's work at the Rand Corporation. He was addressing the problem of how to achieve reliable communications under conditions of system failures. He put forward the notion of developing redundant communications networks (that is, networks with more than one path between the origin and destination points) and then sending the messages divided into transmission packets. Each of the packets would contain standard header information: the destination of the packet, its origin, its sequence number, and the total number of packets in the message. This structure allowed redundant transmission of the same packets over the network, with the packets taking different routes through the network. The destination unit receiving the packets acknowledged receipt of undamaged packets and assembled them into correct order. If the sending unit did not receive an acknowledgment for a packet within a reasonable period, it would re-send the packet. As a result, as long as some path existed between two points, a message could be sent between them—and the sender could know that it was received successfully.

Baran's solution was brilliant—it separated an intractable problem into simpler components, each solvable with existing technology. It is hard to convey how radical this solution seemed to the professionals in the telecommunications industry at the time because computers and associated concepts have become such an integral part of our society. However, at that time, digital telecommunications did not exist; instead, the telecommunications systems were analog, and there was little understanding of the concepts on which digital computers were based. Of course, the people in Bell Labs had been working with computers since they were first developed, but that was Bell Labs, not the rest of AT&T. In addition to the conceptual gap, there was the very real problem that the analog telephone system represented a huge investment that had been made over a fifty-year period. Although the superiority of packet switching had been recognized, and packet switching networks were in common use by the end of the century, analog communication was not totally obsolete. For example, analog systems were the first mobile cellular telephone systems installed, and some regions of the country still did not have digital cellular service (indeed, many areas still had none). And although most of the long-distance services were digital, most local connections to private residences were still analog. The handsets in use were analog, and modems (i.e., Modulator-DEModulators converting analog to digital and back) were commonly used to connect computers to the switched voice network of the telephone system.

Given the reluctance of the telecommunications community, it was nearly a decade before Baran's ideas were put to the test. In 1969, the Advanced Projects Research Agency (ARPA) set up the first network based upon Baran's concepts, ARPANET. ARPANET connected Stanford Research Institute; the University of California, Los Angeles; University of California, Santa Barbara; and the University of Utah. Its connections expanded throughout the 1970s, primarily in the university computer research community and in institutions engaged in defense-related research. At that time, ARPANET was used as a research vehicle for studying the organization of computer networks. Beyond that, it was of limited utility because a researcher had to want access to information maintained on a computer at one of the other network sites. Since rapid remote access to large-scale computer files had never before been available, researchers did not immediately re-organize their work to take advantage of this capability.

In the late 1960s, Xerox decided to enter the computer business. As part of this strategy, the corporation set up a long-range research group, the Palo Alto Research Center (PARC). Although Xerox did not become a dominant company in the computer field, the innovations at PARC laid out the direction of development for individual workstations and networks through the end of the century. Bob Metcalfe, one of the PARC researchers, defined a transmission technique, carrier sense multiple access/collision detection (CSMA/CD), that he called Ethernet. Ethernet is a "free-for-all" transmission method that doesn't depend on any central control or synchronization of the message traffic. Should signals collide, making them impossible to decode correctly, they are retransmitted. Network interface cards (NICs) using the Ethernet protocol were immediately important for communications between computers. Metcalfe left PARC and formed 3COM to manufacture network equipment, particularly Ethernet NICs. By the late 1980s, Ethernet cards were the dominant NICs. It's interesting to note that in the late 1990s, Metcalfe pointed out that Internet traffic had expanded to the point that a new transmission protocol was needed; otherwise, further growth would be severely limited. At the end of the century, a new standard had not been defined, and the Internet has continued to grow rapidly. The forecast capacity problem was put off primarily through the use of faster equipment. For example, when Metcalfe defined the Ethernet, the transmission speed of the individual card was 1 or 2 mbps (million bits per second). By the beginning of the 1990s, standard NICs were 10 mbps. By the end of the century, the least expensive network PCs were supplied with standard 10/100 mbps NICs for less than $100, and those users wanting higher performance could buy giga-bit (trillion bits per second) NICs for less than $900 (3COM: 3C985B-SX).

During the 1970s, the language for discussing network communications between computers was refined by separating the communications process into layers. The bottom layer was the hardware layer, and it was this layer that CSMA/CD operated, translating a message into electronic signals to be sent out or decoding an incoming signal into a digital packet and forwarding it to the next layer. At the next layer, the Transport Control Protocol (TCP) and the Internet Protocol were defined. Then in the 1980s, these two definitions (TCP/IP) were adopted by ARPA as the standard for communication on ARPANET. Given its position as the premier network for connecting computers, this became the de facto standard for Ethernet networks.

In the 1980s, the universities became restive. By then, it was reasonably clear to academic administrators that networks represented the future of computing. At the same time, ARPANET was considered expensive, and it was felt that a network was needed that was not so closely tied to defense research. Several small networks were tried out, but the National Science Foundation (NSF) brought these independent efforts back into a common network by setting up a "high-speed backbone," NSFNET, between the NSF-funded supercomputer sites and then allowing other networks to connect to this backbone. Thus, all computers connected to a network that was connected to the backbone were automatically able to communicate with each other.

By the end of the 1980s, the term "Internet" had entered the common vocabulary of computer users to refer to the network of networks that had resulted from NSF's action. At that time, there were about 100,000 computers acting as hosts—that is, computers whose data and/or programs were being made available to other computers on the network. Two applications generated most of the interest and drove the expansion: e-mail and newsgroups. While e-mail was an improvement of an existing service (teletype), newsgroups represented an entirely new method of communication. Members of a newsgroup did not need to know each other, yet they could share information, ask questions, and provide answers to (or comment on) questions asked previously. Thus, newsgroups had aspects of both broadcast and point-to-point communications. That is, one could send one message that could get to all users (like broadcast), but those users could also reply (as with point to point). At the end of the century, both e-mail and newsgroups were important, standard fare of the Internet. For example, ACQNET has been a boon for the communications of acquisitions librarians. It is a controlled newsgroup for the exchange of acquisitions-related information and ideas. This newsgroup started with a group of twenty-five librarians in 1990 and had more than 1,700 subscribers by the end of the decade.

http://hegel.lib.ncsu.edu/stacks/serials/acqnet/
http://hegel.lib.ncsu.edu/stacks/serials/acqnet/acq-about.txt

The 1990s were the decade of the World Wide Web and the entry of for-profit companies to the Internet. Tim Berners-Lee, at the CERN physics laboratory, is credited with the definition of the World Wide Web (WWW or simply the Web) and for the first "browser" program displaying the data encoded using the Web standards. Until the appearance of the Web, Internet applications were mostly character-oriented and driven by a standard computer keyboard. The Web standards used the HyperText Markup Language (HTML) and made it easy to mix character and graphic data and to use mouse clicks to move between Web pages, each separately addressable. Berners-Lee then followed up with the development of the Wide World Web Consortium (W3C) to provide an open forum for discussion and to lead the continuing technical evolution of the Web.

http://www.3com.com/
http://www.w3.org/People/Berners-Lee/
http://www.w3.org/

The National Center for Supercomputing Applications (NCSA) at the University of Illinois was immediately interested in the Web and set up a project to develop a browser. Marc Andreason is the person most closely associated with the development of this public-domain Web client, NCSA Mosaic, which became the first widely used Web browser. Andreason subsequently left NCSA and was one of the founders of Netscape, Inc. In the mid 1990s, Netscape was responsible for about three-fourths of all Web browsers in use. In 1995, Microsoft released their 32-bit operating system, Windows 95 and included their Web browser, Internet Explorer, as a component of the operating system. Although this may have been the last straw for the U.S. government, which filed suit against Microsoft under antitrust law, it also had the effect of focusing Microsoft's future development on Internet-related computing. At the end of the century, although the first court had found for the government, the case was still on appeal, and it was likely that it would be appealed to the Supreme Court before it was finally resolved. And at that time, Microsoft's Internet Explorer was the most commonly used browser. Also, by the end of the century, AOL had purchased Netscape, and then merged with Time Warner, Inc. (although that merger was still under antitrust review).

http://www.ncsa.uiuc.edu/SDG/Software/Mosaic/Docs/help-about.html
http://www.darien.lib.ct.us/webclass/timeline/part1.htm
http://www.darien.lib.ct.us/webclass/timeline/part2.htm
http://www.darien.lib.ct.us/webclass/timeline/part3.htm
http://www.gwu.edu/~etlsl20/inet_refer.htm
http://info.isoc.org/guest/zakon/Internet/History/HIT.html

In 1991, NSF removed the restrictions on commercial use of the Internet. This was a major stimulus to the growth of the Internet into areas having little or nothing to do with science. This growth, in turn, greatly expanded the Internet administrative duties. Throughout the 1990s, steps were made to transfer the administration of the Internet away from NSF and to other more appropriately structured bodies, thereby allowing NSF to return to its traditional focus on science. By its nature, control of the Internet is very limited. It consists primarily of setting technical standards for connections to the Internet and assigning and maintaining address information about the Internet participants. Doubtless the arrangement and scope of the organizations was logical, but there is some difficulty in tracking the sequence of organizations and the scope of their activities. For present purposes, it is enough to list some of these organizations and indicate the nature of their activities:

- Internet Society (ISOC) coordinated use of some applications and protocols.
- Internet Engineering Task Force (IETF) defined the Internet Protocol Suite.
- Internet Assigned Number Authority (IANA) was chartered by the ISOC and the Federal Networking Council and was the central coordinator for the assignment of IP addresses and management of the Root Domain Name Service.

- Council of Registrars (CORE) provided international governance framework for policies related to administration and enhancement of the Internet's global Domain Name System (DNS).
- Network Information Centers (NIC) performed Domain Names assignment.
- Commercial Internet exchange was a trade organization of commercial Internet providers.
- Internet Corporation for Assigned Names and Numbers (ICANN) controlled space allocation for IP addresses, assigning protocol parameters, and managing domain names.

Three Supporting Organizations (SOs) were set up to develop Internet policy and structure recommendations in the following areas:

- Address Supporting Organization for the system of IP addresses uniquely identifying the Internet's networked computers;
- Domain Name Supporting Organization for the domain name system (DNS) used to identify Internet resources and translating them into IP addresses for specific computers; and
- Protocol Supporting Organization for the technical standards that let computers exchange information and manage communications over the Internet.

http://backofficesystems.com/tips/internet/backbone.htm
http://www.icann.org/general/abouticann.htm
http://www.icann.org/support-orgs.htm

By the end of the century, the Internet had grown and changed to such an extent that measures previously used to indicate its size were no longer useful. For example, at the end of the 1980s, perhaps 200,000 computers were connected to the Internet. In the following ten years, huge numbers of personal computers were connected to the Internet, both through the local networks of individual institutions and through dial-up connections to Internet Service Providers (ISPs). At the end of the century, the number of computers connected to the Internet at any given moment was probably more than 1 million and less than 100 million.[8] As another measure of size, the Internet Software Consortium sponsored The Domain Survey, which searched the Domain Name System (DNS) to find every host on the Internet, that is, every name set up as a host to provide one or more services to other computers on the Internet. At the beginning of 1999, the survey identified 43 million hosts advertised in the DNS. One year later, the number had grown to more than 72 million, giving an increase of nearly 30 million named hosts, a growth rate of more than 70 percent in the last year of the century. There were 24 million commercial (.com) hosts, representing one-third of the total hosts.

Although numbers such as these indicate that the Internet was continuing to grow rapidly, they do not show the growth of those hosts actually connected to the Internet and ready to provide service. At the beginning of 1999, the Domain Survey "pinged"[9] a sample of the hosts identified, and only one-fifth responded to the ping. Unfortunately, the survey did not also ping the hosts in 2000. But given the DNS numbers, there were probably between 9– and 10 million hosts providing service on the Internet at the end of the century. Because many of the commercial names were being reserved for future use, there were probably no more than 4 million, but surely more than 1 million commercial hosts online at the end of the century!

http://www.stevens-tech.edu/~chose/history.html
http://www.isc.org/ds/
http://www.isc.org/ds/WWW-200007/index.html

The growth of the Internet, particularly in the 1990s, changed it from a limited information resource to one of great importance to virtually everyone. But just as a library's collection must be cataloged or indexed to be useful, so too, it was necessary to develop methods for "cataloging" the Internet. The major response was the development of search engines. The appearance to the Internet user of these search engines was similar to search interfaces commonly used for keyword searching in online database systems and in catalog systems. The critically different portion of the search engine was the part that provided the index structure to be searched. In advance of specific searches, the search engines routinely found new or changed pages on the Internet and automatically indexed these pages according to the rules used by the particular engine. Normally, search engines were searching for and indexing the content found on host computers on the Internet. At least one website, Pointera.com, blurred the line between host and client computers on the Internet by providing a service of indexing the content of client computers. At the end of the century, it was unclear whether a sufficient number of users would want to make their content partially available through a service of this nature, but if so, it would expand the number of potential information sites into the hundreds of millions of computers.

http://www.access-search-engines.com/
http://www.pointera.com/
http://ixquick.com/
http://www.asis.org/annual-96/ElectronicProceedings/chu.html

Electronic Journals

Throughout the twentieth century, there was relentless pressure to reduce the time between the authoring of a work and the publication of that work to the interested public. Even before the advent of computers, this pressure resulted in reducing the size of the individual work and focusing relatively more attention on journal publication and less upon monographs. As the Internet became more generally available in the academic community, it was natural to move to the electronic publication of journals, especially those concerned with science and technology. During the 1990s, it was unclear how electronic journals would be delivered to end users—the readers of the journal articles. Access to full-text journal articles was a logical extension to the searching already provided by the database vendors such as Dialog, LexisNexis, and others. But they were not alone in their wish to have a position in this distribution. Most academic libraries had worked with a few subscriptions agents to purchase their print journal subscriptions through annual subscriptions, the issues of which were then shipped direct from the publishers. Would this same model obtain with respect to electronic journals? The subscription agents were certainly interested in maintaining a position in the sale of subscriptions to electronic journals. To that end, various strategic arrangements were tried. For example, EBSCO and OCLC undertook a joint development to provide articles from 1,000 general interest journal titles. At that same time, OCLC introduced its Electronic Journals Online (EJO) service with Applied Physics Letters and also entered a joint marketing arrangement with Elsevier Science for electronic delivery of all of its titles.

http://www.oclc.org/oclc/new/9274rn26/9274rna.htm
http://www.epnet.com/
http://www.rowe.com/

At the end of the century, it was still an open issue whether there would be a fee for access to online journals or whether it would be free, and the costs of providing access would be covered in some other manner. For example, the American Association for the Advancement of Science (AAAS) produced a weekly *Science Online* in addition to its printed *Science* magazine. Members of AAAS received the print version as part of their basic membership, but obtained full access to the online version only by paying an additional annual fee of $12. By contrast, *British Medical Journal* (BMJ) chose to make access to its entire website, including archive searching, free to all.

http://www.aaas.org/
http://www.bmj.com/misc/subs.shtml

Electronic Monographs

As was mentioned earlier, publishers began using computers in the 1960s. Even so, new monographs in electronic format were relatively slow to make their debut. There were both business and technical concerns that contributed to this. The two primary business concerns were, first, how to avoid large-scale theft in the electronic environment, and second, how to price for the one-time display of the book. The technical concerns were primarily concerned with developing an electronic device that people would actually prefer to a printed book. These issues were not resolved by the end of the century.

In the late 1990s, netLibrary began a program for online access to scholarly and academic press books. Their approach was interesting because it concentrated on a class of books with very specific characteristics. First, these books have a relatively narrow market, primarily academic institutions and research organizations. As a result, netLibrary's pricing and marketing could be narrowly focused on these institutions. And second, use of these books within these institutions tends to have an educational or professional purpose; therefore, the relative inconvenience of reading a book on a computer monitor is less important than it would be for discretionary use. NetLibrary chose to sell access to the electronic books on a subscription basis and used a circulation model for its pricing. That is, when a client is using a particular book, it is "on loan" and thus unavailable for use until that client is finished. This means that if an institution signed up for a single "copy" of the collection, then one and only one client could use a given work at a given time. If two "copies" were purchased, then two clients could use the same work at the same time. By 2000, netLibrary was providing access to some 10,000 books under these arrangements. Other vendors, for example, Ingram, were watching netLibrary to see what success they might experience with this approach and gearing up to compete if it proved successful. Not surprisingly, publishers took the approach of working with all interested distributors (rather as they did with print media).

http://www.netlibrary.com/
http://www.lightningsource.com
http://www.wiley.com/about/corpnews/netlibrary2.html
http://som.csudh.edu/depts/cis/lpress/articles/ebook.htm

Electronic Archives

Electronic publishing of journals and monographs in high demand—essentially, new materials—is all very well, but what of all of the past printed publications, what was to become of them? Soon after computers began to be used for text manipulation, books began to be converted to computer form. Later, they were placed in electronic archives from which they could be made accessible. One of the first of these efforts began in the late 1950s as a byproduct of the French government's decision to have created a new dictionary of the French language. To support this program by providing a database of word samples, a selection of French texts was converted to computer form.

In the early 1980s, a joint project was established between the Centre National de la Recherche Scientifique and the University of Chicago, the American and French Research on the Treasury of the French Language (ARTFL). This collaboration continued, and by the end of the century, ARTFL had a website available to subscribers and gave access to a database of nearly 2,000 works that ranged from medieval texts to current science.

http://humanities.uchicago.edu/ARTFL/artfl.flyer.html

Project Gutenberg was the pioneer of public-domain e-books and is the oldest publisher of such texts in the world. The project began in 1971, when Michael Hart was granted $100,000,000 worth of hours of time on the main-frame computer at the University of Illinois' Materials Research Laboratory. As described in the history and philosophy section of the project's website, Hart's insight was that he could best use this time for the "storage, retrieval, and searching of what was stored in our libraries." Hart based the project on the premise that whatever could be entered into a computer could be "repro-duced indefinitely," what he termed "Replicator Technology." The first doc-ument entered was the *Declaration of Independence.*

Hart is now the project's executive director, but it flourishes based on the efforts of many people. Relying on volunteers to identify, scan in, and proof-read public-domain works, the project had over 2,000 e-texts at the end of the century. Essential to the project's philosophy is the notion that the texts should be freely available to as many people as possible; thus, format is a key variable. Project Gutenberg uses "Plain Vanilla ASCII"; this permits an esti-mated 99 percent of computer users to have access to the material. The goal is to make the site easy to use—to read, to search, and to quote.

The texts chosen fall into three categories, termed:

• Light literature, such as *Alice in Wonderland*
• Heavy literature, such as the works of William Shakespeare
• Reference, such as *Roget's Thesaurus*

The project does not aim to include authoritative texts nor does it seek the esoteric; rather, the emphasis is on what a large percentage of the audience will find useful. Users may access the project through several URLs: the best starting point is its official home page lists all of the publications to date.

http://promo.net/pg/

ftp://metalab.unc.edu/pub/docs/books/gutenberg/GUTINDEX.ALL

Though Project Gutenberg was the first major effort to provide free access to books in the public domain, by the end of the century, there were other websites that were also providing free access. The following are some of the sites that were linked from the Tulane University Library:

http://www.lib.ncsu.edu/stacks/alex-index.html
>   Alex: Catalog of Electronic Texts on the Internet

http://etext.lib.virginia.edu
>   Electronic Text Center (University of Virginia)

http://digital.library.upenn.edu/books/
>   The Online Books Page

http://ota.ahds.ac.uk/
>   Oxford Text Archive

http://www.perseus.tufts.edu/
>   Perseus Project

http://www.bartleby.com
>   Bartleby Library

>   http://www.tulane.edu/~html/tulaweb/book.htm

In contrast to Project Gutenberg, whose initial objective was to make books freely available as widely and inexpensively as possible, the original purpose of the project that became the not-for-profit organization, JSTOR, in 1995 was to reduce the library space requirement for universities holding serial backfiles, thereby reducing capital and operating costs. This idea was developed by William G. Bowen, president of The Andrew W. Mellon Foundation, which then funded a pilot project to convert the backfiles of ten journals in economics and history into electronic formats. Some three-quarters of a million pages were scanned into 600 dpi (dots per inch) bit-mapped images. OCR software was used to generate computer text from these page images; the text was then loaded into a searchable database. With both the bit-mapped images and the database, an individual could remotely search and find desired material and then have that material displayed in its original printed page format.[10]

In 2000, JSTOR provided access to its collections by providing site licenses to more than 800 academic institutions, four-fifths of them in the United States. Initial and ongoing annual fees were based upon the size of the institution and the collections to which access was to be provided. For access to the Arts and Sciences I collection, the smallest institution was charged an initial fee of $10,000 and an annual fee of $2,000; the largest institution, $45,000 and $8,500, respectively.[11]

JSTOR worked with the publishers of the journals covered in order to establish the time delay between publication of the print version and the appearance of that issue in the JSTOR archive, usually from three to five years. JSTORE's Arts and Sciences I collection had complete runs of 117 titles in fifteen disciplines; two additional collections were in preparation: General Science and Ecology and Botany.

http://www.jstor.org/about/background.html
http://www.jstor.org/about/phaseI.pricing.html

At the same time that JSTOR was being incorporated, The Johns Hopkins University Press (JHUP) and the Milton S. Eisenhower Library at The Johns Hopkins University launched Project MUSE, to offer the full text of JHUP journals via the Web. In contrast to JSTOR, the Project MUSE was set up to make the journal articles available as soon as they're published—the archive would be built by keeping the material entered into the database. As a result of this policy, Postmodern Culture is the oldest, with coverage from 1990.

Institutional subscriptions to the titles published online were provided either individually or as a package price, and electronic-only subscriptions cost less than print. Under standard pricing, there was no limit to simultaneous access by members of a subscribing institution, while second-tier pricing was available for smaller institutions at fifty percent off the list price, but workstations were limited to twenty-five (IP addresses), all within one building. In 2000, Project MUSE was expanded to include other scholarly publishers, including Duke University Press, Indiana University Press, Pennsylvania State University Press, and University of Hawaii Press. Full database access to 113 journal titles for the largest institution was $8,000 for the year.

Http://muse.jhu.edu/proj_descrip/gen_intro.html

Introduction and Growth of Electronic Universities

During the 1990s, it became commonplace for academic libraries to set up websites, subscribe to various fee-based information services and then make both fee-based and free services available to the library's clients through links from the library's website. For example, the University of York Library provided links to more than 100 sites, representing among other things, library catalogues, library Web services, publishers, and online booksellers.

http://www.york.ac.uk/services/library/subjects/libint.htm

Once the academic library had its website set up, it was a short step to offer services to the library's clientele outside the walls of the library. Separately, the concepts of "distance education" and of "universities without walls" had been steadily gaining reality. All of these concepts coalesced when the Internet was able to serve as the basis for remote, online education. Though maintenance of the site ceased in late 1999, UNESCO's Learning without Frontiers website gives a useful starting place for exploring this area. In 2000, MindEdge, Inc. claimed to list more than 4,500 online college courses and 257 online degrees offered by American universities over the

Internet. Even if the numbers are overstated, it signals the direction of academic development.

http://www.unesco.org/education/educprog/lwf/links/learn.html
http://www.mindedge.com/home/home.phtml?sID=806ad606b67adb8668e7

Speculations about the Future of Electronic Products in Libraries

As we speculate about the future, let's return to the library's purpose as reflected in Ranganathan's five laws:

Books are for use.

Although libraries are making ever-increasing use of electronic resources, the methods for rating academic libraries still place great emphasis upon the size of the printed collection and relatively less emphasis upon the library's ability to provide its clients with the materials they need and use. As a practical result, there is a general preference for buying printed books (instead of access) and then using compact storage instead of weeding, even though the computer records of the last thirty years could readily identify materials with virtually zero likelihood of use. Of course, there is some merit to the argument that the greater the collection size, the greater the likelihood that the reader will find his book, and his time will be saved. However, this argument is weakened when an e-book is available as an alternative. Since an e-book takes up less "real estate" than a comparable printed one and it can be used anywhere, purchasing of printed books by academic libraries will drop rapidly, but only if the rating of academic libraries is changed to deemphasize collection size and to emphasize reader convenience and success.

Every reader his book.

Provided that the reader has the requisite knowledge to make use of the resources of the Internet, the number of books available to him is greater now than it has ever been. The costs of electronic publication, storage, and access will continue to decrease. As more books are stored on the Internet, the potential availability will increase. But since the reader has about the same amount of time available each year to obtain the correct books from the ever-larger collection, the system for retrieval must become more efficient. And because not all readers understand all languages in which the books of interest are written, there will be an increase in the use of computer translation of text from one natural language into another.

Hidden behind the objective of providing every reader with the books needed is the requirement that these books be produced and distributed, regardless of the specific format used. In turn, this raises the questions of copyright and of compensation for the authors and publishers of those books. At the time of this writing, copyright and compensation were by no means settled. Looking forward, even if the ASCAP/PRC model were accepted for electronic republishing, it ignores other issues. For example, in the Internet environment, there appears to be overlap between ASCAP, CCC, and PRC; they use different principles of reimbursement, and they address electronic publication and republication tangentially. And perhaps most critically, they ignore the explosion of Internet publishers—perhaps everyone with email, but most certainly everyone with a website, over 10 million and counting! The PCs, themselves costing on the order of $1,000, outfitted with flat-bed scanners costing less than $100, can be connected to the Internet, thus making it possible to scan and images in color and distribute worldwide virtually instantly.

Should the creators and distributors of an intellectual work be reimbursed in proportion to the use that people make of that work? There are a significant number of people whose behavior can be construed to answer this question in the negative. These people do not consider themselves thieves, yet they make copies of intellectual works for themselves (or others) without paying those who produced and distributed the works. If the producers are not paid when their work is used, then I can think of only two other methods of compensating them: charity and loss leaders. Under both methods, the work is shared without charge. Under charity, the author/publisher requests contributions to support ongoing work. This is the method of authors of shareware computer programs; it is also the method of the Public Broadcasting System (PBS) and other not-for-profit broadcasters. Under loss leaders, the producers do not expect to receive any more revenue for work already produced; rather they hope that knowledge of the work already produced will lead to commissions or contracts to produce new work. This is the method of architects and consultants and essentially anyone else whose work cannot be protected from copying. These two methods are similar because both provide revenue in advance of creation, and neither provides additional revenue for work already produced. The amount of money conveyed by charity tends to be smaller than that conveyed by commissions and contracts, and the latter tend to define the objectives of the new work to be performed.

A final question with respect to the compensation of authors: are they being repaid due to their having made an investment in their works, or are they being rewarded for their creativity? Copyright law has been based upon rewarding creativity. Looked at in this light, fair use can be seen as not rewarding a current author in order to stimulate the creativity of future authors.

Every book its reader.

I am not optimistic about our ability to make progress on this. Although the purpose of the selective dissemination of information (SDI) systems is to alert the reader to the existence of information likely to be of interest, these systems have been of limited success. E-mail and newsgroups have provided some relief, in that they make it far easier to stay in touch with others with similar interests. Word does spread easily and quickly among these cohorts. What is now needed is improved automatic indexing and abstracting of these materials.

Save the time of the reader.

There is much that can be done to save the reader's time. Speech recognition and speech synthesis will improve the interface between patron and machine. It can simplify this interface, reduce error, increase comprehension, and make retrieval more flexible in time and location. It's a wonderful idea to be able to control a database search by voice, instead of having to use a typewriter-style keyboard. Today, you can dial directory assistance, speak the name of the city and the name of the person or organization desired, then hear a synthesized voice giving you the number that you want. In the near future, it should be just as easy to search for books by voicing the titles, authors, or subjects.

It is time to apply the results of research on natural language question-answering systems and incorporate them into search systems. Certainly, most searches of the Internet are likely to demonstrate the need for improvements beyond the simple use of keywords—even in Boolean formulations.

The Library is a growing organism.

LIBRARIES WITHOUT WALLS
Although the physical campus will continue to be important, a greater proportion of education and research will take place outside the campus. As this occurs, the academic library will also shed its walls; it will "collect" its books by making them available without bringing them into the physical library, and it will provide the books to its patrons, regardless of whether the patrons are in the physical library or even on campus. As a result, the library staff will become more focused upon external collections, most of them electronic, and less focused upon acquiring, organizing, and delivering books and journals within the walls of the library.

CATALOGING
Cataloging cannot continue to be a manual process. Internet access must be improved, and the dynamic, decentralized nature of producing and distribut-

ing books via the Internet demands that indexing and cataloging be automatic and continuous. Library research has clearly demonstrated that simple keyword indexing, while useful, is limited in its retrieval success. Given that keyword indexing is the current mainstay of Internet searching, there is a lot of room for the application of improved automated cataloging techniques.

The accumulation of nontext "books," that is, sounds and visual images, has long exceeded our ability to catalog them using traditional manual means. Yet the academic enterprise will rely on such materials more and more heavily. To date, the most efficient method of retrieval has been to ask for the help of a person familiar with the collection. As collections grow, the relative level of familiarity must go down. Therefore, to meet the challenge of organizing and retrieving these materials, entirely new nontext methods of indexing, classification, and searching are required. Of course, once we can catalog/index sounds and graphics, we'll be in an excellent position to catalog/index the content of the Internet!

LIBRARY AUTOMATION

With the increasing use of electronic books, traditional automation becomes less important. For example, use of electronic books and printing of copies on demand will reduce both interlibrary loan and circulation of physical books held in the library's collection. Instead of being used by the library staff and concentrating on the internal operations of the library, the library's future automated systems will need to be operated by the library's clients and support their use of remote resources.

OUTSOURCED SERVICES

Outsourcing of library services occurs automatically as libraries shift to reliance on external resources. For example, if a library signs up with netLibrary, the selection, acquisitions, and processing of more than 10,000 books is done by netLibrary, not the client library. As outsourcing increases, library staff will concentrate more on vendor selection and on quality assurance to make sure the needed services are delivered.

AUTHENTICATION

Electronic books present a problem that I shall call "authentication." Although it can be a problem for any activity, authentication is a particularly important issue for scholarship. I can put the authentication problem in the form of a question: Is the information conveyed on a given Internet page the same as when I last read it? When published in traditional print form, a book is produced in multiple copies, and so we can be reasonably sure that the copies will not all be changed after publication. As a result, the work can be cited with reasonable assurance that the work will be stable and not altered at some future time. This is not the case for electronic information. Although great care has been taken to avoid unintended changes of data within computer systems, it has also been an objective of the computer community to make it easy to change data intentionally. Thus, in the case of an electronic book, it's a simple matter for the author to change the content, even to the point of changing meaning in the process. For example, by judicious editing after the fact, a page of predictions could always be true. An author may go further than changing a page; it may be removed entirely.

How can Internet information be used as the authoritative source if the information cited may disappear entirely? Indeed, at the time of this writing all web pages cited were valid; it will be amazing if that is still true in three years! Before we can rely exclusively upon electronic information for our scholarship, there must be at least one generally accepted and implemented method for authenticating the data, so that in effect it has been cast in stone and can neither be changed nor removed. This is not the Internet as we know it today.

Summary

Throughout the twentieth century, academic libraries became more important to the processes of education and research. The invention of computers in midcentury provided libraries with a new tool to use in the organization and delivery of its services, and at the same time, it significantly increased the need for library services. Innovations in computers and communications provided the ability to store and transfer data, worldwide and virtually immediately. At the same time, the increasing importance of the knowledge component of human activities provided the funding to make these capabilities a reality. At the end of the twentieth century, academic libraries were providing the best service ever; the challenge now is to make it 1,000-fold better!

Notes

1. References that begin "http" are Internet addresses (URLs).
2. At the same time, through its on-going support of research, the federal government remains important to future development. For example, in 1999, the Department of Computer Science of North Carolina State University reported computer science research projects totalling over $7 million. Of this total, nearly one-half (49 percent) was supplied by the National Science Foundation and over one-third (35 percent) came from the combination of the Defense Advanced Research Projects Agency (DARPA), the U.S. Army and the U.S. Air Force, leaving less than one-sixth (15 percent) for all nonfederal sources.

   http://www.csc.ncsu.edu/research/projects.htm

3. Fayollat, James, "On-Line Serials Control System in a Large Biomedical Library," was referenced in two searches, but the following URLs were not found:
   slis6000.slis.uwo.ca/601/test/documents/doc0617.html (Alta Vista)
   http://slis6000.fims.uwo.ca/601/test/documents/doc0620.html (Lycos)

4. Buckland, Lawrence F. *The recording of Library of Congress Bibliographic Data in Machine Form.* Washington, D.C.: Council of Library Resources, 1965.

5. Avram, Henriette D., John F. Knapp, ; and Lucia J. Rather. The MARC II format: a communications format for bibliographic data. Washington, D.C.: Library of Congress, 1968.

6. University of California Union Catalog, Berkeley, Institute of Library Research, University of California, 1972.

7. This is not Innovative Interfaces, but a different company.

8. The number of computers is so imprecise not only because so many client computers were connected to the Internet through dial-up connections, but also because there was no one to one relationship between a Domain Name and a physical computer acting as host for that name. On the one hand, many ISPs provide web-hosting in which one physical computer provides hosting services for many different Domain Names. On the other hand, multiple physical computers could be connected to the Internet and involved in providing the services for a single domain name.

9. Response to a ping is automatic; if available for any manner of service, the host would have to respond to the ping.

10. This approach is similar to the system implemented in the late 1960s, at MIT's Project Intrex. Of course, it was a research prototype; the computer capacities and communication rates of the time made response time slow by today's standards. One solution that Intrex used to improve throughput: a workstation with dual displays and separate communication paths, one for the keyword searching and one for the source images retrieved.

11. It is interesting to speculate about this pricing policy in relation to the expected utility of the archive access to the institution. Throughout most of the twentieth century, larger libraries often helped smaller libraries by supplying services at prices that did not even cover the marginal costs of the services. If that policy were to be at work in the present case, then the amount of usage at the largest institution is expected to be less than 4.5 times greater than that of the smallest.

·13·

The Economic Crisis in Libraries: Causes and Effects

Michael Gorman

How pleasant it is to have money, heigh-ho!
—ARTHUR HUGH CLOUGH

Librarians and libraries have lived in a state of economic crisis for so long that only the oldest among us can remember that times were different once. Most would say that our economic decline began in the early 1960s, a statement that can be substantiated by careful analysis of the figures. I would maintain that the decline turned into a crisis some time between the energy crisis of the Carter administration and the first Reagan recession in 1982. In turn, that crisis became a catastrophe sometime between the late 1980s and the early 1990s. Catastrophes have a long half-life. Just as countries once at war, winners and losers, suffer for years after the armistice is signed, libraries that survive economic catastrophes have to deal with the consequences years after their budgets improve. In writing about libraries in an economic context, as in any other context, we have to recognize the pitfalls of generalization. Libraries come in so many types and sizes, and exist in so many different places subject to different forces, that there is a real danger of oversimplification and generalizations so extensive that meaning is drained from almost any statements. This article concentrates on academic libraries (recognizing the enormous range of diversity of size and mission that term encompasses), but an attempt is made to include libraries of all types.

Whether your library has been experiencing a decline, a crisis, or a catastrophe, is a matter of local circumstance and definition. After all, it is well known that a recession is when your neighbor loses her job, and a depression is when you lose yours. Despite these difficulties of definition, it is possible to say that libraries of all kinds, with precious few exceptions, are worse off today in financial terms than they were twenty-five years ago, even though they may be better off than they were five years ago. What happened?

Causes

The simple answer is that libraries received less money than they had before and/or a smaller share of the total resources allocated by their funding agencies, often dramatically fewer dollars or greatly diminished percentages of the institutional pie. One can be a fatalist and say that it was our karma, or we can be more occidental and ask why that happened.

The answers to that question have many dimensions—social, economic, political, global, technological, and cultural. It is impossible to say that any of these factors is more important than the others or, in retrospect, that anything could have been done to prevent the decline, crisis, or catastrophe entirely. I do believe that, if librarians and their professional associations had more political savvy, some of the details of the crisis could have been ameliorated. In particular, I believe that had different types of library (academic, public, school, etc.) worked together more, we could have achieved more than we did, feeling various degrees of security in our own library environments.

Here are some of the things (in no particular order) that brought about, or affected, the economic travails of libraries:

The energy crisis of the 1970s

There is little doubt that the psychological malaise (as, despite the mythology, Jimmy Carter never called it) that contributed to two decades of financial ill health began with the inflation that was worsened by the energy crisis of the mid to late 1970s. The ability of working people to travel, heat and ventilate their homes, and otherwise use the benefits of cheap and seemingly inexhaustible energy lay at the heart of the American Dream. The ideas that working people might not be able to afford those benefits and, worse, that the sources of energy were controlled by alien and inimical forces, struck a devastating psychological blow to a society that, uniquely, was fueled by optimism and a sense of limitless possibilities. I believe that the energy crisis was the first mortal blow to the consensus view that public policy could eventually solve all problems and symbolized the end of the Roosevelt Era of which Lyndon Baines Johnson was the last great figure.

The "tax revolt" that began (as all things—malign and benign—do) in California in the late 1970s

If you were to go to library journals of the late 1970s and early 1980s, you would be struck by the absence of substantial comment on the likely effects of the Great Tax Revolt (typified by, but not limited to, the infamous "Proposition 13") on libraries in California. The tax revolt made it possible for an indifferent property-owning minority to restrict spending on public services of all kinds and set up a cramping and confining system of public financing that rules even now. It all but destroyed what was once the finest system of primary through university education in the world and, to this day, it is having a malignant effect on public policy in the Golden State. In terms of libraries, school libraries in California now rank fiftieth out of fifty states by all important indices; public libraries have been so battered that whole county library systems have been shut down; and the level of library knowledge and familiarity in California's colleges and universities would be laughable, if it were not so tragic. Here we see a prime example of what happens when librarians act parochially. I am not saying that a united front of all kinds of librarians in the early 1980s would have halted the tax revolt, but I am persuaded that such joint and forceful action would have mitigated its effects and alerted librarians in other states later infected with tax revolt fever.

Reaganomics

President Reagan chose to combat the malaise caused by the energy crisis and to restore a sense of optimism ("morning in America") by an unprecedented program of cutting income taxes, increasing military spending, and running huge and increasing budgetary deficits, which were the inevitable results of the first two strategies. Spending on social services, notably education and libraries, went down in real terms as state revenues also declined (their income taxes being linked to federal taxes) and as federal contributions, other than on military expenditures, were cut. That diminishment was mitigated by the Democratic congresses of the Reagan era refusing to allow the full effect of Reagan's strategy of starving government to take effect, but the already fraying consensus that governments at all levels were duty bound to provide for the greater good became tenuous indeed. Many people still find it hard to imagine a society without publicly supported libraries, but the infamous Howard Jarvis (the Sauron of the tax revolt) declared notoriously and with psychologically interesting imagery that "you could fire a machine gun in most libraries and not hit anyone." *He* could imagine a society without publicly supported libraries ... and *his* side won.

The rise in, and demand for, electronic resources and services that began in the mid to late 1980s and erupted in the early 1990s

One of the great and painful ironies of library history is the way in which libraries of all kinds were simultaneously trying to deal with cuts in their budgets (particularly materials budgets) and with paying for the hardware, software, and access to electronic resources that were demanded by library users, politicians, the educational establishment, and by, say, 1996, the *Zeitgeist*. It is hard for any librarian to rejoice in the wonderful, free world of the Internet when she reflects on how much it costs to provide the terminals and the systems support to provide that "free" and mandated access. Those reflections are rendered even more painful when we consider the sources of the money spent on that free access. For many libraries, access to the Internet for their users has been an unfunded mandate sucking money from personnel, materials, library hours, and other key services Then, of course, there are the expenditures on subscriptions to CD-ROM and online services. Not only are these, in effect, expensive serial subscriptions amounting to hundreds and, in some cases, thousands of dollars, but these services are rarely *replacements* for their printed analogues (with the shining exception of CD-ROM and online indexes). A particularly flagrant fiasco—-the California State University "Journal Access Core Collection (JACC)" project, now mercifully dead—promised permanent access to an *eighteen-month* archive of the online versions of printed scholarly journals. Which librarian with even the vaguest interest in access to scholarly literature could cancel subscriptions based on such a vapid and evanescent scheme?

The metastatic growth of scholarly journals (particularly in scientific, medical, and technical disciplines) and the steep annual increases in their prices

The much written about "serials crisis" is real enough, even though much misunderstood. For example, there is no economic crisis involved in the publishing and acquisition of journals in the arts and humanities. Those journals are reasonably priced and are not subject to unwarranted steep increases in price. Scientific, technical, and medical journals are quite another matter. Many academic libraries have responded to the high subscription prices and the 10 percent plus annual increases of STM serials by cannibalizing their book and other materials budgets, the serials budgets in other areas, and by across the board cuts that unfairly penalize arts, humanities, social sciences, and professional disciplines. Many proposals aimed at ameliorating this disastrous situation have been advanced. They range from reliance on online serials (ignoring the fact that the vast majority of online serials are wholly dependent on the print serial industry) to a complete overhaul of scholarly communication and, while we are at it, of the promotion and tenure system. Unsurprisingly, the crisis continues. What can librarians do to arrest the trend of specialized areas of study splitting into ever-smaller subspecializations, each with its own journals? It is hardly for us to state that only broad areas of study deserve journals or to say whether micro-astronomy or the socio-economy of fourteenth century Finland are legitimate disciplines. It is also hardly for us to intervene in trying to change the promotion/tenure system, particularly as many of the forces that will probably change the tenure system anyway are antithetical to academic freedom and the culture of learning.

The belief that books and reading constitute but one means of acquiring knowledge, with no more legitimacy and importance than many others

The continuing vogue for compounds using the word "literacy" (computer literacy, visual literacy, etc.) should send a signal to those who care about true literacy. Having a facility in the use of computers, or having a facility to decode the meaning of graphic images, are equivalent to literacy at only the lowest level of the meaning of that word. If, as many people do, you believe that "literacy" is simply a matter of being able to read, then reading literacy, visual literacy and computer literacy are on all fours. If, I would suggest correctly, you understand literacy as a life-long process by which the individual interacts with progressively more complex texts, gaining knowledge and wisdom in the process, then it is clearly absurd to equate true literacy and "computer/visual literacies." It is a hard truth for today's society, but reading and learning are uniquely intertwined, each inconceivable without the other. Harold Bloom in his *How to Read and Why* (Scribners 2000) states "Ultimately we read—as Bacon, Johnson, and Emerson agree—in order to strengthen the self, and to learn its authentic interests." Could there be a better definition of education through reading?

The much-derided cliché about academic tenure is "publish or perish," but there is a good reason why the positive alternative is publishing. There is no better way for an academic or researcher to demonstrate her learning and ability to create knowledge than by submitting the fruits of her learning to a rigorous review process leading to the dissemination of those fruits to the benefit of scholars and students, present and yet unborn. The fact is that such publishing is the only way known to ensure that human knowledge cumulates and is transmitted to future generations. Let me repeat: The sustained reading of complex texts is vital to the life of the mind and to the advancement of a civilized society. Any attempt to deny this, on economic or technological grounds, is either ignorant or a contemptible *trahaison des clercs*. The rise of for-profit, proprietary "universities" without libraries is the clearest example of a denial of the fundamental connection between reading and education, in that a degree from such an institution guarantees that its recipient is not educated in any sense that would be recognizable to previous generations.

Television and the Internet, both leading to a decline in reading as a preferred leisure activity

"The student at Yale today, apart from the few intensively literary, has read far fewer books than the student of twenty years ago." (Harold Bloom, interviewed on C-SPAN, 9/3/00.) It is decades since Newton Minow lamented the vast wasteland of television, and it is not now fashionable to concentrate on the effects of tens of hours weekly spent in the passive enjoyment of pabulum and trash. We have now had at least two generations of children grown to be adults whose mental environment has been saturated with television, whose interaction with the outside world is almost entirely visual (rather than textual) and dependent on visual stimulation. Small wonder that contemplation and reading are low on their scale of patterns of living. The consequence of a television-dominated culture in which reading is unimportant and difficult for most is that teachers at all levels give up on imparting knowledge by steering their pupils toward reading, relying instead on visuals and easier ways of transmitting information. In fact, many give up on imparting knowledge and the means to gain knowledge entirely, settling for information and the ability to pass informational tests (multiple choice rather than essay exams, for example). To quote Harold Bloom's *How to Read and Why* again: "A childhood largely spent watching television yields to an adolescence with a computer, and the university receives a student unlikely to welcome the suggestion that we must endure our going hence even as our going hither: ripeness is all. Reading falls apart, and much of the self scatters with it." When children cannot or do not read, why pump money into children's libraries? If students entering a university are incapable of profiting from a well-stocked library (or, more likely, are deemed to be so incapable), why fund the college library at the levels of yesteryear?

The commercialization of education—by which I mean that academia is losing interest in producing educated men and women and concentrating increasingly on producing employable men and women

If university education is coming to be seen as a species of vocational education with a veneer of something higher, and university programs are to be judged by the earnings of their graduates, then the link between learning and reading will suffer as each is devalued. It is a fact that employers are complaining that younger employees, including university graduates, lack the ability to read and analyze complex texts, to do relatively simple mathematical computations, and to write simple declarative English sentences without egregious spelling and grammatical errors. This is not to say that those employers wish their employees to be truly educated, but that they wish them to have basic, useful skills that can make the company profitable. Thus, the desire to produce employable graduates and the need for basic skills in the workplace will not combine to produce an educational Renaissance, but will reinforce the slide to commercialization of all levels of education. In such an environment, it is easy to see the library as an area ripe for fiscal cutting.

The decline in municipal institutions and of faith in government

The steady rightward shift in American public opinion has not been halted by the collapse of the Gingrich radical right. Distrust of "government" and "career politicians" are embedded in the common rhetoric to the point at which people seek to be successful politicians by pretending not to be politicians. Judging by the rhetoric, you would think that the great majority of Americans were philosophical anarchists seeking the ideal of communes of individualists linked only with other communes in terms of barter and trade. "The best government is the one that is closest to the people" and "Why should I send my money to Washington?" lead to a climate of opinion that regards taxation as theft and any government money spent on something that does not immediately and obviously benefit an individual taxpayer as waste. In such a mental climate, the notion of the common good is akin to communism, and people can describe mainstream Democrats as "socialists" without being laughed off the screen. What better embodiment of the common good is there than the library? To someone who hates "government" and the idea of paying taxes and who does not read or care if his children read, the library is clearly expendable.

Effects

The economic crisis in libraries had many causes but relatively few results and responses. Though I realize that the focus of *Against the Grain* and the interests of its readers lie in the effects of crises on materials budgets, I think it is important to see the wider picture and realize that, in a very real sense, any cuts *not* made to materials budgets in times of crisis are at the expense of other aspects of library service.

Broadly speaking, libraries spend their financial resources on materials, staff, and operating expenses, and these are the only areas in which major economies can be made. Different users of libraries value different aspects of library service. For example, the average faculty member of a university is far more likely to be distressed when scholarly journals are cut than when library hours are cut. The opposite is true for the average undergraduate student. Similarly, within the materials budget, present and future students are badly affected when book purchases decline but feel little pain if the more rarified scholarly journals are cancelled. Another important variable in the economic crisis is the amount of autonomy that libraries have had in choosing where cuts are to be made. At one extreme, a library might be given a fixed sum that is, say, 90 percent of the previous year's budget and has complete freedom in choosing what to maintain, what to cut, and what to eliminate. At the other extreme, a library might be given the same 90 percent budget together with specific instructions on which cuts to make and in which areas. It is rare for library administrators to have no autonomy within areas (e.g., which hours to cut within a mandated cut in hours; which books to buy within a depleted book fund), even when the areas in which cuts are to be made are specified. Autonomous or not, the 10 percent reductions in our 90 percent library are overt cuts known to the funders of the library, the librarians, and the library's users. There are also "silent" cuts, generally known only to the library, consisting of those enforced by price inflation and/or other changes in the library's environment. To take our 90 percent library, it will not only have to deal with the overt 10 percent cuts, but also with, in a typical academic library:

- 5 percent increases in average book prices,
- 10 percent increases in average journal prices,
- Increases in the cost of subscriptions to electronic resources,
- Increases in staff and librarian salaries,
- Minimum wage increases for student assistants,
- Increases in the price of maintenance contracts
- Unfunded increases in student enrollment
- New graduate courses demanding new materials

At the end of the day, the 90 percent library is, in fact, more like a 75 percent library when the actual purchasing of materials and services is compared with the actual expenditures of the previous year.

How have libraries dealt with these unpleasant economic facts?

Cutting Hours of Opening

It costs a lot of money to open a library and to keep it open. Even a one-room library must be attended all the time, which means two people on duty. Larger, more complicated structures may require many employees just to staff each of the service points and to provide the other services required by a large building. In addition, heating, ventilation, lighting, and other necessary uses of energy are significant expenditures during the hours that a library is open. Cutting expenses during a budget crisis by reducing the hours of opening may be either a planned decision or an inevitable result of other fiscal decisions. The former is also subject to another constraint. One may plan to reduce expenses by cutting hours without being able to realize those savings immediately or at all. For example, a library that is staffed entirely by full-time permanent employees will only be able to realize savings by cutting hours if it is willing to lay off employees or mandate that full-time employees convert to part-time. Either of these actions may well be difficult or impossible because of union contracts, tenure obligations in academic institutions, and the like. Libraries may have shortened hours forced upon them:

- if staff leave and there is, as is very common during budget crises, a hiring freeze;
- if, in an academic library, large cuts in student wage expenditures are mandated by the university administration; or
- if cuts in materials budgets are not permitted although the overall budget has been cut.

Reduced hours, for whatever reason or however they come about, affect different library users differently. In academic libraries, a reduction in hours is a great hardship to students but may pass virtually unnoticed by faculty. In public libraries, such limited hours weigh heaviest on the young, the old, and the poor (almost any budget reduction is felt most keenly by those classes of public library users). In school libraries, limited hours may be fatal to the educational mission of the library.

Closing Branches

Many public library systems reacted to the budget crisis by closing branch libraries. Why? Because, in the words of the philosopher Sutton, that is where the money is. Rationalism and the weighing of cost-effectiveness, without reference to the human context or to cost-benefit, point inevitably to such closings. Their effect on library users has little to do with the weighing of options and the adding up of figures, but with the impoverishment of the cultural life of a small community or a locality in a city. Some of the people who live in such places may be mobile. There may be good public transportation from such places to the location of a central library. The reality of life in modern America in small rural towns and in poor city localities (far and away the most likely to lose their public library branches) is that young children, old people, and those without personal transportation are likely to be denied library service. In the case of young children, the habit of library use may be gone forever. The latter are, of course, the ones most affected by the closing of school libraries in some of the schools in a school district. This has been a regrettable result of a shortage of funds for librarians or even library aides and the consequent concentration of those remaining in the larger schools.

Then there is the question of academic library branches. Large research universities almost invariably possess a library system consisting of a central library and numerous departmental/branch libraries. The latter can range in size from large undergraduate, law, and medical libraries to what are, in essence, reading rooms. Such systems have every conceivable disadvantage—economically and in terms of overall library service—but one; their most influential users (departmental faculty) love them. Departmental libraries are almost insanely wasteful when it comes to duplication of materials, deployment of library staff, and consumption of all aspects of the library's budget. However, they are usually very responsive to faculty needs (if less so to student needs) and are usually conveniently situated for those same faculty (a matter of no small importance on a large campus). One of the least explored realities of research university life is the fact that talk of closing, amalgamating, or otherwise rationalizing departmental libraries is the third rail of academic politics—touch it and your career dies. The result is that, during even the hardest times, the money to staff departmental libraries and to keep their often-duplicative collections going is sacrosanct, while other aspects of library service suffer.

Materials

The term "library materials" has always denoted a somewhat diffuse concept. In olden times, libraries had "book budgets" or, if very modern, "book and journal" budgets. The term "library materials" came in when those simpler times became more complicated, and libraries bought and collected books, journals, maps, sound recordings, scores, films, videos, audiovisual materials of all sorts, realia, manuscripts, and on and on. It is psychologically, as well as fiscally, interesting to note that, to this day, many libraries do not purchase access to electronic resources from their materials budget but from some other source. It will be much healthier for us all when we see electronic resources for what they are—library materials that have to be purchased or to which we have to subscribe, each from the materials budget. At that point, the relative value of these resources will have to be weighed against other competing means of communicating recorded knowledge. In practical terms, this sequestration of funds for electronic resources has, in many instances, left them virtually immune from cuts and, thus, placed a disproportionate burden on other library materials in times of crisis.

BOOKS

Another danger is that of the book budget being the lonely child in a materials budget cutting exercise. The tendency is to have a book budget that is, essentially, what is left over when all the other materials budgets are determined.

This is exactly the opposite of the result of a rational approach to this matter. A library's, particularly an academic library's, book collection is still its central reason for being. Only a few of the wilder-eyed technofanatics believe that the book is "dead" or that the book will be superseded as the main vehicle for the study and onward transmission of recorded knowledge and the records of humankind. Book publishing is flourishing in all areas of study and literature. Moreover, a book not purchased in one year may not be available for purchase in the next year. The days of warehousing long print runs for years are over, and books go out of print far more quickly than they once did.

The rational approach to planning materials budget cuts is to devote *at least* as much care to preserving the book budget as is devoted to the preservation of the journals and electronic resources budgets. If you look at the way in which the percentage of research library materials budgets devoted to books has declined over the last fifteen years, you will see that the rational approach has not dominated. Because expenditures on serials are annually recurring costs and because journal prices increase at twice the rate of book prices, it can readily be seen that a shift of resources from books to journals carries a financial poison. Put simply, $100 left in the book budget will demand $105 dollars the next year to ensure a steady state of acquisition; whereas $100 transferred from the book budget into the journal budget will demand at least $110 next year if subscriptions are to be maintained. Add the compounding factor into the process and you will see that the $100 left in the book budget will demand $122 in the fifth year, and the $100 transferred into the journal budget will demand at least $146 in the fifth year. In the worst case (and there were many worst cases in the 1990s), that extra 46 percent will also be transferred from the book budget. The net result will be that our $100 "left" in the book budget would actually be $60 with the purchasing power of $45, since nothing will have been done to cover book price inflation.

JOURNALS

In studying the journal cancellations that were so common in the 1980s and 1990s, the alert observer will notice at least two common practices that have led to malign results. Both are in the interest of a superficial equity of treatment and both make the painful process of cutting journals easier for the librarians administering the process. One is cutting journals by a set percentage (either of expenditures or of numbers of titles) across the board—that is, across all disciplines. The second is basing the cuts on likelihood of future use as predicted by language or other objective criteria or as predicted, in academic libraries, by the faculty (usually some faculty) in the discipline to which the journal principally applies.

What could be, on the surface, fairer than a, say, 10 percent cut across the board? Well, lots of things, actually! To begin with, journals are priced in a predatory manner in the areas of science, technology, and medicine. This is true to a lesser extent of some areas of the social sciences, and not at all true of the arts and humanities. It is, therefore, unfair to penalize disciplines with reasonably priced journals in order to protect other areas of study. Let us take a hypothetical library in which the budget for arts and humanities journals shows that each $10,000 buys 400 journals, the budget for social sciences journals shows that each $10,000 buys 125 journals, and the budget for science journals shows that each $10,000 buys 40 journals. A 10 percent cut (in total titles or in expenditures) would leave 360 arts and humanities titles, 113 social sciences titles, and 36 science titles. That is, of the 56 lost titles, 40 (71.5 percent) would come from the arts and humanities, 12 (21.5 percent) from the social sciences, and 4 (7 percent) from the sciences.

In most academic libraries, cuts in journals are made in consultation with the faculty of the area to which the journals "belong." This is supplemented, if at all, by librarians looking out for journals of general interest. I am not sure that this approach is, or has ever been, the best way to approach this painful process. The problem lies in the fact that we live in an age of intense and narrow specialization—more and more people knowing everything about less and less—which has led, in many instances, to faculty who can barely communicate their interests, even to others in the same department. We also live in a time in which the novel and the up-to-date are prized above the time-tested and the enduring. This leads us, inevitably, to the dilemma of wishing to consult the faculty, on the one hand, while having very little faith in their ability to see beyond their own specialized interests; value journals written in languages that they do not read; and to assess the long-term value of titles that they do not use. Another increasingly difficult issue in collection development and management is that of the diffusion of the borders of canonical disciplines and the consequent rise in interdisciplinarity. Examples abound and are not limited to the obvious scientific examples such as biochemistry. This is a time when academic psychology is as much a matter of mathematics and neurology as it is of the id and the ego. The creation of multimedia art may require the collaboration of musicians, performers, and computer scientists. In such an intellectual climate, traditional departments mean less than before, and even the boundaries between colleges are crossed with frequency and ease. All this means that it is hard to assign lists of journal titles to particular faculty groups, and the results of those assignments may be quite unsatisfactory. For example, the Mathematics Department may recommend an expensive mathematics journal for cancellation, either not knowing, or knowing but not caring, that journal is important to the research of a professor of psychology.

The essence of the problem is that a journal collection, indeed any collection, is more than the sum of thousands of individual, unrelated decisions—many taken in the light of a particular time and personality. Large collections can be built by the accumulation of such decisions in the first instance, but they need an animating philosophy and an overarching policy carried out consistently over many years if they are to achieve greatness. I have become convinced that there is only one way of carrying out journal cancellation projects in such a way that damage to the collection is minimized. That is, for faculty recommendations to be just that and for them to be accepted or rejected within a policy and a vision that sees far further than the exigencies of the moment and the cumulation of narrow interests.

OTHER MATERIALS

Times of financial stress are especially dangerous for collections of nonprint materials. The problem is that, with few exceptions, libraries (and certainly academic libraries) lack the history of commitment to videos and sound recordings (and even maps and scores) that they have to books and journals. A library that would not dream of cutting the book budget by more than a mandated minimum will cheerfully abandon the purchase of videos for an entire financial year, or cut 75 percent of the sound recordings and map budgets. Specialized libraries within libraries have commonly received far deeper cuts than have been made to the general collection budgets. These are despite the fact that such materials have assumed a far greater importance to students and scholars in the last two or three decades. The sad fact is that nonprint materials have less political clout because they are used and valued by far fewer people than the general collection and, with rare exceptions, lack the deep roots that sustain the book and journal budgets. As with the book and journal budgets, they should be considered in the library's collection development policy and allotted their place of relative importance to the institution, the library, and the library's users.

ELECTRONIC RESOURCES

As I have stated before, I believe strongly that electronic resources should be bought or subscribed to in the context of the library's materials budget and the policy statements that cover that budget. It is psychologically and practically important that we see electronic documents as the latest manifestation of the long history of human communication and the way in which libraries have incorporated each innovation in communication into their intellectual architecture. That being so, there is no reason why libraries should seek ever-expanding access to electronic resources without reference to the toll that ever-expanding access takes on other parts of the materials budgets. The time has come for libraries, particularly libraries in purchasing consortia, to reject "bargain" offers of electronic resources that are of less usefulness to the library's clientele than other materials costing the same price. That is not the attitude of many libraries, obsessed as they are by the new and the drive to appear modern and innovative, but it is an attitude that must come if we are to deal maturely with electronic resources. One interesting aspect of library provision of access to electronic resources is the near universal rise of interlibrary lending and borrowing of tangible library materials. Close examination of this phenomenon reveals that libraries that spend a higher proportion of their budgets on electronic materials are also high net borrowers of books and articles from other libraries. Exactly the reverse is true for libraries that devote a smaller proportion of their budgets to electronic resources. What this tells you is that the priorities as between electronic resources and print materials in the first class of library does not match the expectations and needs of those library's users. Moreover, the library that spends more on electronic resources is spending money for now and not the future—in ten years time the money will be spent, and the electronic resources, for the most part, no longer available. The library that spends its money on books, journals, videos, and other tangible works, will still possess those materials in a decade and for decades to come.

The Future

It is hard to guess what will happen in the future in any field of human endeavor and predicting the future of library budgets seems particularly hazardous. The financial decline/crisis/catastrophe of the past couple of decades seems to be receding in the new economy, but its effects are still being felt, and it is doubtful that most libraries will ever be back to the purchasing power of the distant past. This is not all bad. Financial exigency has brought reconsideration of all library operations and a focus on the real needs of the library's user. However, years of financial exigency have led, in many cases, to a mindset that is defensive and reliant on the provision of electronic documents to justify increased expenditures. Academic libraries and librarians have almost come to feel grateful if the cuts in their budgets are not too severe and pathetically grateful for a few extra crumbs on the annual budget plate. The libraries of the California State University made a detailed and rigorous study of the effect of the swinging cuts of the early and mid 1990s on their collections. A conservative estimate of the one-time money required to remedy the depredations of the cuts on the twenty-three libraries was $12 million, together with major increases in individual campus materials budgets each year. A request was made for this sum, accompanied by ample documentation. At the same time, a request was made for an additional $3 million for electronic resources, with very little justification in terms of need or importance. No prize for guessing which request was funded. Not only was there no money allocated for repairing the book and journal budgets, but the $3 million for electronic resources was granted for one year, turned into a permanent increase the next year, raised to $4 million in the third year, and will be increased to $5 million in the next budget. Such stories have been repeated with variations all over the country. Faced with a complete indifference to the documented real needs of students and faculty, it is only human for librarians to complete the cycle and ask only for what they think will be funded—electronic materials.

I believe that our present economic good times will continue for a while and that libraries will not suffer overall as they do. I think it extraordinarily unlikely that libraries will be made whole from the last crisis or they will be immune in the next. I trust that the hype over electronic resources will die down and that future budgets will take a balanced view of all library collections. I foresee endless struggles, skirmishes, forays, battles, and wars in which those who care about the library will have to fight with skill, cunning, political *savoir-faire*, and a trust in their beliefs to sustain them. Nothing will be easy for us, but nothing could be more important to culture and society than that what we do and the values we hold. Reason enough to uphold the truth and to seek adequate resources to serve our users, our communities, and the common good.

◆14◆

The Impact of the Library Budget Crisis
on Scholarly Publishing

Jack G. Goellner

When the Soviet Union launched its first Sputnik in October 1957, it unwittingly set in motion a "butterfly effect" that eventually showered good fortune on academic libraries and scholarly publishers in the United States. The federal government, embarrassed that Soviet scientists and engineers had beat their U.S. counterparts into space, responded by throwing money at the problem. Largesse to the nation's colleges and universities was aimed principally at developing more and better scientists and engineers, but the dynamics of trickle-down economics would now come into play long before that concept became politically fashionable. Not surprisingly, some of the new federal money found its way through fattened university budgets into the budgets of academic libraries, and some of *that* money trickled down into academic publishing.

If it is an exaggeration to say that academic libraries were awash in cash during the early 1960s, it is at least true that most had acquisitions budgets they had hitherto been able only to fantasize. Lists of "must have" books were compiled and widely promulgated to guide librarians in spending their acquisitions budgets. In the publishing sector, reprint houses blossomed and flourished in their business of making out-of-print books and journals available again now that an eager market made reprinting not only affordable but profitable. "Books by the yard" was a commonly heard, if jocular, phrase. Licenses to reprint entire back runs of scholarly journals were negotiated—for hundreds of issues in scores of serial volumes. Scholarly publishers, especially university presses, likewise flourished in this early 1960s heyday. New presses were established. Existing presses expanded their lists and augmented their staffs with new positions. It was a good time to get into publishing. One uni-

273

versity press director, now retired, tells how in 1961, without a single day's experience in publishing, he wrote letters of application to six university presses and received four job offers. At no time since has the job market in scholarly publishing been so receptive.

What were the kinds of books that fed the federally financed market? Press directors within their own councils referred to themselves as "pure tobacco growers." The pure tobacco they published was the scholarly monograph— pure in that it sought to advance the boundaries of knowledge, however narrowly, however incrementally, without respect to salability. Such nobility of purpose was of course easily attained in a time when scholarly monographs found an eager market among academic libraries. Marketing staff in scholarly publishing houses referred comfortably to "the guaranteed library market" for each new monograph, the guarantee coming in part from standing orders, if not for every new book in a university press's list, then at least for every new title in specified subject areas. A retrospective look at the new-title output of The Johns Hopkins University Press list—in no way an atypical list—revealed that for several years in the 1960s the average first printing of a hardcover book was 3,400 copies. Today librarians, scholars, and publishers express concern about the monograph as a vanishing species, predicted by some to become extinct. New monographs being published today are coming out of binderies in print runs as low as 750, 600, even 400 copies.

By definition, no heyday lasts. In the late 1960s, as the U.S. commitment to the Vietnam War ballooned; federal largesse to colleges and universities diminished. By the early 1970s many universities were in serious financial difficulty. Funding for libraries was curtailed, book-buying budgets were cut back, and the trickle-down to university presses, whose imprints were then on one out of every ten new books published in the United States, pretty well dried up. A few universities closed down their presses altogether, and most made steep cuts in the operating subsidies they had been providing to their presses. Times were tough, and at meetings of the Association of American University Presses the buzz was about "the crisis in scholarly publishing."

For many libraries, as for many scholarly publishers, the crisis was real. There was no longer any "guarantee" of being able to sell new scholarly monographs to libraries. Their acquisitions budgets strapped, academic libraries were buying fewer books. Wishing to continue breathing air instead of water, scholarly publishers found it necessary to raise book prices. The higher prices further eroded sales to libraries. A vicious circle indeed.

The situation worsened for libraries as subscription prices for scholarly and scientific journals were increased, some of them hugely, some even—in the opinions of librarians—unconscionably. The ratio between serials budgets and book acquisition budgets began a shift toward journals that is unlikely ever to reverse. For book publishers, not only did the library pie get smaller, but the slice for books got narrower.

Eventually bits and bytes barged into scholarly publishing, but before their advent, the technology of film images, especially microfiche, tantalized academic librarians with the promise of reduced shelving requirements for archival storage—even though no one except the apostles of microfiche seemed confident about the longevity of images on film, whether text or graphic. Some presses tried publishing documentary materials directly on fiche; others inserted microfiche adjuncts into pockets inside the back covers of hardbound books; but not much came of these experiments. Even today microfilm has its uses, but it was not to prove truly helpful in dealing with the whipsaw of increasing prices for scholarly books and journals and diminished acquisition budgets for purchasing them.

Enter now the electronic media, ripe with promise for the dissemination of scholarly information. Every academic librarian will acknowledge that—woe to the printed page, woe to the monograph—an ever-widening slice of the library budget is being consecrated for the acquisition of materials in electronic format. First on the scene was the CD-ROM, able to store and display what then seemed a prodigious amount of information. Like microfiche, it found its adjunctive way into and alongside scholarly books. Like microfiche, it still has its uses. But its day was short, for CD-ROM has for the most part been superseded by the technology of online communication.

Much sorting out has yet to be done of what serves well electronically and what doesn't. Some foundation-funded experimentation with publishing scholarly monographs on line has come up empty, perhaps because of trying to impose the traditional book format—front matter, chapters, back matter—on the electronic matrix. But the publication of scholarly journals online, when done simultaneously with publication of their print versions, has met with quick success among academic libraries. And why should it not? A library subscribing to the widely known Project Muse, for example, whether individually or as a member of a consortium, can at once offer its patrons online access to more than a hundred scholarly journals, and with enhanced search capabilities. Providing such service to a library's patrons makes minimal demands on the acquisition budget and zero demand for shelf space.

To date, librarians have been consistently ahead of their counterparts among scholarly publishers in adapting to and exploiting the electronic environment. But the publishers are sure to catch up, some sooner than others. One leading university press, MIT, has announced publicly that it is in the business of publishing bits as well as books. But, significantly, MIT has emphasized that its publishing program will continue to embrace books as well as bits. As indeed it should, for it is still books that pay the bills.

One prediction that can be made—perhaps the only one that can be made with assurance—about the foreseeable future of academic libraries and scholarly publishing is that it will divide along the fault line between information and knowledge. As foreseen more than a decade ago, the various electronic media will always excel in the ordering, storage, and dissemination of scholarly information; and books as we know them will remain the primary repository of scholarly knowledge. The debate about the dichotomy between information and knowledge is old and ongoing.

•15•

The Place of Scholarly and Scientific Libraries in an Increasingly and More Widespread Competitive Information Knowledge Marketplace

Charles Hamaker

As we look back to the twentieth century and forward to the twenty-first century, we need to recall the major forces that created academic library collections. The chemists' war (World War I) and the physicists' war (World War II) and their aftermaths shaped library collections and scientific, technical, and medical (STM) publication and pricing practices as much as any other events during the century. Today, financial limitations and user demands shape collections.

Following World War I, German scientific publications emerged as the most critical journals for scientists worldwide. After that war, however, librarians around the world began complaining about the price of German journals, and ultimately, Charles Harvey Brown at the end of the interwar period wrote:

> The responsibility for the high cost of German periodicals was by inference placed on the shoulders of American librarians. We have been the ones who have been ready to pay these high prices. If we had not continued to purchase scientific books and periodicals at prices far greater than ever charged in the history of the world, some means would have been found to reduce the size and price. American libraries, by their ability and willingness to pay have enabled the publishers to persist in charging exorbitant rates. (Charles Harvey Brown. 1933. "German Periodicals in American Libraries: Deflation or Extinction?" *Library Journal* 58: 526).

One firm, that of Julius Springer, by their own account handled 90 percent of German scientific periodicals just before World War II. Barely was World

War II over when Robert Maxwell, who ultimately became a media baron of mythic proportions, took over a fledgling operation from the British government and created Pergamon Press. Before that, he handled the worldwide distribution system for Springer journals out of war-torn Berlin. (For an overview of this period and its subsequent rediscovery, see Deana Astle and Charles Hamaker. 1988. "Journal publishing: pricing and structural issues in the 1930s and the 1980s." *Advances in Serials Management: A Research Annual* 2: 1–36. For a history of periodical pricing from a library perspective, see Ann S. Okerson. 1986. "Periodical prices: a history and discussion" in *Advances in Serials Management* 1: 101–134; http://www.library.yale.edu/okersonforicin.html.)

The Servicemen's Readjustment Act of 1944, better known as the GI Bill, meant that the arrival of 2 million ex-soldiers doubled undergraduate enrollments on campuses in the United States and "increased student-fee revenues on some campuses as much as fivefold" (David A Hollinger. 1996. *Science. Jews and Secular Culture: Studies in Mid-Twentieth Century American Intellectual History*. Princeton, N.J.: Princeton University Press, p. 9). In addition, two Cold War projects were begun, the National Science Foundation's funding of science and the foreign area-studies programs. These three developments had an enormous impact on U.S. libraries.

The Gerould Statistics, which are a continuous collection of data from academic libraries from 1907–1908 until 1961–1962, report on twelve libraries comprehensively. They show significant increases over the decades in terms of the average number of volumes added in those libraries. (See Robert E. Molyneux. 1998. 2d ed. *The Gerould Statistics 1907/08–1961*; http://fisher.lib.virginia.edu/gerould/.)

By 1961, the average number of volumes added was about 76,000 for the twelve libraries (Berkeley, California; Minnesota; Illinois; Kansas; Washington; Michigan; Wisconsin; Missouri; Indiana; Iowa; and Ohio State).

In 1963 the Association of Research Libraries (ARL) became the standard source for statistics in the large research libraries. From that date, net volumes added climbed to over 90,000 volumes per year from the late 1960s to 1973, when numbers began dropping. In the early 1980s, member libraries of ARL added on average 64,000 to 67,000 volumes annually. That number has very slowly increased, until today slightly fewer than 73,000 volumes on average (books and journals) are added in an ARL library. (For a comprehensive file and interactive version of the ARL statistics from which this summary and all ARL statistics referenced here are drawn, see *Association of Research Libraries Statistics;* http://fisher.lib.virginia.edu/newarl/.)

The two Cold War initiatives created funding and opportunities for libraries in the United States that led to massive infusions of funds for creating library collections. For scientific publications in particular, however, they created an almost unending fountain of money for American university libraries. From the 1960s on, they also meant funds for creating area-studies collections. Although expenditures for academic library collections did not decrease at any point in the last half of the century, and in fact increased well above any measures of inflation, and even above levels of increases in NSF funding for research, the increases were insufficient to provide sustained funding of both these initiatives. As the Cold War wound down, a casualty was the funding for areas-studies collections and the diversity of materials that such collections brought to U.S. libraries. In fact, the average number of books purchased by ARL libraries now stands at fewer than 25,000 titles per year. In 1986 the number was about 33,000 titles.

For most of the late 1990s, the ARL institutions awarded an annual average of approximately 280 PhDs with reduced collecting. The late 1960s to early 1970s saw comparable numbers of doctorates awarded, but a substantial increase in the average number of volumes being added to collections.

It seemed inconceivable that serials, which for most of the decades of this past century represented less than 30 percent of a library's materials' budget, would take on such incredible significance in the last twenty-five years of the century and mark the end of global collecting. It was not until 1976 that ARL began reporting serials expenditures as a separate category for its member libraries. The emphasis for academic librarians in training through much of the last half of the twentieth century was on building and managing research collections, which primarily involved selecting books and cataloging books (and, of course that dreadful stuff, microform). For those with a bent toward cataloging, the last twenty-five years have been ISBD (that's punctuation to the rest of us), MARC format, the various incarnations of AACR, such mind-boggling concepts as desuperimposition, latest versus successive entry for serials, OCLC, and the agonizing of the profession over moving collections from Dewey or homegrown classification systems to Library of Congress system. Then there were the inevitable "which library system" decisions to be made.

Meanwhile, the collecting community was filled with dreams of becoming the keepers of the cultural patrimony of the word for whole nations. By the late 1970s, many members of this community recognized the problem of the slow self-destruction of the paper on our library shelves.

Who could have believed this vast enterprise of erudition and selection and cataloging and preservation would have as its nemesis the lowly serial? Except in pure science and medical collections, serials were almost an afterthought. You selected them, you got them, then serials' departments figured out what to do with them. Until the 1970s the primary issue was selection. And even after that, we kept hoping it would all go back to "normal," and we could get on with the business of building great collections.

Ignorance of the underlying nature of serials had not always been the case; a period of upheaval and challenge and proposals for radical change had occurred earlier in the century. A primary issue for academic libraries during the years between the wars was the behavior of commercial publishers of international scientific and technical serials. But the excesses of pricing from those publishers were a dim memory when the heady collecting days of the 1960s were upon us. With a mandate from governments to catch up with the Russians (Sputnik) and dollars flowing freely to create instant institutions and collections, the "heart" of the university was in grand shape, and libraries and librarians were ready and willing to create true world-class collections.

In those dreams of great collections, the Alexandrian vision ran deep even in the smallest of libraries claiming to serve research and scholarship. And from the 1950s to the 1970s, when small collections became great by any standard (in terms of size of collection, size of buildings, and numbers of staff), we did not, even in our nightmares, think that the impulse and the funding to build ever more comprehensive collections would end. The profession created a new category of professional, the Collection Development Librarian. Librarians became bibliographers, a time-honored term that in new hands meant not the people who were truly specialist bibliographers, but those who selected materials for libraries for whole categories covering the human experience. They seemed to be the new experts, or at least acolytes of the great mission of collecting the human patrimony of the word manifest. Like members of the priesthood, they gathered to themselves priestly functions. In library after library, bibliographers held sway over large sums of money, commanding down to the minutest detail the care and feeding of collections of global scope. However, the language began to shift, perhaps ahead of the reality. Instead of collection development, the issue in the mid 1980s became collection management.

Few individuals did more to systematize collecting of the output of book publishers than did Richard Abel, whose dream it was to bring regularly and predictably the output of whole areas of scholarship into libraries. His dream foundered by 1972 and was picked up by larger booksellers who had the capital needed to make that particular system function. In the end of the century though, only two U. S. firms could sustain the process on the scale that Abel pioneered. Where many labored, few survived.

Other vendors worked in other areas. Firms like Blackwell's, Otto Harrassowitz, Cassalini, Swets, Nijhoff, and many others helped systematize and standardize processes that ensured a steady flow of international publications to America's libraries. The antiquarian and out-of-print dealers also played significant roles in building collections. As a result of both the funding and the systems that vendors developed to service libraries, between the 1930s and the 1990s membership in the ARL, which quite frankly used size of collection as a key membership criterion, almost tripled.

The first inklings that the spree was over began in the early 1970s. By 1973, many libraries were experiencing their first real need to cancel serials in almost two generations. Fluctuations in the cost of serial publications became so great that what had never been dreamed of in library schools, what had never been whispered in corridors of the new priesthood, became the most important skill librarians could develop: how to handle serials reviews.

This wasn't new, but it was an area that had last been a priority in the years between the two world wars. The lessons learned then had all been forgotten. In that prewar era, even the collecting ideal of the Farmington Plan had been considered. Librarians had forgotten about the risks of currency exchange, had not foreseen that the STM mandate would become the dominant force in this new world that had been forged from Sputnik fears and the postwar educational boom, and they had never really developed truly cooperative institutions. The Conspectus was a sophisticated attempt to develop a common comparative language for collections. But we were caught unawares. The international library community too had forgotten the lessons of the 1930s, when librarians and their organizations had joined forces to examine and challenge practices that submerged during World War II, but were re-invented or perhaps just re-learned by such publishing barons as Robert Maxwell, or the grand conglomerate that Elsevier represented, or the tradition that Springer-Verlag sustained.

In the United States, several commercial publishing houses came into existence as a result of World War II that owed their practices and understanding of how STM was published to the prewar years in Europe. Academic Press was founded by two refugees from Academische Verlagsgesselleschaft and the current (at least as of 2000) head of Academic Press spent time with both Pergamon (and Robert Maxwell) and Elsevier, headquartered in the Netherlands, which owed much of its STM core and practices to the German publishing exodus. After the war Springer-Verlag itself came back to prominence. In fact, the system that Springer perfected continued to serve the company, as well as all these various offspring of the European scientific publishing tradition, very well through most of the century. Maxwell, who was probably the most interesting character (in all senses of the word) in STM publishing in the century, led a massive shell-game of funding, slipping finds from one company or account to another to gather a large empire to himself. This empire evaporated at his death, but continued, at least the STM section, which merged with Elsevier. In the United Kingdom, the longest-running scientific publisher, Taylor & Francis, reinvented itself in the last quarter of the century, stretching into new publishing areas in scholarly journals.

We should have known something was wrong with the system from the library community's experiences with academic publishers in the 1930s. In 1931, Charles Harvey Brown, one of the great American librarians, wrote an article whose title could just as easily be from the 1990s: "A Hazard to Research: The Danger to Research through the Increasing Cost of Scientific Publications" (*Journal of Higher Education*. 1931. 2). Beginning before World War II, Brown was involved in calling attention to the problem of the pricing of German periodicals. At his institution, Iowa State, serial subscriptions represented, in the late 1920s and early 1930s, between 25 percent and 30 percent of the materials budget.

Robert B. Downs was perhaps as responsible as any single person for the great buying bonanza that American libraries experienced after World War II. His reports for fledgling libraries are still cited. In 1947, after the war and during his early years as director of the library and the library school at the University of Illinois, he documented the battle of libraries and publishers in the 1930s in a classic summation of issues. His article, "Problems of German periodicals" (*College and Research Libraries*. 1947. 8: 303–309) should be taken as a base point for describing and understanding the problems not only of German periodicals, but for documentation and proof that the problems of the last fifty years dealing with commercial STM titles are inherent in the systems used for creating, publishing, and selling such titles.

At the height of the Great Depression, countries around the world were desperately trying to find buyers for the goods that they produced. But publishers of literatures that were in and of themselves the gold standard of the scientific world did not lower prices—they raised them. They finagled prices: used predepression valuations, value-added taxes, and artificial currencies. They created publishing mills centered on critical research cores from Europe, stuffing their journals with dissertations, through payments to writers based on the number of pages they wrote, refusing to even set a specific price for a year's output of a specific title. And they invented twigging, that bane of the twentieth-century serials world.

What scientific publishers learned and continued to practice after the war in the new publishing centers that developed was that a few good articles in a journal could be used to sell a lot of less important, even bad, articles at the same high prices that the good articles commanded In fact, the bibliometric dispersions that Eugene Garfield and others documented continue to hold sway—even in the "new" electronic environment, but statistical analysis has thus far yielded no practical change in an antediluvian system. Garfield's creation, the Institute for Scientific Information (ISI) and its great citation indexes, are one of the few systematic overviews available of the scientific and medical literature. Librarians ignored what Garfield's statistics and methods found (at their peril, it turned out) in the name of "we know what's best," or "this is what the faculty want."

Richard Trueswell "codified" on a general level for librarians, the so-called 80/20 rule. But Garfield, in indexing the articles that were cited in the journal literature, identified accurately, especially in the sciences, the journal titles that provided the "80 percent of use." Once ISI began producing the *Journal Citation Report*, the information was available. Librarians had the basic tools to identify the most important literatures and could have created cost-effective and cost-efficient collections that would have met most of their users' needs in journal areas.

One of the more interesting arguments I've ever had was with Edwin Shelock, who published for the Royal Society of Chemistry. He laid the blame on librarians. You have to decide what's the best, and only buy that, he told me repeatedly at an early NASIG conference. Because of our neglect of statistical tools, our refusal to ask and learn how to answer the question of quality in scientific publishing, he was perhaps not too far off in his accusation. Only at the end of the century did we get from Stephen Bensman and Stanley Wilder a comprehensive statistical understanding of bibliometric distributions in terms of what they meant for an actual library collection. They described this in their article "Scientific and technical serials holdings optimization in an inefficient market: An LSU serials redesign project exercise" in *Library Resources and Technical Services*. (1998). 42,3:147–242; http://www.lib.lsu.edu/collserv/lrts/ST1.html.

What Shelock understood and Bensman and Wilder demonstrate is the same insight that Brown had: for much of the debacle of STM publishing's impact on other collecting responsibilities, the library profession failed itself and its primary vision. The response that faculty members had to the study, which demonstrated the skewed nature of the price and value of the literature, is epitomized in the article by a professor who was defending a highly priced, specialized foreign, commercial journal and told Bensman: "When it comes to my journal, your damn statistics mean nothing!"

Libraries continue to buy a lot of insignificant literatures in packages that contain a few grains of excellent articles. The packaging and selling of scientific literatures, a few good and a lot not so good, continues as the modus operandi of scientific publishing. Package sales of "all" of a publisher's journals in the electronic environment continues the support of a system that is and has been repeatedly demonstrated as noneconomical, destructive, and artificially high priced, one that limits distribution of scientific and technical information. Selling the good, the bad, and the ugly under the same package continues unabated. Package deals let publishers protect their income streams and permit librarians to avoid the problem of identifying high-quality publications.

German scientific journals were sold at premiums, even as the German currency itself was devalued again and again. This should have alerted the world to the fact that these titles did not behave like normal economic goods, that the journal system was not only immune to more common economic forces, but operated under its own laws, its own rules. Only recently has an economist looked closely enough at pricing behavior of large STM firms to document just how distinctly these "goods" behave. Mark McCabe has documented pricing behavior that doesn't fit any standard model. He has demonstrated that pricing behavior in STM publishing is sui generis. (See his article "Academic journal pricing and market power: a portfolio approach," which was presented at the Economics and Usage of Digital Library Collections Symposium at the University of Michigan, March 23–24, 2000 and is available in an Adobe PDF file format at http://www.prism.gatech.edu/~mm284/JournPub.PDF.) He also noted that libraries, in making choices among journals, actively seek a cost-effective mix, from a group of titles, expanding our understanding of what motivates cancellations and purchases from a one-title-at-a-time approach to a coverage-of-the-literature approach.

World War II brought the German journal commerce almost to a standstill. After the war, in the rush to repair library collections, to handle the onslaught of GIs and take on new challenges, cost was almost not an issue. In the heightened collecting opportunities caused by the war, collections moved across national boundaries guided by book dealers and librarians and sometimes-unscrupulous adventurers. Librarians and vendors assiduously filled "gaps" in serial collections. The grand vision of collecting on a global scale, and the appetite and will and systems to do it, roared to life.

What brought the great dream almost to a stop was a change in the way the world's currencies were regulated. The collapse of the Bretton Woods Accord exposed the world once again to the reality of the unchanged, wasteful, and out-of-control cycle of scientific publishing. I did not realize the international currency exchange standard was critical for stability in purchasing by academic libraries until I began to try to understand what had happened to what I had been taught to believe about libraries and collections and collecting, to what, as a professional librarian, I had expected my daily occupation to be.

The Bretton Woods agreement, which was formalized in 1944, had the goal of stability in international exchange rates. The world's key currencies were pegged to a gold standard. In 1971 Richard Nixon took the United States off the international gold standard and abandoned the Bretton Woods' system of currency regulation. He announced that the United States would no longer buy and sell gold with foreign central banks. This marked the end for price stability that had been enjoyed since World War II in terms of the dollar's international value. And because scientific publishing was (as had always been true) an international enterprise, all libraries were as much at the mercy of the dollar's fluctuations as they were at the mercy of publishers with a product and process that had not changed since the beginning of the century. It was the end of the grand collecting schemes, the Alexandrian dreams.

Libraries in the 1970s began experimenting (albeit crudely) with many of the tools that have become standard in serials reviews. One librarian in the sciences told the tale that he personally had taped shut bound volumes of certain journals to ascertain if they were *really* used. That and the so-called white-glove test became standard stories told around library conference tables— library legends.

The problem was, of course, that they weren't just legends; almost every library had at least one bibliographer or collection development officer who tried the same thing. They learned that this "evidence" wasn't convincing to university faculty who as much, if not more so than librarians, believed that the institutions they worked in owed them subscriptions to their journals and the right to have any piece of information they demanded. Faculty defended the retention of second- and third-tier journals controlled by invisible colleges to which they belonged. Cost, as it had been for the bibliographers, was no issue. The next two decades of the century were to be a lesson not only to librarians but also to scientists that there was something radically wrong with the system of publication.

Use studies in the 1990s became almost the final word in deciding what to retain and what to cancel. Tina Chrzastowski, the librarian at the chemistry library at the University of Illinois in Urbana-Champaign, reported a longitudinal study of use of chemistry journals that has become a classic in the literature (Tina E. Chrzastowski. 1991. "Journal collection cost-effectiveness in an academic chemistry library: results of a cost/use survey at the University of Illinois at Urbana-Champaign." *Collection Management* 14: 85–98). Another study by two Canadian librarians took a no-nonsense approach to evaluating the cost-effectiveness of journals in their library. Their report at the NASIG conference in St. Catherines, Ontario, was published in the annual conference volume: Dorothy Milne and Bill Tiffany. 1991. "A cost-per-use method for evaluating the cost-effectiveness of serials: a detailed discussion of methodology." *Serials Review* 17 (Summer): 7–19. This was in contrast to countless surveys of faculty that asked what titles to keep and which ones to cancel. Bensman and Wilder combined the two approaches, looking at a faculty survey that asked faculty to rank journals, as well as the use surveys that

Chrzastowski reported. Combining these with Garfield's Journal Citation Report, they identified the cost-effective core of areas in the STM literature. The most famous study surveying the cost of a specific literature was that of the physics literature conducted by Heinz Barschall. Because those articles have been the source of continuous litigation in four countries, librarians are keenly aware of the impact of publishing studies that list specific publishers. Barschall's work is documented at http://barschall.stanford.edu. The earliest article, "The cost of physics journals," published in the December 1986 issue of *Physics Today,* was an early warning not only to publishers but also to librarians that cost-effectiveness was a rational means of measuring the value of STM literatures. It is perhaps this article that really launched the methodologies that struggled to create cost-per-use impact studies. Barschall used a surrogate, ISI data. Individual libraries used that source as well but believed that they needed to determine local variants, if any.

Several interesting experiments outside traditional publishing schema are in development. The ARL has become an activist organization on behalf of research libraries, and its SPARC project is at least an effort to affect the current publishing systems. Stanford University Libraries' Highwire Press is another experiment, and there are others.

At some point, and I am at a loss to put an exact period for this development, access to information for faculty and students became not a privilege, but a right. Circulation librarians saw it in daily contact with faculty who had never been asked to return books they checked out, who at least in my experience at a number of libraries, believed that the books in their office were almost their private property. The library could have them back when they died! (And many of us have come across library books as we process "gift" collections from old campus offices). The move toward making faculty members responsible and require the return of such materials is still not universal. There are academic libraries that still do not charge faculty book fines. It's one of the fading privileges that is most reminiscent of aristocratic privilege among those in the ivory towers.

Much like faculty who believed that getting what they wanted was a right, many librarians who were employed as bibliographers said to their institutions in the boom years, "I'm the expert, and I say we need to purchase x, y, or z." There are even proud statements in the literature indicating the bibliographer's sole job was selection. Payment, ordering, even identifying if the darned thing really existed, were mere mundane details, someone else's responsibility. Collection development librarians made the "intellectual" determination of items' value to the collection. The rest of the library's processing systems did their biding. However, some institutions never made the transition to library responsibility for collections. The tradition of faculty control continues in a surprising number of libraries even today.

I select, and someone else finds the money and pays the bills: this was almost an anthem throughout much of the last thirty years for the bibliographic theocracy that was created in many libraries. Is it too much of a step from the situation in which the bibliographers select, and the library does their bidding to the situation today, when we have shifted emphasis from the library and the librarian to purchasing on demand in response to users demands? Is that famous dictum of industrial sourcing introduced to the library community by Dick Rowe, of Faxon and Rowecom fame, just-in-time-not-just-in-case anything other than our new anthem? Could it be that as libraries have stopped believing in their mission to collect and preserve the world's patrimony that we have substituted a new charge? Could, within our tradition of intellectual freedom, the right to seek information lead to the responsibility for librarians to become guarantors of access to information at any price?

Many of my peers express the belief that the library has the responsibility to pay the bills and provide the means for what they term free access to all expressions of ideas. Much as Al Henderson might say, the only responsibility librarians really have is to go get more money. ALA's Office of Intellectual Freedom, in its definition of freedom of information, might not have meant free in the sense that someone else pays the bills, but this meaning is almost explicit in ACRL's Intellectual Freedom Principles for Academic Libraries

> Whenever possible, library services should be available without charge in order to encourage inquiry. Where charges are necessary, a free or low-cost alternative (e.g., downloading to disc rather than printing) should be available when possible. ["Intellectual Freedom Principles for Academic Libraries: An Interpretation of the Library Bill of Rights." Approved by ACRL Board of Directors: June 29, 1999 Adopted by ALA Council July 12, 2000; http://www.ala.org/acrl/principles.html.]

To demonstrate how radically the landscape of libraries has changed, consider this: the new power base in libraries is no longer the collection development librarians, no longer bibliographers. Collection development librarians have had to add other tasks or become redundant. They manage technical services and oversee payment systems and OPAC selections. They worry about workflow and efficiencies. In many libraries, they have been relegated to secondary importance if collection development is all they do.

The new authority I would suggest is the public-service librarian, and it is their credo that is taking central importance in library after library. Many of them do not count the cost anymore than the bibliographers used to. They can speak authoritatively (as bibliographers used to). Their motto is, "The patrons want, the patrons need," and they see themselves as the interpreters for the library of what users demand. Instead of the traditional way that we interpret the library to the users, the mandate is reversed: It's not the collection, it's the service, and service means anything (or everything), anytime, anywhere.

For those still concerned about collections, the question has stopped being about collecting or even selection, but about what is "needed." The first need that has become the new prime directive is what the faculty needs for teaching. And secondarily, what does the faculty need for research? These two needs are not distinct, at least in universities with the expectation of research from faculty. One of the more interesting findings early in our attempts at serials review at Louisiana State University was exactly this question. We asked the chemistry faculty to list first the titles they needed for teaching and second, those needed for research. What we found was that the lists were almost identical. What this means for librarians trying to figure out how to spend scarce resources is that they still must learn subject areas, must still use judgment to determine the best use of resources. The responsibility cannot be delegated without extreme danger to the constituents of the library, the very people we are supposed to be assisting, or the long-term collecting mandate.

There is no simple or even final answer and the faculty's answer or the students stated need is always conditional for the librarian. This lesson alone is probably an impossible one to expect new librarians and many of those who have worked a long time to fully understand without a solid grounding in the way disciplines really work and how information is really used. The responsibility for collaborative decision making, with a lot of information going both directions, cannot be delegated, shifted, or given away.

One of the casualties in the new electronic paradigm, one that is most disquieting to collection development librarians, is the traditional selection processes. Library after library is documenting the failure of traditional selection patterns. This is a variant on what the LSU serials redesign project discovered. Beyond a core level, faculty (or any users) are not very good at predicting their own information needs. This is because they know their own fields. They don't know what they don't know. And that is why librarians need to learn and constantly apply the basic understanding of how information is used, how it behaves, in order to make consistently good choices about resources.

Although faculty may not predict their own needs very well for materials the library does not have, almost invariably when they use materials *not* in the collection it is from key journals in other fields, in cognate fields, in fields that cross their own. Faculty in the social work department with a strong collection in-house wanted the secondary and tertiary journals of their own field added to the LSU libraries' collections. What they actually used, when given the opportunity to access those titles, were *not* the less important journals they wanted subscriptions to, but the *more* important journals in medical and nursing fields that crossed their particular subject areas—titles they would not normally demand for subscriptions. This phenomenon, repeated throughout the academic support system, has left many librarians wondering what they were doing wrong. John Cox, in a recent ALA presentation, noted that one university in Australia that was making full-text journals available from a large publisher found that about half of the journals used heavily were not in the local collections. And about half the journals barely used at all were in the local collections. What this means is that faculty and librarians have been very successful in pushing material in their special interest areas into collections, and at the same time been very unsuccessful in identifying important material that they need outside their own fields.

My conclusion from this is different from the what-the-faculty-say-they-need-we-must-get-them philosophy or the belief that we have to buy it all because we can't predict what we'll need. The librarian responsible for expenditure decisions must balance needs both inside and outside of the traditional collecting areas in any library, especially when the collection is a virtual one. We will be known by the quality of our wares.

The damage done to librarians' egos over the discovery that people need (and sometimes need very much) what was *not* in our collections is a fact that had been buried in interlibrary loan statistics. With data from interdisciplinary full-text resources that demonstrate unanticipated needs, the profession is being forced to rethink its modus operandi, perhaps even its rationale for existence.

In place of the priests of the collection (Librarian as god), we are seeing a rise in the librarian as facilitator, as provider And this role that we are rushing into is as welcome in its own way to many library users as the collection priests of other years.

Some of my experiences with the "new" library users reinforce this. I recently called a student who had submitted requests for twenty-five interlibrary loan articles. The first four articles checked were from journals that were in my library's collections. When I suggested that since the first four were in the library, that we should send back all of requests to be checked against the library's OPAC, the student accused me of being abusive. I've been charged with that before (most often by publishers). It turned out that half of the articles were available in the library. Not only did the student have a right to the articles requested, the library did not have the right to request that a thorough search be conducted first. (We normally send back to the requestor a screen print of the bibliographic record for any "haves"—proving that we had what they want—and have been soundly reprimanded by at least one student in the last year for not returning the original request—a phone call repeating the title was insufficient.) Because of the multiplicity of choices, of sources, I, in fact, sympathize with the student—figuring out what is in or not in the library today is a task even hardened professionals will fail at more than they did in the environment of ten years ago. Unless the profession moves quickly to integrate finding tools, the failure rate at discovering what libraries *have* will increase. Thus far, the cataloging community has moved at a glacial pace to create tools that integrate both stand-alone titles and aggregator titles. Similarly, the publishing community, with its CrossRef initiative undertaken without involvement of the library community, is contributing to a potentially significant failure of an information-rich environment to provide access to its content. And system and aggregator vendors and publishers, by not moving rapidly to create and maintain dynamically updated pointer or bibliographic systems, are adding to the problem.

For the immediate future, increased failure rates, frustrated librarians, and ever more strident patrons are awaiting the profession. And something very like a battle for the soul of academic libraries is underway.

In the mid 1990s, shortly after the Web began to mean something, I walked down an aisle in the vendor area of an American Library Association annual conference. A periodical vendor almost breathlessly said to me, "Do you know what the really big sci-tech publishers are going to do? They are going to sell their articles to the end-user." As far as I can tell, this continues to be the exit strategy for any number of today's large STM publishers. They believe that with the Web providing a road to their doors, individual users can't wait to get at all that information that they have. And once they break the pay-per-use barrier for individuals, then, yes then, they will have arrived at Nirvana. Library budgets will no longer be their regulators, their barriers to another level of profitability. But in fact, that vision, although premature, may not be all that wrong. Brokers, specialized database providers, specialized search services—all are moving rapidly into areas that once were the sole purview of libraries.

Libraries were the only source for most of the world. No longer. Magazines with their own websites are providing backfiles of what people want to use. Have you visited the *Consumer Reports* site lately? It's a lot faster than trying to find a five-year-old report in any traditional library. With projects like netLibrary, which at least for the time being has been focused on library sales instead of individual use, and Questia media, which aims at students, the complexities of library information navigation are something many students and, in fact, many faculty are not interested in learning. As I was recently informed, if they can't find what's in the library, that's a reference desk problem. In other words, library users don't want to learn *how* to find information, which is what we have specialized in providing, they want the information itself. They have very little patience in learning to read an abstruse library OPAC screen display. If it isn't intuitively obvious, it won't mean much. Recently, I've been noticing that those ubiquitous dashes in library holdings statements don't communicate much to the current generation of college students. You know what I mean: vol. 42(1975)–45(1978) doesn't mean anything to anyone but a librarian that the library *does* have volume 44. And the idea of searching in several places to find out if they can get something from the library—well, that's a really funny thought. If at first you don't find it, then let somebody else figure it out. In that kind of market, it doesn't take much before someone else will figure it out, and it's not necessarily going to be libraries. Using Trueswell's rule, and Garfield's findings, there is no reason a savvy bunch of entrepreneurs (does that mean publishers??) will figure out how to meet that 80 percent of the need and leave libraries with the slim and very expensive "other" pie—of the institution's information needs. Perhaps that great story circulating at library conventions about the administrators who wanted to cancel the library's budget because everything was on the Internet wasn't about administrators who were naive—just premature.

In the last century libraries moved from a Victorian perspective on collections, a prescriptive approach towards collections at the beginning of the century (a hangover from the foundations in the United States of the Christian university and in loco parentis), to a collect-everything dream, to the perspective that we are merely the assistants ready to get you whatever you want. (And when you want it and how you want it.) None of these attitudes or approaches will work in the new century. There will be too many options for identifying and acquiring information that's needed when it's needed to continue either patriarchy or free gifts on demand—we'll get whatever you say you need (we probably can't afford that approach if the last fifty years are any guide). As questions of selection, of collocation or organization of information are answered, the library profession and society will know whether anything recognizable as either libraries or librarians will survive.

Conclusion

Richard E. Abel and Lyman W. Newlin

When we sat together in Charleston, two years ago, to frame the outlines of this Special Millennial issue of *Against the Grain,* we formulated what has proved, in the event, to be one of the most decisive editorial principles in the evolution and forging of this issue. That decision was to turn to the "old hands" in the world of the book and the journal as the authors of the essays that make up the volume. Our reasons for formulating this principle were several:

1. Those who had spent long and productive careers in this unique world of the book and journal had lived and created much of the history of the century. Further, they had learned firsthand, from their immediate predecessors, the history, philosophies, and practices of the first decades of the century. As a consequence, the contributors we would seek out had either directly inherited the accumulated understanding of their part of the book/journal world or had been directly involved in the framing of the subsequent history, philosophy, and practices thereof. They were, thus, able to reflect well the portrait of the century.

2. Although the editors had framed a rough outline of the topics that we thought should be addressed, we well understood that the veterans of the discrete and distinct métiers making up this world would have distinct and well-formed views of that aspect of it to which they had devoted all or much of their life's work. We encouraged them to range freely within the broad topic area—and, if needs be, simply to disregard our suggested outline to best communicate what they knew of the history and evolution of their area of specialization.

3. Given these other, but related considerations, we concluded that authors of this class would give the Special Issue, when it appeared, an authenticity that could not be achieved so successfully in any other way.

It is virtually axiomatic that the advancing years of "old hands," many in retirement, lead to all manner of unexpected disabilities. Indeed, both of the editors had to deal with such more or less serious although passing setbacks in the course of the shaping of this issue. But far more unhappily, several of the essay authors initially identified were forced in the early days of their undertaking for this issue to withdraw due to serious adverse misfortunes. And to our great sorrow, several more developed grievous difficulties that compelled their withdrawal at various stages. We deeply regret the assorted difficulties that obliged old, long-time friends and associates to discontinue their participation in this venture. And we wish them well and hope for brighter prospects in the near future.

Happily, there were other "old hands" out there who most generously agreed to pinch-hit for their temporarily afflicted associates. As a result the utility of this Special Issue to its readers has not been compromised in any meaningful way. Some of the unique vantage points of those who were compelled to leave the field can only be regretted. But by way of compensation, other equally valuable and unique vantage points have found a place herein.

The second notable consequence of the decision to turn to "old hands" as the writers of the essays was the sheer quality of their contributions to the world of the book/journal during their active years. The editors had turned to these people because we had grown to trust their insights and to respect the contributions they had made to the world of the book/journal. As noted above, we had supplied each with a broad-brush outline of the content we believed that each essay should address. In every case the writers departed more or less markedly from the outlines we had furnished. And in every case, the final essay better dealt with the substance that the essay was meant to address and the way in which it was meshed with and supported the other essays making up this account of the past century of the book/journal world.

To not put too fine a point on it, the authors of these essays have provided what might prove, in time, to be the most comprehensive and faithful account of what genuinely happened in the world of the authentic book and serious journal in North America in the twentieth century. The outline, as originally constructed by the editors, was neither a shabby nor a cobbled-together piece of work, but the essay authors have taken the objective of this exercise and its outline and run with it to fashion a first-rate history of this unique corner of the cultural world. And beyond that, they have infused it with a verisimilitude that only those who have been "in the trenches" can conceivably do.

We trust that present readers and future researchers will find this assessment of the worth of the authors' hard and diligent work not wide of the mark. Given so vivid and full a recital of the forces, events, and people, all profound influences in what is surely one of the most remarkable centuries in the history and evolution of the world of knowledge, the serious book/journal, and their associated organizations/institutions, it is hardly the editors' place to somehow summarize what has been recorded herein. But it does seem worthwhile to endeavor to put these recitals into a larger historical context and to then raise some questions about how the remarkable advances in the discovery of data and information of the century just past can be sustained but fruitfully augmented in the present century.

America (and Canada must surely be included in this term, whatever the common usage) only fully came into its own in the community of nations worldwide in the twentieth century. Following World War I and more markedly following World War II, America became the intellectual leader of the world. This ascendancy was manifestly the consequence of multitudinous historical forces that had been at work, often over several millennia. But within the past century itself, many of the most powerful of these forces came into being. Leaving to others the delineation of these historic forces and the preponderance of the outcomes thereof, we seek to deal with only the single most relevant of these outcomes to the world of the serious book/journal. That outcome turns on the fact of the increasing volumes of data/information that were generated in the past century—and the likelihood that this trend will continue into some indefinite future. This reality leads, in turn, to several genuine and major conundrums. The latter have, unfortunately, preoccupied and perplexed only a handful of observers. And their voices have been little heard above the din surrounding the more visible, because immediate and/or voguish issues of the day.

The first, and arguably, most important of these conundrums is the vexing matter of converting these monstrous accumulations of undigested, discrete bits of data/information into knowledge concepts. This problem, which is of truly awesome magnitude, has whimsically been epitomized in the expression "We work harder and harder to learn more and more about less and less." But such a jocular observation fails to even remotely convey the genuinely incredible magnitude of the problem with which we, at least in the West or the developed world, are faced. The continued churning out of discrete and separate bits of data/information, fueled by the ever-increasing funding of research, by both the private and public sectors, can only lead to a kind of intellectual bloat or constipation that makes the bulk of such expenditures uneconomical and hence irrational.

What is called for is the funding of knowledge synthesizers who expend their time and energies in libraries rather than in laboratories or field studies or other kinds of narrowly defined research venues and are concerned with only limited, short-term objectives. What is needed is the return to a large cadre of "library scholars." The function of the latter, long the preserve of distinguished and meaningful scholarship and in the recent past itself a sclerotic and largely vacuous endeavor, to sift through these mountains of data/information to retrieve the valuable bits and forge them into useful and defensible knowledge concepts. The most compelling evidence in support of this assertion is the continuing superior citation rankings of the various Annual Review series. Although no editor or reviewer for such a publication series would claim that the writings that appear therein even approach that level of synthesis that full-blown knowledge syntheses embody, they clearly represent the first major and significant cut at such synthetic knowledge formulations. But as virtually all Annual Review writers and editors will also confirm, such endeavors yield precious little return, economic or in terms of prestige, for the level of informed effort involved in the present grossly imbalanced allocation of resources and prestige between research and scholarship. This unhappy observation is but a pale reflection of the critical imbalance that presently exists between the churning out and reporting of raw research data/information and the ongoing synthesis of this raw material into useful and, more important, meaningful knowledge concepts and the subsequent publication thereof.

The second, but associated, conundrum relates to the integration of the knowledge concepts adverted to in the preceding paragraph into the inherited body of knowledge. It is simply not enough to ground human understanding merely in the accumulation of another, although substantially smaller, mountain of discrete and disparate knowledge concepts, analogous to the present menacing towers of raw data/information. Knowledge concepts must be integrated into the larger bodies of accumulated knowledge to make them culturally useful. This task is again the province of the "library scholar." The roles of the "library scholar" in creating new knowledge concepts and of integrating these concepts into the body of accumulated knowledge overlap to a significant degree and can be usefully separated only conceptually, not operationally.

The third conundrum that requires resolution is that of purging the enormous volumes of sheer intellectual "garbage" that now permeates these mountains of raw data/information. Those responsible for the integrity of the journal literature seem quite unable to police their own premises. As a result, in the interests of intellectual honesty and integrity, this job must migrate elsewhere. This seems another critical cultural function best entrusted to the "library scholar" at both levels of abstraction. The task of identifying and publicly repudiating the vast mass of redundant, useless, ill-conceived, poorly executed, and false research "results" that so widely disfigure the present research data/information literature seems to naturally fall within the purview of the "library scholar."

It must be noted here, based upon the history of the intellectual odyssey of the West, that these processes of knowledge concept creation and knowledge concept integration do not result in eternally firm and fixed intellectual and ethical structures. Rather, all being successively closer approximations to the true and the good, they are perpetually subject to re-examination, reappraisal, and reformulation as new knowledge concepts are created and older concepts ultimately found insupportable or indefensible. In short, the work of creating and disseminating knowledge is a never-ending cultural enterprise.

The varied functions of the "library scholar" will require not simply significant funding for the conduct of this genus of tasks, although but a modest fraction of the resources presently expended on the discovery of data/information, and the status presently accorded the researcher but a renewed commitment to restoring the funding of libraries to that level required to maintain widespread local currency with the data/information output as well. Local currency must be stressed, for the research activity implicit in "library scholarship" is so indeterminate and random that a generous and wide-ranging collection of not only the most current books and journals but a rich accumulation of older material is dictated by the very characteristics of the task and must be available in a large number of locations. In-depth library collections are, after all, the very raw material or life-blood of "library research."

It is perfectly clear that the genus of the journal, whether print or electronic, can provide neither the environment nor the incentive nor the forum for the creation or distribution of the outcomes of the ongoing knowledge concept and knowledge integration functions. This assertion can in no way be construed as a criticism or diminution of the journal as a form of publication. The journal was from its founding largely devoted to the dissemination of research results of data/information. The subsequent evolution of this publishing genus resulted in its continuing refinement and as such an intellectual vehicle of the first order. Its great strength and proper function, however, was, and remains, the timely dissemination of discrete bits of data/information.

In contrast, the codex/book genus of publication originated and has continued to be the form of communication medium tailored for and devoted to the dissemination/publication of bodies of knowledge. It, therefore, follows that book publishers must be intimately involved in the incubation and development of a properly balanced process of knowledge concept creation and integration. What shape this relationship will take will, in substantial measure, is dependent upon the species and levels of intellectual impulse and initiative authentic that book publishers are prepared to venture. Should they adopt the high-risk and immediately involved role of their predecessors of the fifteenth and sixteenth centuries, they will prove to be movers and shakers of the first order in the onward progress of the culture. Should, on the other hand, they adopt an all-too-convenient supine and reactive stance, the role of the book publisher will continue as a comfortable, reflexive "occupation for gentlemen." In short, the options open to publishers in a regime of "library scholarship" boil down to electing to return to the model of "publishing scholars" or continue as "financial-marketeers."

One last conundrum deserves attention here. That is the far from trivial matter of relaying knowledge concepts and integrated bodies of knowledge to that small group of interested layman who might best be characterized not as "the general intelligent reader," a term and identification so beloved by those in the present anemic book-world, but rather as "lifelong learners." Because the overwhelming mass of society in any era has consistently manifested a near-total disregard for matters of the intellect and cares hardly a whit for cultural fare of any significant substance or weight, the sheer difficulty of identifying and maintaining contact with lifelong learners immersed in a sea of near-indifference is, to say the least, challenging. Publishers, booksellers, and librarians have sought more or less successfully for centuries to ferret out this *rara avis*. The task has become more difficult due not only to burgeoning worldwide populations but the distressing upsurge of wide-scale indulgence in popular folkways, customs, and practices that apportion no respect for matters intellectual, ethical, or remotely mentally taxing. The haystack has grown not only in magnitude, but also in the percentage of populist thistle, thorn, and assorted other debris contained therein, making the finding of needles geometrically more difficult. Here is one place that the Internet could prove genuinely valuable. The latter has been touted for all kinds of bizarre roles in the information/knowledge transfer process. The locating of and maintaining continuing contact with the population of "lifelong learners" is one of those things the Internet could do exceedingly well.

The other related difficulty in relaying the results of knowledge creation and knowledge integration into existing bodies of knowledge to the lifelong learner is largely the book publishing community's problem. This observation has to do with the willingness of the publisher scholar to make a significantly larger investment in list-building and editing than is now commonly the practice. In the first case, list-building, the publisher scholar has to be continually identifying those places in the existing bodies of knowledge where new knowledge concepts need to be formulated and/or integrated. And after having identified such gaps or lacunae, undertake the search for a suitable author to write a book on the topic and then encourage that author in the lonesome business of writing a book-length manuscript so that in due time the lacunae is closed. Editorially, the publisher scholar must work in tandem with the author to make the final manuscript accessible to the "lifelong learner." This is a major necessity not only because most scholars are not skilled writers, so their writing is commonly far from clear, but also because they tend to load it with disciplinary jargon. Such jargon can, in fact, be translated into the common language without any loss of meaning in the hands of an intelligent editor. In short, the publisher scholar must help the writer prepare a clear, understandable manuscript cast in the language readily comprehended by the sophisticated reader. Books of such qualities will reward the publisher scholar by reaching a wider audience than is now generally reached by scholarly publishers.

These conundrums will be resolved in the due course of affairs by people of the stature and steadfastness that has characterized the authors of the essays constituting this publication. They were some of the wheelhorses in the solving of some of the conundrums that beset the century just past. Indeed, the accomplishments of these "old hands" set the tone and the confidence that what is recorded herein is the promise of the next century.

Coda

"What's done is done." The twentieth century is over. For those of us—authors, publishers, vendors, librarians—working in the world of the scholarly book and journal, incredible changes took place which impacted not only the production of the scholarly archive, but also the very fabric of that archive for posterity.

In college, we loved the term *fin de siècle*. It had that feel of mauve decadence and forbidden sybaritic Yellow Books of the dying Edwardian Age. Then the *fin de siècle* actually turned up, and we lived it without any sense of history, just a melting of one year into the next that petered out in a debate over which year was actually the start of the twenty-first century.

The last years brought with them the knowledge explosion and a torrent of innovations so fabulous as to seem to spring out of the kingdom of the imagination—which in fact they had. In a growing numbness we adapted to a technology so all-pervasive it seems to have taken possession of us, leaving us nostalgic for the leisured Great Book, the professor who produced one magnum opus in his career, the small Greek revival county library with its shelf of dog-eared who-done-its.

We feel old, having been born on the cusp of the midcentury. We recall the advent of Xerox copiers and IBM selectric typewriters. But to get the full perspective, we had to turn to Newlin and Abel, two garrulous old gents who have truly been there and done that. And they set to and put together a work of authority and clear vision out of the foggy landscape of the past.

Richard E. Abel and Lyman W. Newlin assembled an impressive cast of players to record what happened as they saw it. Among those selected are "old hands," persons of position, including John Dill, Hendrick Edelman, Robert Follett, Jack Goellner, Ralph Shoffner, Sam Vaughan, Alan Veaner, and Richard Zeldin. Also selected are those who are currently working in full-

301

time positions in the profession, including Peter Adams, Barbara Dean, Peter Givler, Michael Gorman, Chuck Hamaker, Albert Henderson, and Stephanie Oda.

From the efforts of their toil, we can look back on the last hundred years with a coherent wonder.

And we salute them.

Bruce and Katina Strauch
Against the Grain
Charleston, SC,   September 8, 2001

Index

Contributors

Richard E. Abel
Retired
Consultant
1730 S.W. 90th Avenue
Portland, Oregon 97225

Peter Adams
President, Mosely Associates
342 Madison Avenue, Suite 1410
New York, NY 10173

Barbara Carol Dean
Acquisitions Librarian, Arlington County Department of Libraries
1015 N. Quincy Street
Arlington, VA 22201
email: bdean@co.arlington.va.us

John Francis Dill
Retired
Previously President of STM Group;
CEO of Times-Mirror Medical Group
2988 Saint Barnabas Court
Kensington Golf and Country Club
Naples, FL 34103
email: jfdill@aol.com

Hendrik Edelman
Retired
Consultant
Previously Director, Rutgers University School of Information and Library
Science; Librarian, Rutgers University
138 Colton Ave
Sayville, NY 11732
email: hedelman@scils.rutgers.edu

Robert J.R. Follett
Retired
Previously President & CEO, Follett Corporation
PO Box 4848
Dillon, CO 80435
email: bob@alpineguild.com

Peter Givler
Executive Director, Association of American University Presses;
Previously University Press Director
71 W. 23rd Street
New York, NY 10010
email: pgivler@worldnet.att.net

Jack G. Goellner
Retired
Director Emeritus, Johns Hopkins University Press
215 Ridgemede Road
Baltimore, MD 21210
email: jgg@mail.press.jhu.edu

Michael Gorman
Dean of Library Services, California State University, Fresno
Malden Library
5200 N. Barton
Fresno, CA 93740
email: michael_gorman@csufresno.edu

Charles Hamaker
Associate University Librarian, Collections and Technical Services
University of North Carolina--Charlotte
J. Murrey Atkins Library
9201 University City Boulevard
Charlotte, NC 28223
email: Cahamake@email.uncc.edu

Albert Henderson
Retired
Previously Editor, Publishing Research Quarterly;
Consultant to STM and journal publishers
PO Box 2423
Bridgeport, CT 06608
email: 70244.1532@compuserve.com

Lyman W. Newlin
Retired
Book Trade Counsellors
PO Box 278
Lewiston NY 14092

Stephanie Oda
Editor & Publisher, Subtext
President, Open Book Publishing
PO Box 2228
90 Holmes Ave
Darien, CT 06820
email: OdaSan@aol.com

Ralph M. Shoffner
President, Ringgold Management Systems, Inc.;
Computing and IT consultant to university libraries;
Previously IT manager at R. Abel & Co.
PO Box 368
Beaverton, OR 97075
email: ralph@ringgold.com

Bruce Strauch
Professor, Law, The Citadel
Publisher, Against the Grain
MSC 98, The Citadel
Charleston, SC 29409
email: strauchb@citadel.edu

Katina Strauch
Librarian IV
Head, Collection Development
College of Charleston Libraries
Charleston, SC 29424
Editor, Against the Grain
MSC 98, The Citadel
Charleston, SC 29409
email: strauchk@earthlink.net

Sam Vaughan
Retired
Previously Editor in Chief at Doubleday;
Editor at Knopf, Morrow
23 Innes Rd
Tenafly, NJ 07670

Allen B. Veaner
Retired
Previously Director, University of Arizona Library
PO Box 30786
Tucson, AZ 85751
email: veaner@worldnet.att.net

Richard Zeldin
Retired
Consultant
Previously President of R.R. Bowker;
Manager, STM Publishing at John Wiley & Sons, Inc.;
Manager, STM Publishing at McGraw-Hill
20 Fairfield Dr.
Tinton Falls, NJ 07724